Technical Editors: Michael Taylor, Bob Levine
Book Designer and Compositor: Pariah Burke
Cover and Interior Illustrations: Pariah Burke and Lina Chekhovich

Published by Pariah Burke, LLC, Portland, Oregon
ISBN: 978-0-9890864-2-4 (print & PDF editions)
ISBN: 978-0-9890864-3-1 (EPUB & Kindle editions)

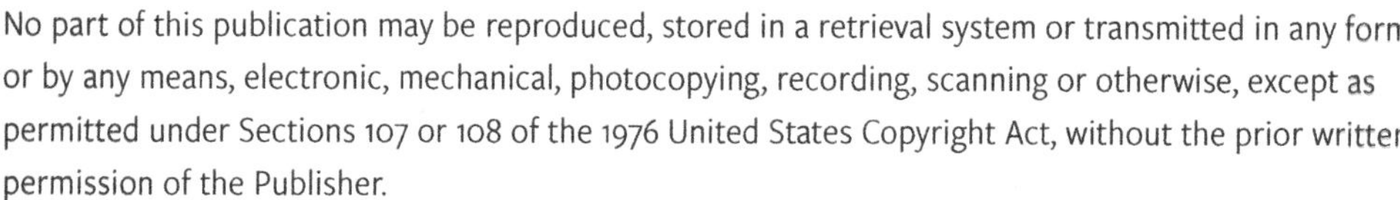

InDesign Masterclass: Text Techniques

For Lori

Acknowledgments

I wrote not one but two books concurrently from late-spring, throughout summer, and into the autumn of 2024. This book you're holding is one of them. The other is *InDesign Masterclass: Type & Tables* (ISBN: 978-0-9890864-5-5). And I did it while also teaching classes eight hours a day, four days per week, plus hosting a weekly syndicated radio show. In other words: for the majority of 2024, I worked very long days, sometimes seven days a week. This book would not have been possible without the love and support of my amazing partner, Lori. Thank you, my love.

My cat, Neytiri, was equally patient and, in her own way, supportive. For all the times I had to say, "Daddy has to work," and all the times you slept on my desk late into the night, thank you, Neytiri. Now it's time for all the play you can handle!

To my family and friends who wondered where I'd disappeared to, why my social media went quiet except for what the radio show team posted, this is where. Thank you for your patience. Thank you for calling and lunching to catch me up on the goings-on in your lives that I missed.

Teri Stone and David Blatner: thank you for letting me write for *CreativePro.com* and *InDesign Magazine* all those years. That was the first place I came up with and wrote about many of the InDesign techniques and tricks in this book.

I also want to acknowledge and thank all the InDesign users I've had the privilege of instructing, speaking before, hanging out with, and interacting with on the Adobe Forums, YouTube, Facebook, Twitter, and other social media. Many of the techniques and tips in this book are the direct result of your questions and project needs.

Thank you to Johannes Gutenberg, Aldus Manutius, Claude Garamond, John Warnock, Chuck Geschke, Paul Brainard, Tim Gill, Steve Jobs, Bill Gates, and everyone else who got us to the Desktop Publishing Revolution.

About the Author

Pariah Burke is a leading expert in digital design and publishing, with a career spanning over two decades. He has authored or co-authored 10 books on Adobe InDesign and related topics, along with producing 26 video courses that have educated professionals worldwide.

As a veteran trainer, Pariah has taught thousands of graphic designers, layout artists, and production staff globally, imparting his deep knowledge of Adobe InDesign, InCopy, Photoshop, Illustrator, and electronic publishing. His expertise also encompasses cutting-edge fields like artificial intelligence and accessibility in electronic documents, making him a sought-after consultant and speaker.

Throughout his career, Pariah has served as an advisor to industry giants such as Adobe, Quark, and Extensis. His extensive client list includes organizations like NASA, Lockheed Martin, Nike, Johns Hopkins University, and several U.S. government agencies, including the Air Force, Army, Marine Corps, NSA, CIA, and the FDA.

At the university level, Pariah teaches graduate courses on InDesign, audiobooks, book production, and ebook production to Masters-level students, preparing the next generation of publishing professionals for the dynamic demands of their industry. His contributions to the Adobe Certified Expert exam and to the actual features of InDesign underline his status as a recognized authority in InDesign, InCopy, and Illustrator.

Beyond his technical and educational pursuits, Pariah connects with a global audience of Rock N' Roll fans as the host and producer of the syndicated weekly radio broadcast, *The Hard, Heavy & Hair Show*, where he interviews Rock legends from across generations.

Pariah Burke is a prolific and respected voice in the digital design community, dedicated to empowering creative professionals around the world. Outside of his professional pursuits, Pariah enjoys exploring the trails, lakes, waterfalls, and other natural beauty of Portland, Oregon, attending concerts, sci-fi conventions, and renaissance fairs, and immersing himself in a good novel or audiobook.

Table of Contents

Introduction

I wrote this book concurrently with another title during the spring, summer, and fall of 2024. Two books at once? Yup. It was insane, but I did it. Moreover, I'm very glad with the way both turned out.

First, you have this book, *InDesign Masterclass: Text Techniques*. At the same time, I wrote *InDesign Masterclass: Type & Tables*. And, to be honest, in the process I also wrote half of my next book, *InDesign Masterclass: Objects & Documents*.

They all started because I wanted to update *Mastering InDesign for Print Design & Production*, which Sybex/John Wiley & Sons and I had published a few editions of throughout the years. I started writing and revising from the last edition of that book, though it quickly occurred to me that the limitation of the book—the "for Print Design & Production" part of the title—was not the direction in which I wanted to go. Yes, of course, InDesign will always be central to print design and print production, but the world has changed since the first edition of that book. The word "print" doesn't just mean ink on paper anymore. Truth be told, it didn't even then. I got around the titular limitation of *Mastering InDesign for Print Design & Production* by also writing books about electronic publishing with InDesign and by creating numerous video courses about using InDesign and InCopy in solo- and team-based publishing workflows that included print, true, but also included EPUB and fixed-layout ebooks, interactive PDFs, Adobe Digital Publishing Solution, and Adobe Experience Manager.

This time, though, I wanted to bring *everything* InDesign into a single book… Which I ultimately didn't. Instead, I'm bringing everything InDesign into a *series* of books: *InDesign Masterclass*.

I'll be honest, I made the decision in part because I didn't want you straining a shoulder carrying around a 1,200 page InDesign book. I knew I wasn't holding anything back from *InDesign Masterclass*. Everything (relevant) that I've learned in more than 20 years teaching and writing about InDesign, I put into the *InDesign Masterclass* series. This first book, *InDesign Masterclass: Type & Tables*, is every piece of information, trick, and best practice I've accumulated from projects I've built, courses I've created, classes I've taught, classes Adobe put me through when I worked there, books I've read, conference sessions I've attended, and your projects and workflows you've shown me or asked for my help in perfecting. This is the no holds barred InDesign book I've always wanted to write… broken up into three books so you don't get rucksack palsy.

InDesign Masterclass: Type & Tables is everything about InDesign's core competency: working with text. Whether you're a 20-year-veteran of InDesign or a brand new user, you'll learn something new from that book. The question is the distance you'll travel. You can go from veteran to master, beginner to master, or to master from any other point in your InDesign experience. You'll learn not only *how* every type- or table-related function of InDesign works, what all the options and subtle changes accomplish, but also the *why* and *when* of using InDesign features. *Why would you choose* this *over* that*? When should you employ this technique or that methodology?* That's what the book is about. It's not just a "click here, click there" software manual; it's an education in InDesign as it's used in real world, professional design and production roles.

InDesign Masterclass: Text Techniques is page after page of step-by-step tutorials, recipes for effects and techniques, and tips for varying my tutorials for your own projects and needs. It's an entire book full of the main reason people buy magazines, read blog posts, and watch YouTube videos. It's all the sidebar tricks and how-tos you'd find in other software books, but expanded to so much more. In fact, that's how *InDesign Masterclass: Text Techniques* began. Several of the techniques are expanded versions of sidebars and appendixes in *Mastering InDesign*, *ePublishing with InDesign*, and my other books. Others are techniques I've shown on stage at conferences and speaking tours, the tutorials that make the audiences' eyes grow wide, their jaws drop, and their hands beat rapidly against one another—sometimes they even stand to applaud after some of what you'll read in this book.

I recommend *InDesign Masterclass: Text Techniques* for advanced InDesign users. If you consider yourself a beginner, intermediate, or self-taught InDesign user, I strongly recommend you first read *InDesign Masterclass: Type & Tables.* Although most intermediate InDesign users can employ many of the recipes in this book immediately, they might find themselves challenged by a technique here and there.

I sincerely thank you for reading my book. Teaching others what I've learned so that they can be more creative without barriers is my life's work and my greatest honor. This book is conceived, written, designed, and laid out entirely by me. I will be honored and grateful if it teaches you something.

Now, design something!

Sincerely,

Pariah Burke
Portland, Oregon, USA

And more, much more than this, I did it my way. ~Frank Sinatra

How to Use This Book

While I suppose you could read it cover-to-cover (it's only 200 pages, after all), I didn't write it in a way that needs to be read linearly. Instead, I recommend you check out the Table of Contents, find a technique that interests you, and use it to help you start creating something cool. The other recipes will be there when you want to create a different cool thing.

When an advanced technique incorporates another, foundational technique, the latter is cross-referenced from within the former. If you're reading one of the electronic versions of this book—PDF is the best version of it, in my opinion—you'll find those cross-references are hyperlinks that jump you directly to the referenced recipe.

Glossary

Glossary terms are linked to their glossary entries for quick click/tap definitions (in the electronic forms of this book). I've also included the full Glossary from *InDesign Masterclass: Type & Tables*, which might help if you run across a term you don't recognize.

Special URLs

Although *InDesign Masterclass: Text Techniques* doesn't include hyperlinks to many external resources, where they are included, they mostly employ a URL shortener service. It's my own, as a matter of fact. URLs that begin with `https://abbrv.it/` use the URL shortening service I own. Their use in this book provides two benefits to you: First, they allow me to present you with Web addresses that are typically much shorter and easier to remember and retype, which is especially useful to readers of the print editions of this book. Because Web-based pages, articles, downloads, and other resources change location from time to time, the second benefit of using my URL shortener is that you don't have to go hunting down content Adobe.com or some other website moved. I do.

If a link stops working, tell me via email to IDMC@iampariah.com. I'll then see if I can find where the resource moved to, and update the destination of the shortened URL to that new location.

How to Contact the Author

If this or any of my books is helpful to you, if you use any of my techniques in a project, or if you have a suggestion to improve this book or another in the *InDesign Masterclass* series, please let me know. I welcome the contact. Although I'm on just about every social media, I often don't open them for weeks at a time writing a book (and I get a lot of DM spam anyway), so the best way to reach me is good ol' fashioned email. You can email me at IDMC@iampariah.com or reach out to me from https://iamPariah.com/contact.

Also by Pariah Burke

Training, Consulting, and Development

Visit https://iampariah.com for the highest-quality, most learner-focused, bespoke training, consulting, and development services.

Training

Timely, tailored, results-oriented Adobe, Microsoft, Canva, Elearning, Section 508/Accessibility, and other software training delivered in a variety of formats: Instructor Led Training, Virtual Instructor Lead Training, On-Site Classroom Training, Private Customized Training, White Label Subcontract Training, and Project-Based Training.

Consulting

Services beyond training and development can include anything from customized hybrid education-development events that result in your team learning to create projects while actually building a deliverable, ready-for-market project, all the way through me spending time evaluating and helping to revamp your creative professional department on-site.

Instructional Design

Adult learning theory-based conception and development of elearning modules and courses, video-based instruction, written education such as manuals, job aids, step-by-steps, and other forms, as well as development of testing and results evaluation systems.

Document Development & Remediation

Learning to develop projects or remediate projects isn't always your goal or an option with a specific deadline. If that's the case, vend the project to me. I can develop many types of print, digital, elearning, audio, video, and Web projects from scratch while working with your SMEs and stakeholders, from a previous version requiring updates, or from an incomplete or falling behind existing project. My most popular development work is to remediate non-accessible PDFs and other documents and make them Section 508-compliant and accessible to people with disabilities.

Books

Pariah Burke, sometimes credited as Pariah S. Burke, has authored or co-authored other books:

- *InDesign Masterclass: Type & Tables*
- *InDesign Masterclass: Text Techniques*
- *Mastering InDesign for Print Design and Production*
- *ePublishing with InDesign*
- *The Business of ePublishing*
- *InDesign: Creating Fixed-Layout eBooks*
- *InDesignSecrets Guide to What's New in InDesign CS5*
- *Adobe Illustrator @Work*
- (co-author) *Real World QuarkXPress*
- (co-author) *Using Adobe Creative Suite: Special Edition*

Video Courses

Pariah Burke has been an author since 2011 with Pluralsight.com, a quality-over-quantity, highly discriminating online learning library, where he has authored more than 30 top-rated video courses spanning dozens of hours.

- *InDesign Tip-o-the-Week: 52 Powerhouse Tips and Tricks*
- *InDesign Publish Online*

- *InDesign Projects: Designing a Flyer*
- *InDesign Projects: Designing a Book Cover and Spine*
- *InDesign Mastering Type*
- *InDesign Mastering Productivity*
- *InDesign Mastering Objects*
- *InDesign Mastering Documents*
- *InDesign Long Documents, Books, Manuals*
- *InDesign Interactive* PDF
- *InDesign Integration with InCopy*
- *InDesign Fixed-Layout eBooks*
- *InDesign* EPUB *Fundamentals*
- *InDesign* EPUB *Building on the Fundamentals*
- *InDesign DPS Fundamentals*
- *InDesign DataMerge and Variable Data Printing*
- *InCopy Fundamentals*
- *InCopy Building on the Fundamentals*
- *Illustrator Typography*
- *Illustrator Pixels to Vectors*
- *Designing in Duotone in Photoshop and InDesign*
- *Creating a Brand Style Guide*
- *Advanced Typography*
- *Adobe Digital Publishing System Designing and Building Apps*
- *Adobe Digital Publishing System Creating Content in InDesign*
- *Adobe Digital Publishing System Adding Content from* HTML *and WordPress*

Non-Design-Related

- *The Hard, Heavy & Hair Show* syndicated radio show
- Podcast: *Hard, Heavy & Hair: The Interviews*
- *The Iron Outlaw* radio show

Character Recipes

Highlight Text at the Character Level

Introducing the **NeuraSync™** ***Smartband***, the ultimate productivity tool designed to sync your thoughts with your devices. With just a tap, you can seamlessly transfer ideas from your brain to your phone or laptop, enabling real-time collaboration without even lifting a finger. Its ergonomic design and AI-driven interface learn from your daily habits to help you stay focused, energized, and productive all day long. Whether you're a busy professional, a creative thinker, or a tech enthusiast, **NeuraSync™** adapts to your workflow for maximum efficiency. Elevate your productivity and unlock the power of your mind with **NeuraSync™**–the future of human-tech integration.

Also known as, *Applying a Highlight Marker to Text.*

This has been one of my most popular tutorials since I first wrote about in 2002 on the very first professional publication devoted to InDesign, my own (now defunct) website *Quark VS InDesign*. Since then, I've probably written about it in a dozen other magazines, and demonstrated it at thrice as many conferences. The simplest techniques are often the most popular because simplicity often equates to versatility.

To highlight text in Adobe InDesign, you can use the Underline Options feature to create a custom underline that mimics a highlighter effect. Here's how:

1 Use the Type Tool to select the text you want to highlight.
2 With the text selected, open the Character panel by navigating to Window ▸ Type & Tables ▸ Character.

3. On the Character panel menu choose Underline Options.
4. Turn on and watch your underline take shape by activating the checkbox controls beside Underline On and Preview.
5. Set the Weight of your underline to be around 120-140% of your type size. For example, if you text is set at 10 pt, the Weight should be 12 pt or higher to account for ascenders and descenders, and to give a little bit of highlight color above and below those. Be careful not to make the Weight so high that the highlight actually underlaps the text in lines above or below your selected text.
6. Leave the Type as Solid (other techniques will show how you can use other line types shortly).
7. Skip the Offset for a moment and set the Color to any color swatch you'd like as your highlighter color. In my effect, I used a modified version of the Magenta swatch to create a pink highlight. Adjust the Tint field, too, if you like.
8. Leave Overprint Stroke, Gap Color, and so on alone, and go back to the Offset field. At this point, you have a thick pink (or other color) line *below* the text you want to highlight. The Offset field is how we make it underlap the text directly.
9. By default, the Offset field is set to Auto, revealed by a value wrapped in parenthesis. Click the down arrow to open the Offset drop-down menu and set it to 0 pt. Your underline should be partly behind the selected text now.
10. Click the down-pointing-arrow button on the left side of the Offset field to go down from 0 pt offset into negative values. Keep pressing that button until your highlight has risen up to fully encompass—and highlight—your selected text.
11. Click OK, and, for best practice, make a character style from your highlighted text.

Highlighter Colors

You can use any color you want with the previous recipe, of course. However, if you want to recreate the effect of standard highlight markers, use the following colors, presented in both RGB and Hex formulas. Just create a swatch from each, and, if appropriate, a character style from each—as I've done (opposite).

Introducing the **NeuraSync**
productivity tool designed
your devices. With just a ta
ideas from your brain to yo
real-time collaboration with
ergonomic design and AI-d
your daily habits to help yo
and productive all day long
professional, a creative thin
NeuraSync™ adapts to you
efficiency. Elevate your pro
power of your mind with **N**
human-tech integration.

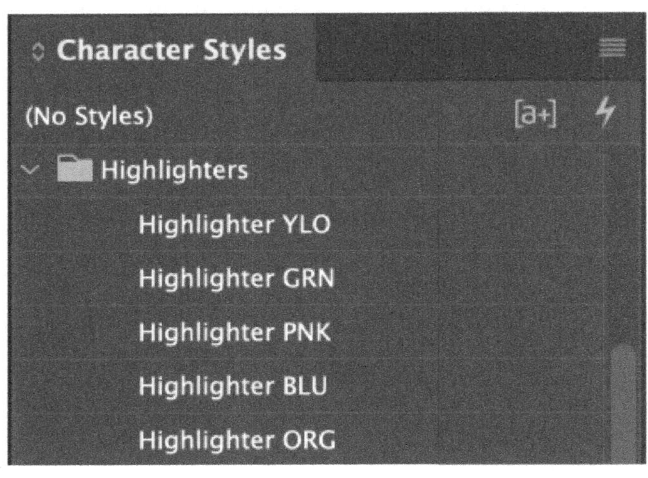

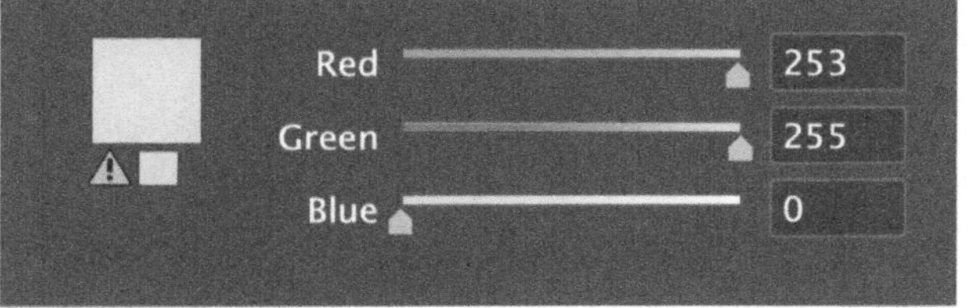

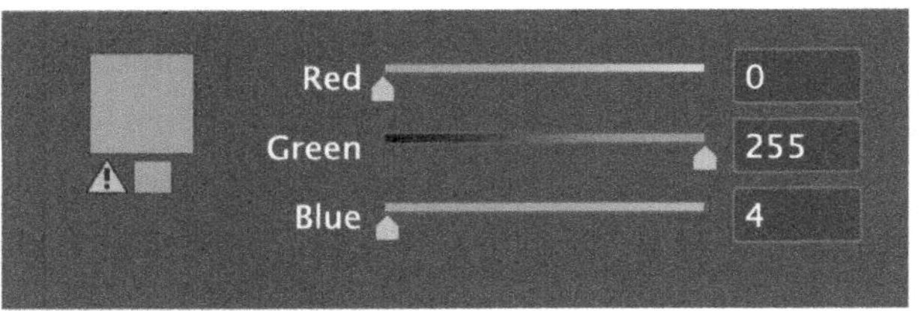

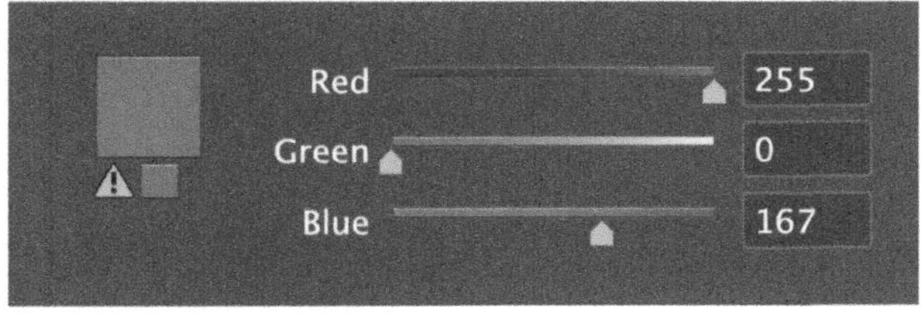

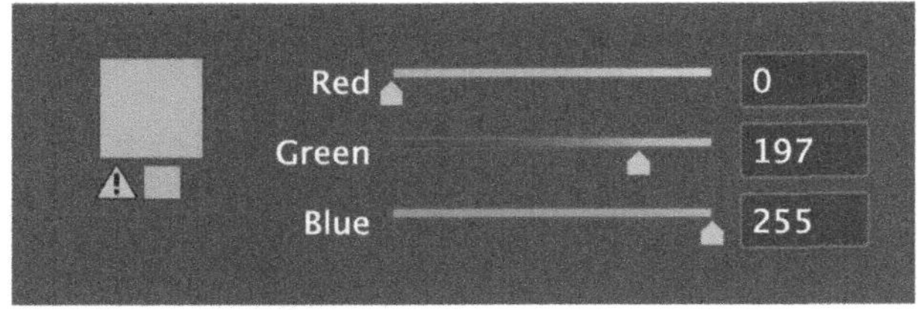

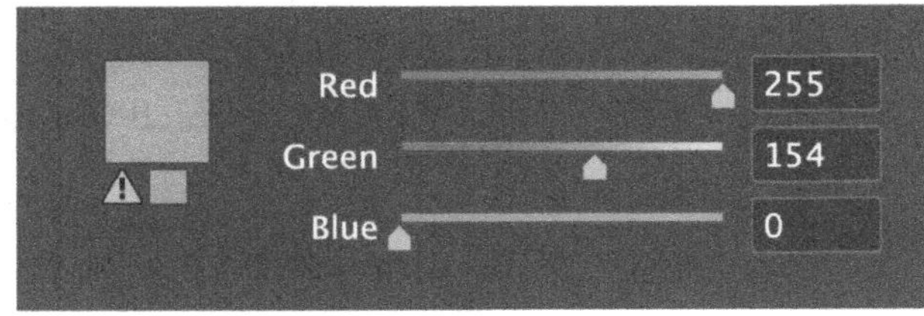

Round End Text Highlighter

Introducing the **NeuraSync™** ***Smartband***, the ultimate productivity tool designed to sync your thoughts with your devices. With just a tap, you can seamlessly transfer ideas from your brain to your phone or laptop, enabling real-time collaboration without even lifting a finger. Its ergonomic design and AI-driven interface learn from

A refinement I came up with to the original highlight marker effect is to round the ends of the highlighting.

1. Follow the steps in the "Highlight Text at the Character Level", but stop before clicking OK.
2. Go back and change the (Stroke) Type field from Solid to Japanese Dots. You should now have a polka dot highlighting, which, by itself, can be cool for the right project.
3. Go to the Gap Color field, which is now active because you chose a (Stroke) Type other than Solid, and set it's color swatch to be the exact same as the Color field above it. If you adjusted the first Tint field, make the Gap Tint filed match.

Now you have text highlighting will rounded ends, creating the classic pill shape.

Note: The rounding often leaves out of the highlighting parts of the first and last glyphs of the selected text. To counter this problem, apply the round end highlighter to the spaces and punctuation before and after that text.

Automatic Hyperlink Character Style

You can save yourself the effort of initially creating a Hyperlink character style by just creating an actual hyperlink *without* choosing an existing character style. InDesign will automatically create and apply the Hyperlink character style, which you can then modify as desired.

Better Hyperlink Underlining

Introducing the NeuraSync™ Smartband, the ultimate productivity tool designed to sync your thoughts with

Introducing the **NeuraSync™ Smartband**, the ultimate productivity tool designed to sync your thoughts with

When you create a hyperlink, InDesign automatically creates a Hyperlink character style. Unfortunately, it's not a *good* hyperlink character style. Note the difference in the underlined text examples in the image above. First, the underline is the same color as the text, which is fine, if that's what you want. Worse, though, is the underline bisecting the descender of the *y*. If your text has multiple descenders, it gets even more cringe-worthy.

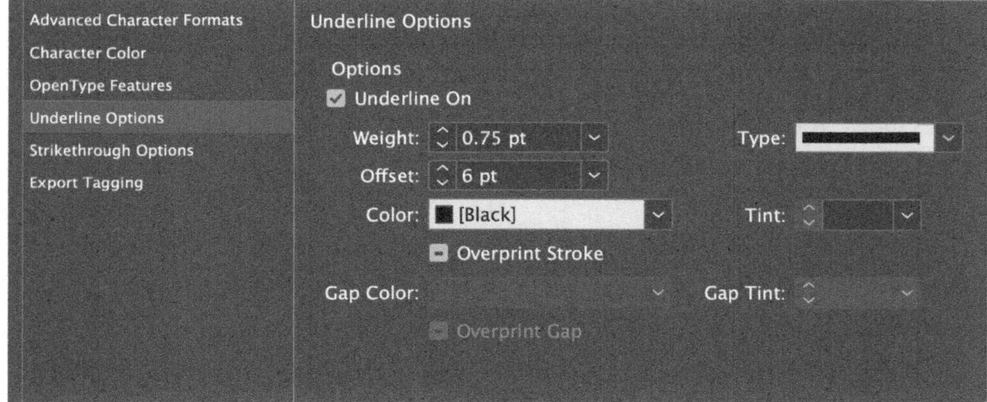

In the sample the top is InDesign's default hyperlink style, the one it makes automatically when you create the document's first hyperlink without choosing a pre-existing character style. The bottom uses my pictured settings better hyperlink underlining, which includes a stronger weight font style, but that's not the big difference. Note the Offset field: it pushes the underline down below the descenders, preventing collisions with lowercase letters like *y*, *g*, *p*, and so on. The tradeoff is a lower underline, which may not be what you want. For that, I have another recipe for you…

Anti-Collision Hyperlink Underlining

Introducing the NeuraSync™ Smartband, the ultimate productivity tool designed to sync your thoughts with

Think of underlines on hyperlinks as the brakes on your car. InDesign's automatic Hyperlink style and its unsightly underline as the first generation of braking technology—pulling a handle to lever a wooden block against the wheel. My "Better Hyperlink Underlining" technique, while an improvement on the block brakes method, is still simple, like mechanical linkage brakes where the force the human driver exerted on the pedal was directly transferred to the brake pads scraping against the wheel (this is why people used to "stand on the brakes," putting their body weight behind their exertions to stop the car). And then we have modern ant-lock braking systems (ABS) that are much, much smarter and don't rely on brute force to underline hyperlinks. This is that ABS technique.

1 Start by creating two character styles. Call the first Hyperlink, and give it an underline—or let InDesign create it and use the default hyperlink underline settings.
2 Create a second character style and name it something like Hyperlink – Anti-Collision.
3 Edit that second character style to open its Character Style options. Set the Based On field to be Hyperlink, inheriting from it settings like Font Family, Style, Color, and so on.
4 On the Underline Options pane turn *off* the checkbox beside Underline On. Click OK to save your style changes.
5 Make a hyperlink and assign it the first Hyperlink character style through the Hyperlinks panel and the New Hyperlink dialog.
6 If you have a collision between a descender and the underline, as does my *y* in the example, highlight the character whose descender hits the line, and apply the Hyperlink – Anti-Collision character style to just that character. The hyperlink will still work, but that one character—or two, three, whatever—will cause a break in the underline, avoiding an accident that old block and mechanical linkage brakes would drive us straight into.

Differentiate Kinds of Hyperlinks

Thank you for completing the *NeuraSync New Employee Orientation Guide!*

Do you have questions about your new position at NeuraSync?

Call:	HR: 503-555-1212, ext 6
	Security: 503-555-1212, ext 2
Email:	hr@neurasyncus.com
	feedback@neurasyncus.com
Intranet:	https://portal.neurasyncus.com

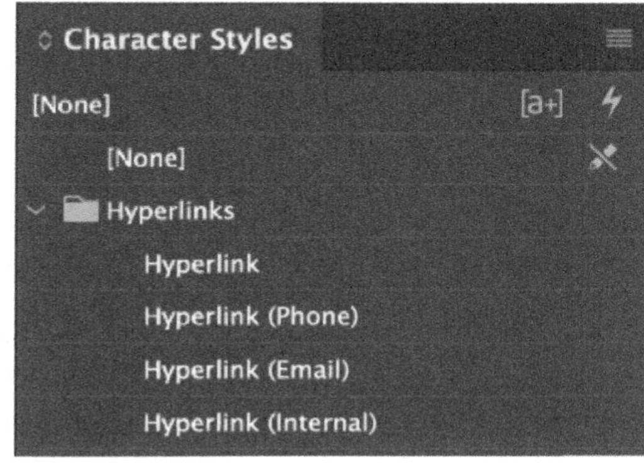

Let's assume you've just landed a plum job as the creative director for your company's newsletter. The newsletter, which is distributed to employees, clients, and vendors as a PDF, is 10 years out-of-date, and your first task as creative director is to redesign it from scratch.

PDF's ability to contain live hyperlinks will definitely help you exploit the power of the newsletter, but how much thought have you given to the types of hyperlinks you may employ? There are many different types of hyperlinks a typical corporate e-newsletter may contain—cross-references and other links to pages within the same PDF, links to the company website and documents thereon, links to email addresses, as well as links to outside resources and partner websites. How are your readers to know which link will do what?

Use different underline styles to instantly identify your publications different types of hyperlinks.

1. Place or type your text—including the hyperlink candidate.
2. With the Text tool, highlight the text to be linked and that will be underlined to show the link.

3 Open the Character panel, and from its panel flyout menu, select Underline Options toward the bottom. This will open the Underline Options dialog box.
4 First, turn on Preview on the right, and then check Underline On. You should immediately see your selected text underlined.
5 Set up your external hyperlink underline how you like. Most users are accustomed to a solid, single underline that is the same color as the text (which you should change from black to a contrasting color like blue, green, or red). When ready, hit OK. Don't forget to actually assign the URL on InDesign's Hyperlinks panel.

Creating the hyperlink underline may not be tough, but it is tedious if you have more than a couple of external hyperlink underlines to format. Save yourself some time and make a character style for this particular underline. Thus, underlining more text is simply a matter of highlighting and then clicking on the style entry in the Character Styles panel.

Set up your other underlines' styles the same way, making character styles for each of them, too. Make them all obviously hyperlinks by changing their text and underline colors from the color of the surrounding copy, but don't go overboard. Thin single, double, dashed, or dotted lines tend to serve readers well.

In Same Document

Intranet/Company Controlled

External Resource

In the corporate newsletter I inherited, I used the following styles:

- Links to other pages and resources within the same PDF were done in blue, with a dashed underline.
- URLs for company-owned resources such as intranet systems (the Acme Customer First Order Center) and links to documents on the company's

public website (the newsletter's first quarter issue) were colored green and given a double underline.

- External resources, such as those for the Albuquerque Gazette review and the partner's site, which take the reader away from company-controlled materials, are styled with a single, solid underline and colored red to closely approximate familiar Web hyperlink formatting.

Hyperlink to an Email Address

You could be 15 or 50 years-old; someone has said to you "email is dead", usually followed by way too many exclamation points. Uh-*huh*. Also, Steve Jobs said "people don't read anymore"[1].

Email is a mainstay of communication. Love it? Hate it? *Who cares?* Email is here to stay with 57% of Gen Z, 79% of Gen Y, 67% of Gen X, and 69% of Boomers preferring email communications to text messages, social media, and (ugh) voice phone calls in a 2024 survey[2].

If you think email is dead… Move on. Find a job in a like-minded startup rather than using InDesign. This section is *not* for you or for any entity you work for who doesn't want to, A) be accessible to people with disabilities (who have a $13 trillion disposable income worldwide, and $21 billion in the U.S. alone), or B) be inclusive of people with disabilities or anyone, self-identifying as disabled or not, born between 1906 and 2018[3].

For the rest of you, here's how you create a hyperlink to an email address in InDesign:

1. Select the text that should be linked to an email address. Remember: *only* the text you hyperlink is likely to be presented to assistive technology. Most static text is skipped upon basic navigation, so the text you choose to hyperlink *must* answer the fundamental accessibility questions of: "what will happen if I activate this hyperlink" and "where will I go if I activate this hyperlink".
2. Go to Window ▸ Interactive ▸ Hyperlinks to open the Hyperlinks panel.
3. Click the plus-symbol-adorned Create New Hyperlink button at the bottom of the Hyperlinks panel.

---

1 January 15, 2008, New York Times
2 https://www.emailisnotdead.com/
3 https://www.rod-group.com/research-insights/annual-report-2020/

4. From the Link To drop-down menu, choose Email.
5. In the Address field, type in the email address to which the message should be sent.
6. Optionally, fill in the Subject Line field to pre-populate the subject line for the email, which helps both senders and recipients, especially if the former has any number of cognitive-based disabilities.
7. Turn off Shared Hyperlink Destination. It's a long-standing, Adobe-ignored complication that will likely cause you problems. (Again, way back in the "Characters" chapter, I did say Adobe hears customer feedback *eventually*. This is apparently one of those things their decades-delayed voicemail hasn't yet transmitted to Adobe Development and QC."
8. Set the appropriate Character Style option.
9. Click OK.

Hyperlink to a Phone Number

Here's a thing, fam. I have a good memory, but I don't remember phone numbers. Once upon a time I did, but, well, I have a cell phone. I know my own number from telling people so often, and I know my partner's from filling out all the "in case of emergency" forms that come with being a freelancer to companies and contract employee to universities and a white-label trainer to the best of the United States government's training companies, but I don't know any other phone numbers. Moreover, I have a terrible memory for phone numbers in general. So, here's what happens when I encounter a phone number in a PDF, web page, or elsewhere that isn't hyperlinked:

1. I try to remember the phone number—*503-555-1212*.
2. I press the Home button my phone, find the Phone app, start to dial—5-0-3-*dammit!*
3. Swipe left. Re-read the number—*503-555-1212*.
4. Swipe right back to the dialer.
5. Tap 5-5-5-1-2... what?!
6. Swipe left. Re-read the number—*503-555-1212*.
7. Swipe right back to the dialer.

8 *1-2*, hit Send, and hope I got it right, that I'm not disturbing some grandpa during his nap or a mom breastfeeding her kid waiting to hear from the father whether they found the right kind of diapers or—*Oh! Hi, um is this Acme Corp. Rocket Skates Customer Servic—Oh, my gosh! I am so, so sorry! Please accept my most sincere apolog*—click.

9 *Sigh.* Swipe left. *5-5-5…*

And I do not have a memory disability.

So, save your users some stress: hyperlink to the phone number for two-tap calling (nothing is one-tap, for security of users).

1. Select the text that should be hyperlinked to a phone number—usually just the phone number or something like "call us at 503-555-1212".
2. On the Hyperlinks panel, click that plus-sign-adorned Create New Hyperlink button.
3. Set the Link To drop-down to URL.
4. In the Destination ▸ URL field, type `tel:` and then the phone number to be dialed. You can enter it with or without hyphens, with or without country code.
5. Again, turn off Shared Hyperlink Destination because Adobe laziness.
6. Click OK.

When a user of your document taps or clicks that link, their device will then open the dialer or phone app, with that number pre-inserted, ready for them to hit Send.

Also note that you can pre-supply extensions and pauses. On the URL line in New Hyperlink, a comma (,) equals a 2-second pause. Therefore, if your automated AI-powered phone tree answers the phone and then asks for an extension number, you just have to enter commas equal to the message and pause length before the system will be ready for caller input, and then enter the number callers should input to reach the desired department or service. For example, if your system has a 6-second greeting and menu overview before saying: "press 2 for account billing," you could enter the following as your hyperlink in InDesign to get someone from your document directly into the billing system:

```
503-555-1212,,,2
```

Hyperlink to Send a Text Message

I was at a concert not long ago. It was one of those outdoor amphitheater concerts with a giant screen on either side of the stage. While we waited for the opening act, and then again between bands, short, uplifting statements appeared on the screens flanking the stage full of techs and roadies breaking down, and then setting up, bands. It turns out, the screen sayings were coming from text messages in the audience, sent to the screens (through a gatekeeper person somewhere, no doubt), via text messaging. The mechanism for this positive, inclusive audience narrative was the email received by ticket purchasers immediately after getting their tickets: "send a text message to this link while you're waiting for the show to start!" That, ladies, gentlemen, non-binary readers, and children of all ages, is a *brilliant* idea, one I've espoused ever since that concert.

You can create a text message hyperlink in InDesign the same way you create a link to dial a phone number. The only difference is the prefix. Instead of starting the hyperlink with `tel:` to activate the operating system's dialer, if it has one, add `sms:` followed by a phone number. Again, the phone number can include or exclude hyphens, a country code, or even comma-generated pauses and an extension number.

Now, now, before you get all judgy, *yes*, I do know that SMS (Simple Messaging System) is an older technology. Sure, RCS *is* the current standard but like most modern technologies, it has a fallback protocol to operate on older network technologies—SMS in this case. And that's by law in most countries to allow for 9-1-1 or 9-9-9 communications on low battery power or signal strength as well as while using older generation cell towers networks.

Therefore, if you create a hyperlink like the following, any text-capable mobile device will initiate a text message, regardless of whether it's using 2027 RCS messaging or 1997 Blackberry protocols, and with equal capability:

1. Select the text that should be hyperlinked to send a text message.
2. On the Hyperlinks panel, click that plus-sign-adorned Create New Hyperlink button.
3. Set the Link To drop-down to URL.

4 In the Destination ▸ URL field, type `sms:` and then the phone number to which the text message should be sent. You can enter it with or without hyphens, with or without country code.
5 Yet again (ugh), turn off Shared Hyperlink Destination because Adobe still hasn't fixed this since I type the instructions 6.25 minutes ago.
6 Click OK.

When your user clicks or taps a hyperlink with the format `sms:503-555-1212`, a text message will be initiated in the device's text messaging app—iPhone Messages, iMessages for older iPhones, Google Messages, Textra for Android users who don't like Google Messages, or whatever—and will be onscreen waiting for the device user to finish the message and press Send.

Hyperlink to Anywhere

Honey badger don't care. Neither do InDesign. Want a hyperlink? Then make a hyperlink. InDesign don't care. Whatever you can hyperlink to outside of InDesign, you can hyperlink to *inside* of InDesign.

How? Simple: InDesign doesn't actually hyperlink to *anywhere.* As you may have realized, InDesign is simply a document creator; very few people actually *view* documents in InDesign (you and me excluded, of course). The rest of the world? They consume our content as PDF, EPUB, fixed-layout ebook, or printed content. Therefore, all InDesign has to do, really, is make sure the formats it outputs are compatible with leading viewing/reading tools, like Adobe Acrobat or Acrobat Reader, Apple Books, Kindle, and so on. Those viewing/reader tools are then responsible for making sure they work with the operating systems that host them—MacOS, Windows, Android, iOS, or what-have-you. That last part? That's easy, especially for you and me, because we have no responsibility there—o *F*s given—about PDF, EPUB, or FXL readers conflicts with their hosting OSes. We only have to use tools that we know (should) work using common technologies Apple, Microsoft, Google, Apple (again), Adobe, and other OS- and tool-makers work very hard (probably) to ensure work as expected.

If you open the Hyperlinks panel from Window î Interactive î Hyperlinks, and then, with text, an image, or some other object selected, click that little plus sign at the bottom of the panel to start a new hyperlink, whatever you hyperlink to will work—in theory. You want to link to a Google search result with half a dozen variables on the URL? Cool. Throw in there a link to an FTP file server behind a login-wall, complete with username and password on the address? Gucci. Going luxe with an email that also puts in a subject line? InDesign is nonplussed. *You do you, boo*, it says. T-rexing an ancient doc for an ancient boss who wants a "dial my digits" phone link? Fire. No cares, dawg. InDesign does it all when it comes to hyperlinks, even the cringe gampa ones, because the operating system is actually handling the call to the hyperlink protocol.

1 Select the text that should be hyperlinked to.... some darned thing.
2 On the Hyperlinks panel, click that plus-sign-adorned Create New Hyperlink button.
3 Set the Link To drop-down to URL.
4 In the Destination ▸ URL field, type.... *whatever! Honey badger don't care!*
5 Click OK.

Table 8.1 shows a few examples of things to which you can link. Note that the following are, except for the Google search and the harmless Adobe Usenet and Duck Duck Go Dark Web links, made-up, non-functioning examples of common types of URLs to which you can hyperlink.

Table 8.1: Examples of some of the hyperlink URLs InDesign will accept

URL Type	Example
Google Search	https://www.google.com/search?q=indesign+tutorial+pariah+burke
BitTorrent	magnet:?xt=urn:btih:123abc456def789ghi012jkl345mno678pqrs90&dn=examplefile
FTP (File Transfer Protocol)	ftp://username:password@hostname/path/to/file
IRC (Internet Relay Chat)	irc://irc.example.com:6667/#examplechannel
Telnet	telnet://telnet.example.com:23
Deep Web (A.K.A. Onion URL)	http://expyuzz4wqqyqhjn.onion/
Usenet, Netnews, Newsgroup, collectively NNTP (Network News Transfer Protocol)	nntp://news.example.com/alt.graphics.adobe

Overscoring

Tēnā tātou katoa

$$\overline{a} + \overline{b} > x = 5.\overline{33}$$

Employment History

In modern typography and publications, overscore, also called overlines and overbars, are used primarily for stylistic emphasis, mathematical notation, and linguistic purposes. They often indicate long vowels in certain languages, such as Māori and Japanese, or are used in mathematical equations to signify repeating decimals or averages. In some cases, overscores add a visual element to headings, logos, or specialized design work. While less common than underlines, overscores can serve both functional and aesthetic purposes, enhancing readability and meaning in various contexts.

To create them in InDesign, follow these steps:

1 Place or type your text—including the overscore candidate.
2 With the Text tool, highlight the text to be linked and that will be underlined to show the link.
3 Open the Character panel, and from its panel menu, select Underline Options toward the bottom to open the Underline Options dialog box.

4 First, turn on Preview on the right, and then check Underline On. You should immediately see your selected text underlined.
5 Set up your overscored text how you like, noting that, initially, the line will appear beneath the text
6 Adjust the Offset field until you have a sufficient negative value offset to place the underline *above* the selected text.

Note that you can also use a strikethrough instead of an underline if your underline is already employed for another purpose.

Redacted Text Effect

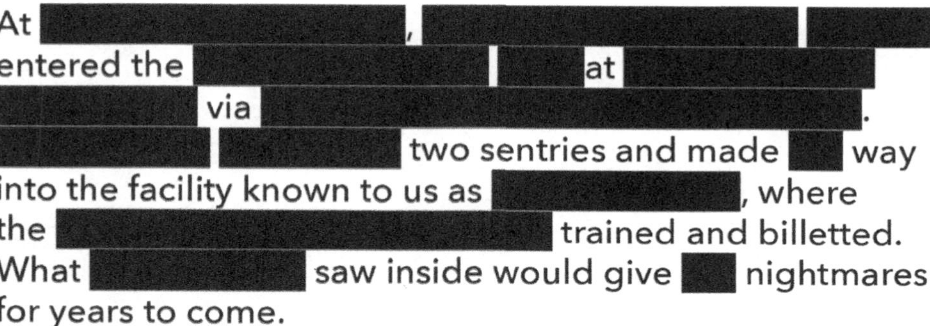

I will be the first to admit, especially under torture (and I'm admitting right here in print, I have no tolerance for pain and…) If you're reading this book, there's a good chance you're from one of the United States' 3-letter intelligence agencies, because I teach them all, but I have to re-iterate what I have undoubtedly told you in class: InDesign does *not* have a redaction feature. Adobe Acrobat Pro does, but that process can't even be started in InDesign.

However, if you want to *simulate* redacted text in InDesign, perhaps for a new Faridah Àbíké-Íyímídé or Jason Bourne novel, follow this recipe:

1 Use the Type tool to select the text you want to redact.
2 With the text selected, open the Character panel by navigating to Window ▸ Type & Tables ▸ Character.
3 On the Character panel menu choose Strikethrough Options.
4 Turn on and watch your strike take shape by activating the checkbox controls beside Strikethrough On and Preview.
5 Set the Weight of your Strikethrough to be around 120-140% of your type size. For example, if you text is set at 10 pt, the Weight should be 12 pt or

higher to account for ascenders and descenders, and to give a little bit of highlight color above and below those. Be careful not to make the Weight so high that the highlight actually underlaps the text in lines above or below your selected text.

6 Leave the Type as Solid (other techniques will show how you can use other line types shortly).

7 Skip the Offset for a moment and set the Color to any color swatch you'd like as your highlighter color. In my effect, I used a modified version of the Magenta swatch to create a pink highlight. Adjust the Tint field, too, if you like.

8 Leave Overprint Stroke, Gap Color, and so on alone, and go back to the Offset field. At this point, you have a thick pink (or other color) line *below* the text you want to highlight. The Offset field is how we make it underlap the text directly.

9 By default, the Offset field is set to Auto, revealed by a value wrapped in parenthesis. Click the down arrow to open the Offset drop-down menu and set it to 0 pt. Your Strikethrough should be partly behind the selected text now.

10 Click the down-pointing-arrow button on the left side of the Offset field to go down from 0 pt offset into negative values. Keep pressing that button until your highlight has risen up to fully encompass—and highlight—your selected text.

11 Click OK, and, for best practice, make a character style from your highlighted text.

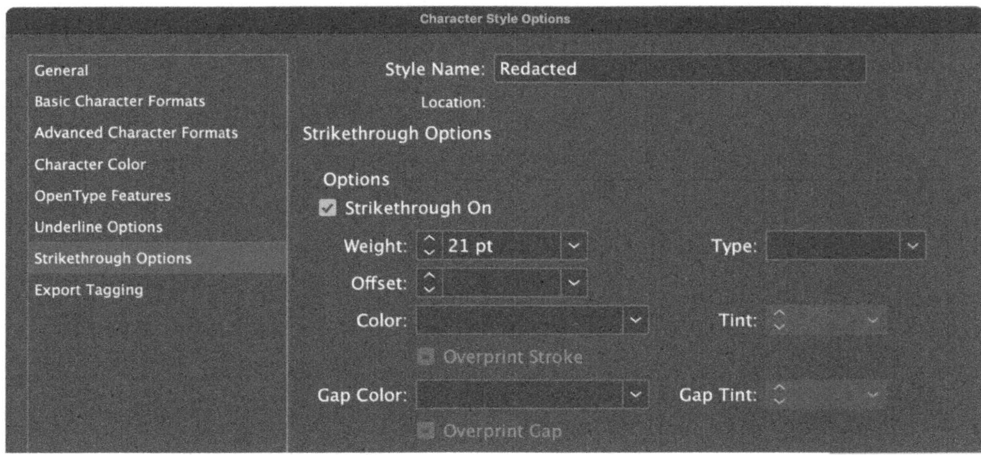

Note that, despite the blackout, there *is* still real text within that black highlighting. Even if you set the text's fill and stroke colors to [None], anyone can find out what the actual text is if they have the advanced counter-intelligence skills of File ▸ Export As from Adobe Acrobat, the old BND and KGB trick of using Acrobat's Select tool to highlight text, or even the Mossad-pioneered specialty skill of copy and paste.

All that said, I've laid out content in InDesign for fiction novels and RPG role-playing games where this sort of faux redaction, and it's methods of circumnavigation, can be significantly fun for the players. While my afore-mentioned intelligence community students might find PDF security laughable (seriously, some of them laughed out loud when I started talking about it), for readers of fiction book and RPG players, this recipe can create an awesome effect that makes them sincerely feel empowered, like world-saving operatives.

Botched Faux Redacted Text

Almost as fun as the discovery that you can, through computer hacking wizardry, thwart secret communiques between the Gray Man and Treadstone, is the hard-earned unearthing that you, the real Jason Dressen have, through your fingerprints and retinal scans, the same unfettered access to Slade Industries as the vile, murderous Jason 2, and that, despite the best efforts of Lovecraftian horrors in Tanis and its various deep state agents, the powers that be… *Have messed up!* What the shadowy organization worked so hard to bury, what it *believed* to be safe from prying, patriotic, *just* eyes, was inadvertently divulged to the worst possible person—*you*—because of an internal mistake!

You're a reporter stalking a life-and-death story that will blow the cover-up wide open.… if you live long enough. Or you're a secret agent disavowed and proclaimed "kill on sight" trying to substantiate your innocence from the frameup orchestrated by your counterpart's intelligence service. Either way, you're *desperate*. You know a FOIA (Freedom of Information Act) request will delivery unto you the records you need to make your case, but they'll be *useless!* Everything that can help you will be blacked out, redacted, and what's left readable in the text will be of use to no one, least of all you. You're a hard-as-nails realist. You *know* how the world works. You try to explain this to your plucky sidekick, but they transmit the FOIA request anyway because, well, plucky sidekicks are always optimistic, that's what makes them plucky… and sidekicks.

Oh. Em (not the measurement). *Gee!*

The Agency traitor screwed up!

The file is delivered under FOIA, but the redaction is only *partial!* There, *right freaking there*, is the information you need to make your story/clear your name/save the free world from the rogue nuke/earn that front row parking spot/whatever *your* win is! The document *proves it!*

Your mission is complete! But it wouldn't have been, if only the idiot at the Pentagon had maintained protocol, if they'd redacted what they supposed to redact, if they'd dispatched Consular Services to deal with you on that bench beside the Potomac before you read the file…

Thankfully for you, the country to whom you've devoted you career and life, and for all of the free world, *someone* made a mistake when redacting that FOIA request!

If you're rolling your eyes, then, well, um, *yeah*. Real intelligence, law enforcement, and information officers do not make such mistakes. But, real-world details need to be set aside for fiction to be engaging and fun.

Maybe you're working in InDesign to layout a thriller wherein the first paragraph's scenarios are part of the story. Or, maybe, it's 600 years in the future and the Earth Alliance isn't offering a high enough salary to attract the top talent in document security, the Sol Conglomerate is a more righteous organization, and you need information from Old Earth… For whatever reason, if you need to recreate the effect of redacted text that isn't correctly, completely redacted, here's several effects you can employ:

Select the text to be (faux) redacted and apply either an underline or strikethrough effect, setting your options as below so that the selected text is readable—just barely. Follow these recipes for different levels of readability, depending on how much you want to challenge your readers to decipher the would-be redacted text.

Slash by Hash (Underline) Faux Redaction

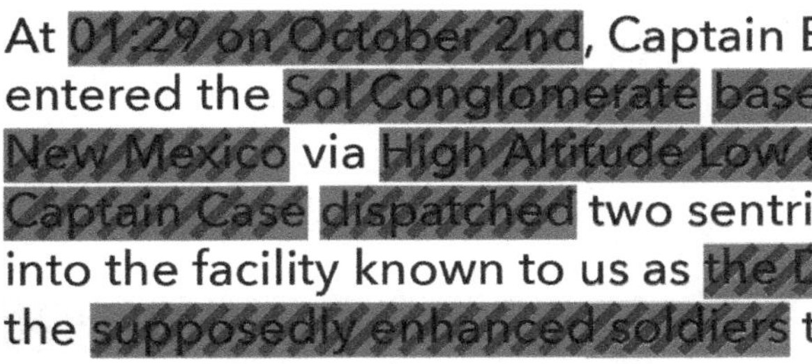

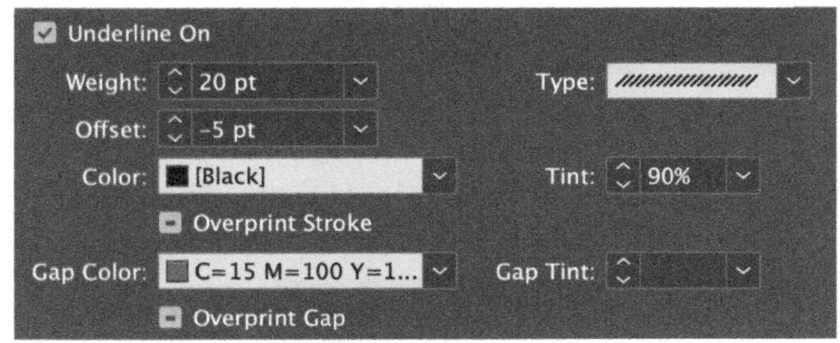

Multi-line (Strikethrough) Faux Redaction

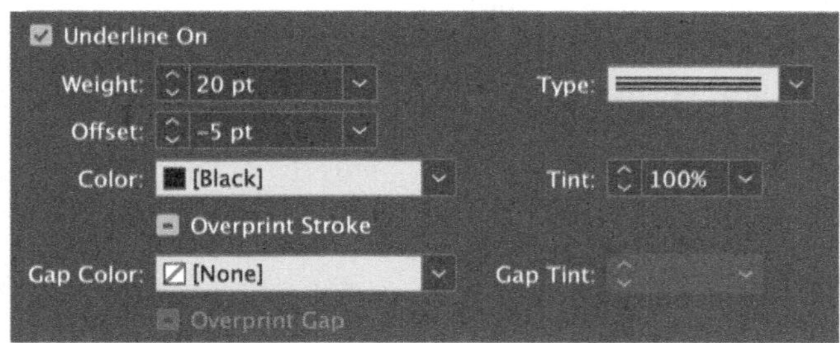

Red Diamond (Strikethrough) Faux Redaction

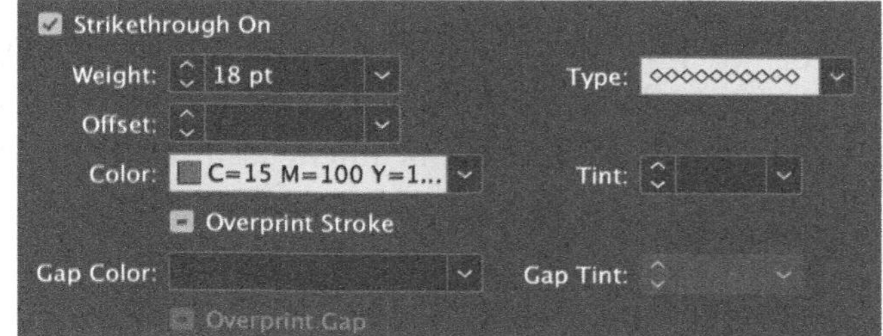

Whiteout (Strikethrough) Faux Redaction

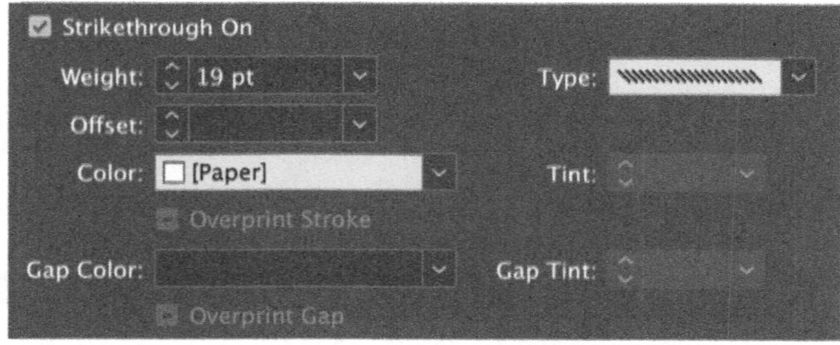

Blackish (Underline) Faux Redaction

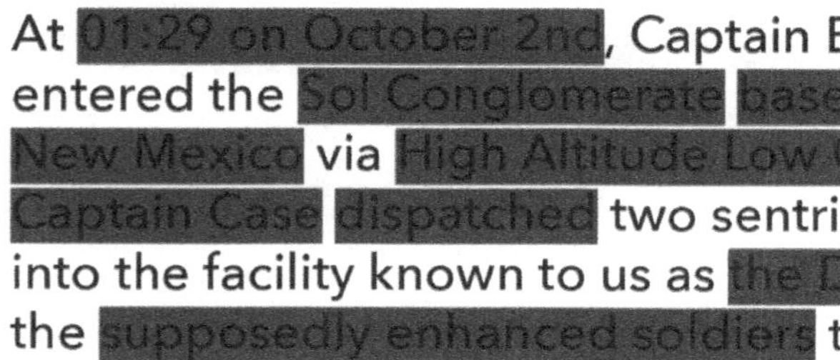

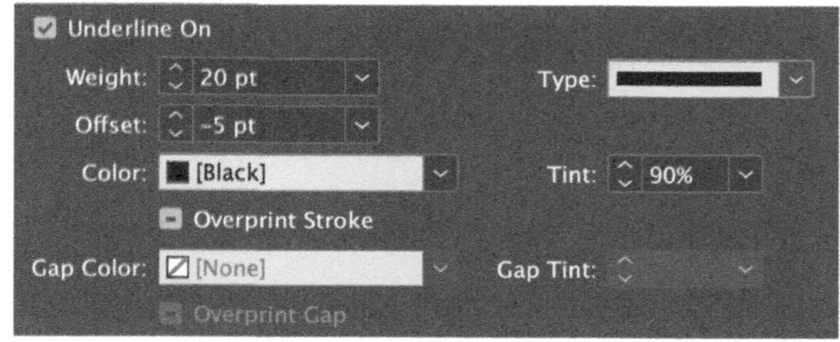

Paragraph Recipes

Reversed, or Negative, Titles

Inctotatem velit, omnistio officatur? Licia ea qui te voluptatum faccus.

Lente conecta cullut officia dolenim illacepudis modit et asit vent odit pro mint quos nos nime mod ea nationsequo volut aliquia tquiatis audandus.

Gita sint quis debit ut dolenimin porendigente odit, sa sunt harum vendi re et estem fugit aut iur?

Or remquia volupti nverume expe cuptibe rchilig nihitamus velecae odisquas es sunt pos maionsequae esti adisciasi tem nam a di se cuscitApit ea sa nonsernatum sedissit quament.

Tem eum sum, con enia cuptur, offictur? Qui cor rehenda eptat.

Int volescipsus ressequi to ommolles net et hil ipsundent, tem quodisi tissinvenit vellam, sitio dest re possi ipsae pro voluptaque ex exceror re sed molupta cus as sant quo voluptat quam que sa que mossequam sit, nonse lam nis qui a sequo id etur aut molute conem natum faciet omnia con eris nos sequamus, as intio. Nem voluptae aceprovid quo et prepe vel in prorumque poritatasit reped ma con pos simi, ilis que pernam es

If you're an old hand at desktop publishing, you may remember that PageMaker and QuarkXPress both had a button that instantly reversed out text—making it white text on a black background. InDesign doesn't have that, but with this short recipe, it's really easy to achieve the same effect, and with greater control. In fact, there are several methods of creating this effect.

1. With the Type tool, select the title or other paragraph to be reversed out.
2. Set the text fill color to white or whatever color you want.
3. Open the Paragraph panel and choose Paragraph Borders and Shading from its flyout menu.
4. Go to the Shading tab and turn on Shading by clicking the checkbox.
5. Set your Shading options to match mine (in the first screenshot) to get the same effect on the white-on-purple text.
6. The fancy gray bar is also paragraph shading—no inefficient management of objects behind titles for me! Those settings are in the second screenshot.

Note that in my settings, the Width field under Top Edge is set to `Text` rather than `Column`. That's what makes the purple background only as wide as the text. If you want the background to be the same width

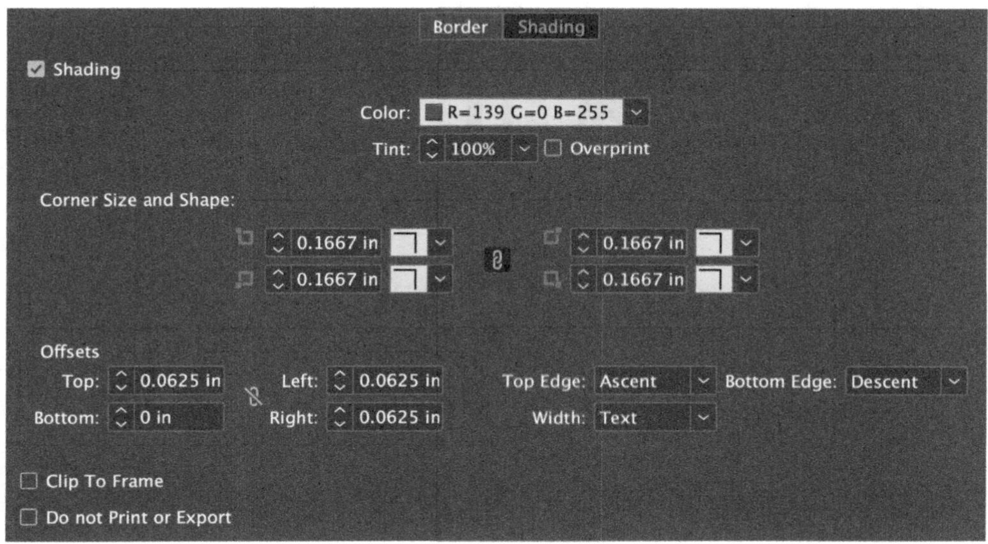

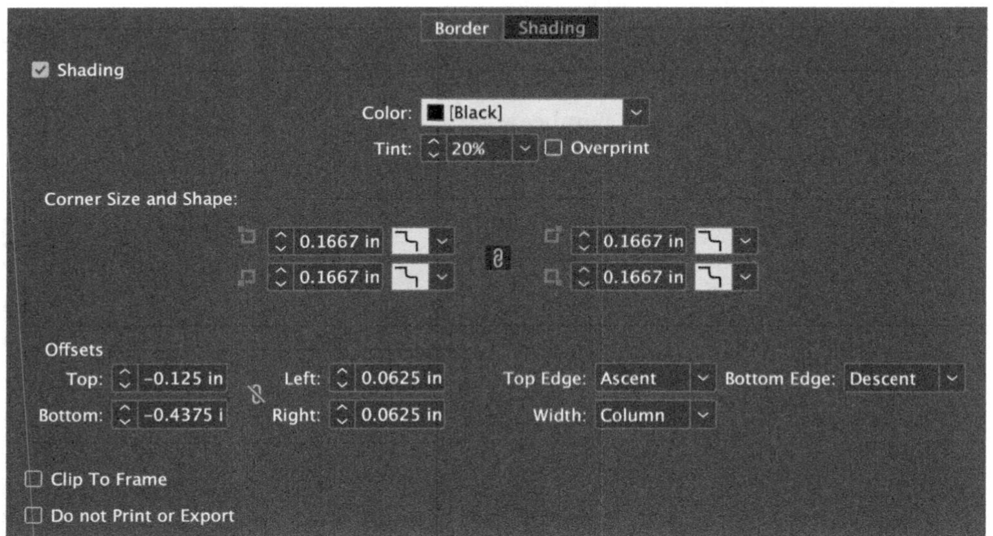

regardless of the paragraph's length, as with the "Atticus Finch" line, change the Width field to `Column`. Also, the Offsets fields are what give the background a little padding around the text so they aren't butting up against each other in the first example, while the second's negative offsets pull the shading inward to make it smaller than the text.

Reversed Titles without Shading

WIZARDS, WITCHES REAL!

A spectular and frightening light show in the early morning sky over downtown could only have been the work of magic, say police. The dazzling fireballs that

If you can't use paragraph shading for some reason—maybe you're already using shading to attain a different effect on the same text—there's another technique just as simple.

1. Select the text to be reversed out.
2. Set the text fill color as desired.
3. Again, go to the Paragraph Panel, but this time, choose Paragraph Rules from the panel menu.
4. Choose Rule Below from the drop-down menu and activate the checkbox control to turn the rule on.
5. Make sure Preview is turn on in the bottom of the dialog.
6. Set the Weight field to a number at least as high as the text's point size (I often use the text's leading size as my starting point).

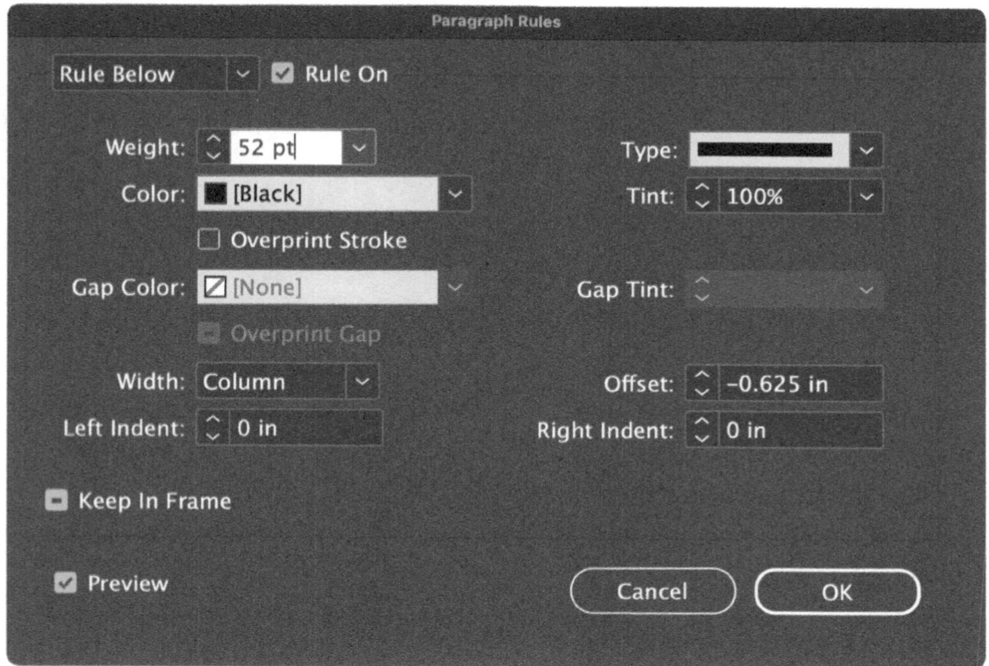

7. Change the Color field from its default of `(Text Color)` to `[Black]` or some other dark color.

8 Set the Width column to `Text`.
9 In the Offset field, lower the value into the negatives. Keep lowing it by clicking the down arrow button until the line moves up and under your text, forming its dark background.
10 The Left Indent and Right Indent fields will also accept negative values to push the background out from either side of the text.

Paragraph (Faux) Redacting

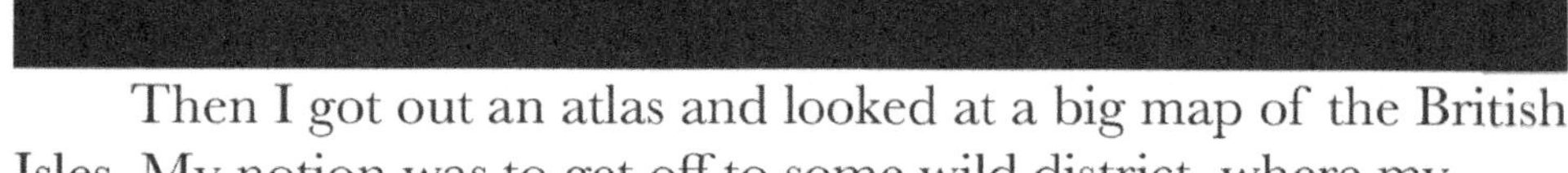

sign of the little black book in which I had seen him making notes. That had no doubt been taken by his murderer.

Then I got out an atlas and looked at a big map of the British Isles. My notion was to get off to some wild district, where my

The "Character Recipes" section ended on various means of achieving faux redaction at the character level. From that you can create a character style and apply it to an entire paragraph, but if you haven't already made the character style, there are easier ways to redact (or fake it on) whole paragraphs. Here's the easiest:

1 Create a new paragraph style for your redacted (or faux) paragraph(s).
2 Edit the paragraph style and make sure it's based on the main, non-redacted style of surrounding text. This will ensure font, size, color, and other changes are inherited by this new style, which we'll call Redacting. Afterall, you want redacted text to look just like surrounding text—except for being blacked out.
3 In the Paragraph Style Options dialog, go to the Paragraph Shading tab and replicate my settings to create the redacted paragraph effect. Reduce the Tint of your shading color if you want to make a faux redaction because paragraph shading, like underlines, appears behind the text (see figure on next page).

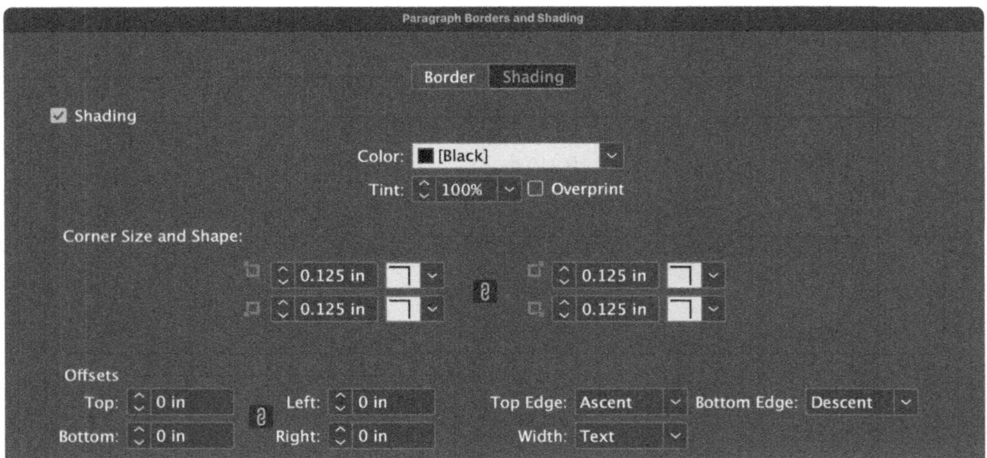

Paragraph Highlighting

sign of the little black book in which I had seen him making notes. That had no doubt been taken by his murderer.

But as I looked up from my task I saw that some drawers had been pulled out in the writing-table. Scudder would never have left them in that state, for he was the tidiest of mortals. Someone must have been searching for something—perhaps for the pocket-book.

Then I got out an atlas and looked at a big map of the British Isles. My notion was to get off to some wild district, where my

Like paragraph-level redacting, you *can* apply a character style to an entire paragraph to create a highlight. That's very easy if you already have the character style for highlighting as we made earlier in this chapter. But, if you don't already have that character style and only need to highlight at the paragraph level, follow the steps for "Paragraph (Faux) Redacting" but set the color of the paragraph shading to something light like yellow or highlighter-green.

Even better, in the Corner Size and Shape area, change the corners to rounded and give them a subtle radius. The result will be rounded corner highlighting, something that's much more difficult to achieve with character-level formatting such as underline and strikethrough (see figure opposite).

Again, paragraph shading is *behind* the text of the paragraph, which means it's a snap to use paragraph shading to call out text.

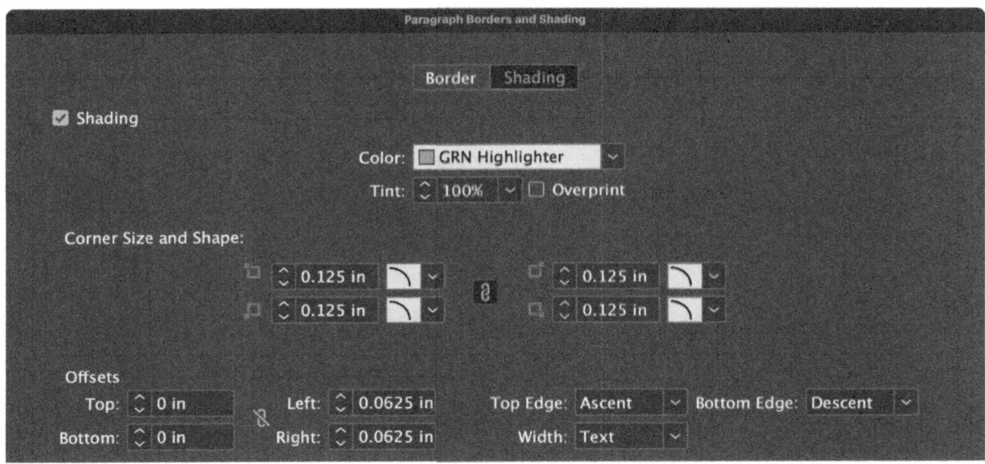

Dyslexic-Friendly, Readability-Enhancing Paragraph Highlighting

There are studies suggesting applying a color filter to text can improve readability of the test for people with dyslexia. This author himself can attest to that. My daughter has dyslexia, and she found it significantly helpful to read text through a yellow-tinted plastic report cover and, later, through yellow-tinted fashion eyeglasses. Whether changing text display from the typical black-on-white to black-on-yellow improves readability for everyone with dyslexia, I don't know. As an accessibility expert for electronic documents, I know what WCAG says, and I've read several studies on the subject, but there doesn't seem to be a widespread consensus so far.

Still, if you'd like to employ the technique to create a version of your document that makes it easier for at least some dyslexics to read, add a yellow paragraph shading or frame fill to your text. The table below shows the best color combinations to try, based on this paper published by, the organization behind all electronic accessibility (https://abbrv.it/IDMCdysHiLite).

Text Color		Background Color	
Hex	**RGB**	**Hex**	**RGB**
#000000	0,0,0	#FFFF00	255,255,0
#0A0A0A	10,10,10	#FFFFE5	255,255,229
#00007D	0,0,125	#FFFFFF	255,255,255

Cast Shadows

Drop shadows are easy and popular. One contributes to the other. They also both contribute to the fact that drop shadows are heavily over-used. Setting that aside, a drop shadow casts a shadow of an object directly behind the object, onto a surface on the same plane. For example, the upper title below is a simple drop shadow. An imaginary light source out front of free floating text causes that text to cast a shadow on the page behind the text. It's a simple faux 3D effect.

The lower title is an example of a cast shadow, a shadow cast by the text but not necessarily onto the same plane. They also create a faux 3D effect, but it's more striking and much rarer, owing in large part to a cast shadow requiring a few more steps than activating a checkbox control on the Object ▸ Effects menu.

Here's how to create a cast shadow on any object:

1. Create and finalize the object that will cast a shadow. In this case, I'm using a text frame containing just a single line of text.
2. Select the object with the Selection tool, and choose Edit ▸ Copy or press CMD+C/CTRL+C.
3. Paste in Place using that command from the Edit menu. An exact copy of the object will appear in front of the existing one. This copy will be what we'll call the Shadow Object.
4. Fill your Shadow Object with a black-to-white gradient using the Gradient panel (Window ▸ Color ▸ Gradient). I recommend using a rich black rather than just the process [Black] swatch.

   In my case, because I'm dealing with text, I'll need to make sure I'm working with the text fill instead of the frame fill.
5. Select the Shadow Object again and set its Blending Mode to Multiply.

   You can do that on the Effects panel (Window ▸ Effects), in the Effects dialog by choosing Object ▸ Effect ▸ Transparency, and by a couple of other means. Whichever route you take, find the Mode menu, which isn't labeled in all places. If you don't see any drop-down filed called Mode, look for a field whose value is currently set to Normal. If you open it, you should see options like Multiply, Screen, Overlay, and more. Select Multiply.

The Multiply blending mode will hide the white in your gradient, effectively darkening everything behind the Shadow Object by the black and different shades of gray.

6 Switch to the Selection tool, and select the Shadow Object again.
7 Go to Object ▸ Transform ▸ Shear.
8 Turn on Preview, and then use Shear controls to distort your object to look like a shadow winding out behind, and away from, your first frame of text. When you're happy, click OK.
9 Finally, send the Shadow Object behind the main text by choosing Object ▸ Arrange ▸ Send Backward. You may have to do this a few times to get it behind the text.

Adjust the location, shear, and transparency until you're satisfied with your cast shadow.

For a little extra realism, blur the receding edges of your shadow with InDesign's Basic Feather, Directional Feather, or Gradient Feather effects from the Object ▸ Effects menu or the Effects panel.

Cast Shadows Forward

Not all shadows fall behind the objects casting them. Drop shadows must, but that's one of the reasons drop shadows are seen as overused even cliché in some circles. If you want to make an object cast its shadow forward instead, you just have to add one more step to your process.

1 Follow the steps in the "Cast Shadows" tutorial, but don't send the Shadow Object behind.

2 With the Shadow Object selected, choose Object ▸ Transform ▸ Flip Vertical. That will make the Shadow Object's a reflection of itself.
3 Line up the baseline of the Shadow Object text, now at the top, to the baseline of the original title text.
4 Now set the shear, location, and transparency as needed.

Dynamic Text Cast Shadows

Let's say we're creating a cast shadow effect on the titles for a series of reports or posters. Rather than employ the previous techniques of duplicating and manipulating for every document's or page's unique title, we can build a single set of title and shadow(s) that automatically stay in synch after a single text change—whatever the main text is changed to say, the shadow (or multiple shadows) will dynamically update to match.

I created and wrote about the following InDesign technique back around 2003. It was my very first assignment for one of the giants in graphic design publications, *CreativePro.com*, which would also launch *InDesign Magazine* a couple of years later. In that piece, I presented the following technique in a way that would be out of place in this tome—I wrote the tutorial like a classic noir mystery.

Although the website has undergone significant changes in the intervening years, many of which were not kind to the pre-WordPress formatting of the article, my original hard-boiled design detective pulp fiction tutorial is still available if you'd like to read it (https://abbrv.it/

IDMCCastShadowsCase). If 1940s detective noir isn't your genre just follow this recipe for dynamic drop shadows on text that automatically match the text.

> She had more curves than a Bezier tool, and she flowed in with the supple grace of a placed story moving through threaded text frames. Her eyes were rich black, a full-on CMYK mix of deep, mysterious ink. Her smooth skin was like aqueous varnish on ultra-smooth paper. Most striking of all were her lips. I knew instantly what must be written on the cap of her lipstick tube: PANTONE 1797C.

The secret to making this technique work is to use text variables.

1. Go to Type ▸ Text Variables ▸ Define.
2. Click the New button and start a new text variable called Title.
3. Set the Type field to Custom Text, and then type into the Text field the title of your first publication. Use the arrow menu to the right if you need special characters.
4. Click OK and then Done to get back to your document.
5. Create a text frame to hold the main version of the Title.
6. With the I beam cursor flashing inside the text frame, go to Type ▸ Text Variables ▸ Insert Variable... ▸ Title. The title you just created will appear.
7. From here, follow the same steps as the "Cast Shadows" or "Cast Shadows Forward" recipes.
8. When done, select the Shadow Object and main title frame, and group them together with CMD+G/CTRL+G to make it easier to keep them together as you make the versions for the rest of your reports, posters, or what-have-yous.

Any time you need to change the title, return to Type ▸ Text Variables ▸ Define, and edit the Title variable. Your edits will instantly apply to the main title and all of its shadows.

Cast Multiple Shadows

Miss Registration

I noted earlier that you can use multiple shadows. I wanted to remind you of that. The real world rarely has a single source of light interacting with a subject. There are usually multiple direct or indirect sources of light, each causing a solid object to cast a different shadow in a different direction. Those shadows also often overlap and mix. You can recreate this greater realism of multiple shadows using the same techniques we've worked through already. Ideally, of course, you should use the "Dynamic Text Cast Shadows" technique so that all your shadows, no matter how numerous they are, can be edited with a single point of text entry. Additionally, if you use different colored shadows, explore other blending modes than just Multiply. You'll get some interesting (realistic and not so much) interactions of shadow colors.

Vertical Side Heads with Tables

1. Overview	The Tables chapter of *InDesign Master Class: Type & Tables* provides a detailed guide on creating and working with tables in Adobe InDesign, covering both basic and advanced features. It explains how to create tables from scratch, convert text into tables, and import tables from external sources like Microsoft Excel. The guide emphasizes the benefits of using live linking with Excel, allowing automatic updates to tables within InDesign. Styling tables is a key focus, with instructions on applying strokes, fills, and borders, as well as controlling text alignment and adding header or footer rows. Advanced table manipulation, such as merging and splitting cells, inserting images into cells, and adjusting row heights and column widths, is covered in detail. The document also highlights the use of cell and table styles for consistent formatting and suggests the use of scripts for more complex tasks. Importantly, it discusses handling large datasets across multiple pages with repeating header rows. The guide concludes with practical tips for working with graphic cells and handling large amounts of data effectively within table structures. Overall, it serves as a comprehensive resource for mastering tables in Adobe InDesign.

Vertical side heads are a unique technique to employ when you're going for a design that is modern, rebellious, sleek, or elegant—and none of those is mutually-exclusive. There are several methods for getting vertical side heads to work, with this being the easiest but least recommended. I don't recommend this particular technique to most people for two reasons: First, it's extremely limited, working primarily when each head and section occupies a single frame. It can work with multiple frames, but it can also get unwieldy just as quickly. The other major reason I usually advise against this technique is that it has a significant impact on accessibility. WCAG and, by incorporation, Section 508 for the Workforce Rehabilitation Act, specifically disallows using tables for primarily layout purposes. That said, there are occasions such as print-only documents when this technique is useful. Moreover, teaching you this first allows me to simply build on it with more flexible and accessible techniques on the following pages.

1. Create a table with a single row for each section and two columns for the entire table. In my example, I need only a single row, so I set 1 and 2 as my values.
2. In the first column, type your heading.
3. Open the Table panel from Window ▸ Type and Tables ▸ Table.
4. Among the four Rotate Text buttons, click the second button, the clockwise-rotated 90-degree *T*. That should rotate your heading such that it starts at the top and reads downward.
5. Click in the second column of your table and type, paste, or place the body copy defined by the heading.
6. Format both pieces of text, adjusting their respective column widths as needed using either the Column Width field on the Table panel, or by hovering your cursor over the dividing line between columns and dragging left or right.

Vertical Side Heads without Tables

The Tables chapter of *InDesign Master Class: Type & Tables* provides a detailed guide on creating and working with tables in Adobe InDesign, covering both basic and advanced features. It explains how to create tables from scratch, convert text into tables, and import tables from external sources like Microsoft Excel. The guide emphasizes the benefits of using live linking with Excel, allowing automatic updates to tables within InDesign. Styling tables is a key focus, with instructions on applying strokes, fills, and borders, as well as controlling text alignment and adding header or footer rows. Advanced table manipulation, such as merging and splitting cells, inserting images into cells, and adjusting row heights and column widths, is covered in detail. The document also highlights the use of cell and table styles for consistent formatting and suggests the use of scripts for more complex tasks. Importantly, it discusses handling large datasets across multiple pages with repeating header rows. The guide concludes with practical tips for working with graphic cells and handling large amounts of data effectively within table structures. Overall, it serves as a comprehensive resource for mastering tables in Adobe InDesign.

- Creating and importing tables
- Live-linking to Excel data for instant updates (and not-your-responsibility data updates)
- Adding, removing, and editing ~~columns~~ and rows and headers and footer rows

As I alluded to previously, tables should be used for tabular data rather than for layout-only purposes. Using a table merely to divide page geometry or get around more complex techniques will almost certainly cause you to bump up against a limitation of the table method at some point, not the least of which is the very real possibility of making your content more difficult to understand for people with disabilities using assistive technologies.

The following is a more flexible, scalable, and accessible method of cleverly creating vertical side heads—especially with multi-page stories—though it does take a little extra work.

1 Place your entire story—heads and body copy—into InDesign, and style them as needed (preferably with paragraph styles).
2 Create a new text frame roughly the size of your first heading-that-will-be-a-side-head (I recommend setting this text frame to auto-size horizontally and/or vertically).
3 Cut the heading from the main story and paste it into that new frame.
4 Switch to the Selection tool by pressing ESC.
5 Select the heading frame you just filled, and choose Object ▸ Transform ▸ Rotate.
6 In the Rotate dialog box, set the Angle to either 90- or -90-degrees, as you prefer. Click OK.
7 Still using the Selection tool on the heading's frame, drag the Anchored Object Control, the little blue box toward the top-right corner of the frame (possibly rotated to a different location), and drop it in the body copy, at the very start of the first sentence of body copy.

That's all there is to it. This method anchors headings into the body copy at the start of the text the header defines, meaning the heading will actually *be* at the very start of the body copy. And, of course, that's where headings belong, logically and for accessibility purposes. Moreover, by anchoring, if the main story reflows, taking that section-starting paragraph to a new location, the heading will automatically follow, sticking with its corresponding body copy. Therefore, you have the flexibility of using this method throughout a longer, threaded story without significant cleanup work every time the story reflows. Also, because the heading is in its own frame, you can apply object effects to the headings that you couldn't (without also applying them to body copy) using the "With Tables" approach.

Here are a couple of tips that might prove helpful when employing this technique:

- Use paragraph styles for everything.
- Build object styles for at least the headings. Object styles can apply and change not just things like drop shadows, strokes, fills, and so on. They can

also apply paragraph styles, set auto-sizing options on text frames, and control the exact placement of anchored heading frames relevant to their body copy text and the frames and page margins containing those frames, ensuring a perfect fit and position even when text reflows. The image at the start of this technique shows the Anchored Object Options I used to keep the vertical side heads in place relative to their modifying body copy.

- Use the following threaded variation if you prefer.

Vertical Threaded Side Heads

Side heads are each in their own frames, which, as you saw, are completely disconnected, non-threaded text frames. You *can* use this technique with threaded frames, which makes some aspects of working with vertical side heads easier while complicating others.

I typically choose to thread my side head frames together when I: First, have enough headings to make it worth the effort—fewer than half a dozen heads is nearly always more easily done with unthreaded text frames, and; second, when I have a reasonable assurance that I won't be adding or removing many sections (and heads), or swapping them around too much. Given a fair number of headings and a belief that a copy editor isn't going to jump out of the shadows waving major changes at me, I'll go with a threaded frame technique.

It's easy, really: I'll leave all the headings in a single list, as a completely separate story (see "Get a List of Only Your Story's Headings"). Then, among the Sidehead paragraph style's Keep Options I'll change the Start Paragraph option to In Next Frame, forcing every hard return-separated item in the headings list to jump to the next side head frame in the sequence. If done correctly, the headings will then land in their appropriate spots, in the correct sequence.

Once you have the disconnected method down pretty well, give the threaded variation a shot.

Get a List of Only Your Story's Headings

If you've got a long document with a large number of headings that you need in their own list (perhaps to convert into vertical side heads) and not too many other paragraph styles in the same story—it will probably be much more efficient to duplicate the story and strip out everything except the headings using Find/Change. To do that, follow these steps:

1. Click inside the story with the Type tool and press CMD+A/CTRL+A to select all text, across all linked frames, even overset text.
2. Still using the Type tool, create a new text frame off to the side on the pasteboard and paste (CMD+V/CTRL+V). You now have a complete copy of the story; don't worry if the frame is overset.
3. Click inside the new text frame and press CMD+Y/CTRL+Y to open the story in Story Editor. Take note of the paragraph styles visible in the left column. If you don't see the Style Name Column activate it by choosing View ▸ Story Editor ▸ Show Style Name Column. Each paragraph that is not styled as a heading must be removed. For that, we'll employ Find/Change.
4. Select Find/Change from the Edit menu to open the Find/Change dialog; switch to the Text tab if it isn't already there.
5. To the right of the Find What field is a tiny menu marked by an @ symbol. Click on it and go to the very last menu, Wildcards, and choose Any Character (see figure on next page). This will insert the special ^? Code into the Find What field telling InDesign to search for any letter, number, white space, and so on.
6. Down in the Find Format section, click the tiny button adorned with a *T* and a magnifying glass. If you don't see the Find Format section, click the More Options button on the right. In the Find Format Settings dialog go to the very first pane, Style Options, and choose from the Paragraph Style drop-down menu the first style of paragraphs to removed from your would-be list of headings. Leave all other settings alone and click OK.

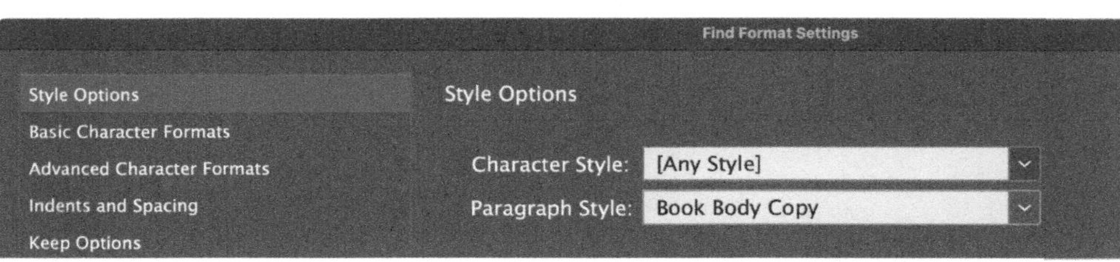

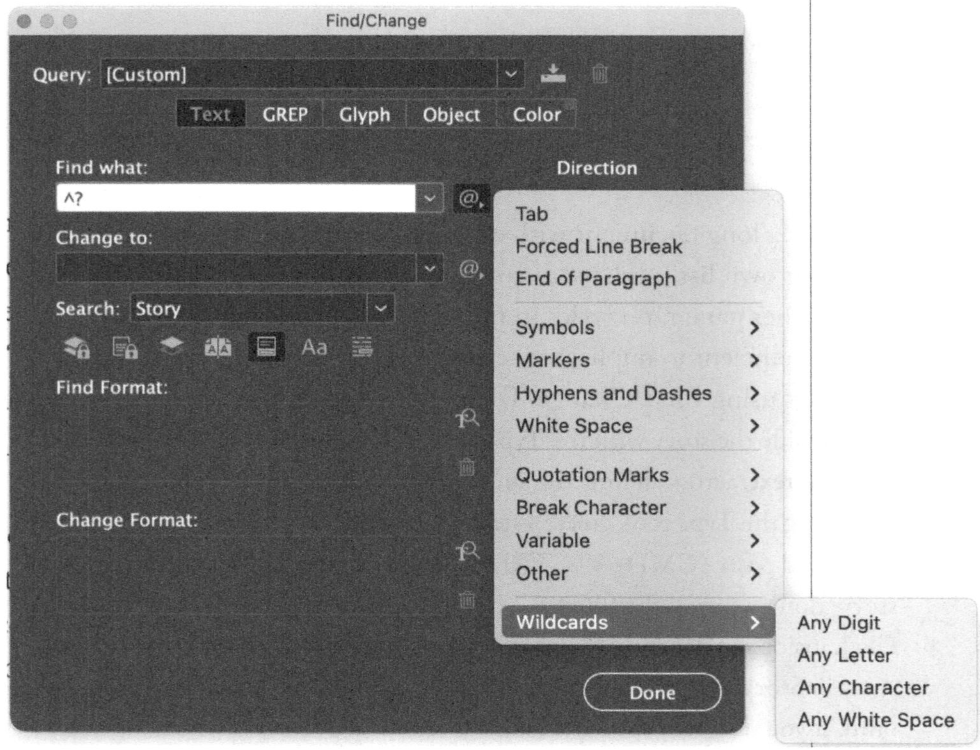

7 Finish the search and replace criteria by leaving the Change To and Change Format fields blank, setting the Search drop-down menu to Story, and deselecting all buttons beneath the Search field. Click Change All on the right and every paragraph, every glyph, assigned the specified paragraph style will instantly disappear from the story.

8 Repeat the above steps until you've completely eliminated all text that you don't want in your list of headings (e.g. text that isn't a heading). In the end, you should have a nice compact list of headings.

Add a Number Before Headings

05 | Stories

Now that you've mastered setting and styling type on a page, it's time to think bigger, about writing,

In many documents, especially academic, scientific, and government white papers, reports, and other documents, headings need to be numbered. Most InDesign users know how to use numbered lists (especially after reading *InDesign Masterclass: Type & Tables*), but don't forget that InDesign can keep track of many different numbered lists. Just because *this thing* is automatically numbered 1 doesn't mean *that thing* after it has to be number 2.

Here's how to number your headings the right (and safe) way:

1 Create a paragraph style for your numbered headings and edit that style.

2 In the Bullets and Numbering pane of the Paragraph Style Options, set the List Type field to Numbers.

3 In the List field immediately below it, choose New List.

4 Up will pop the New List dialog. Set the List Name to Headings, Heading 1, H1, or something similar. I went with the name Chapter Numbering.

New List

List Name: Chapter Numbering

OK

Cancel

Options

Continue Numbers across Stories

Continue Numbers from Previous Document in Book

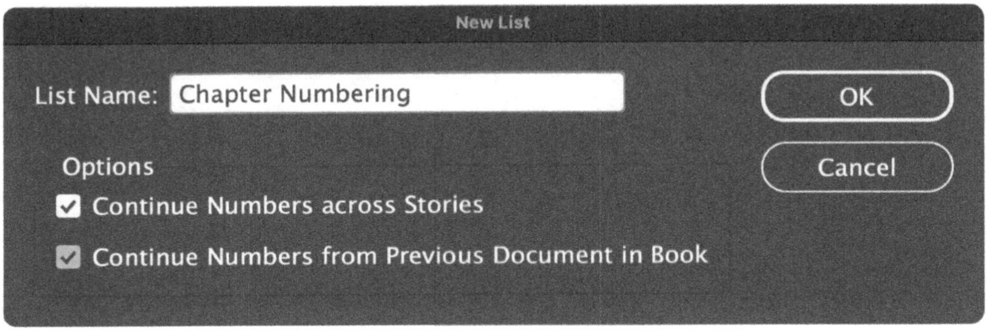

5. Choose whether you want numbering to continue across stories and/or book documents (by enabling the relevant checkbox[es]) or reset at each story or book document (by disabling the relevant checkbox[es]). Click OK when you've made your choices.
6. Configure the Numbering Style and Bullet or Number Position options to taste, and click OK on the style.

Now paragraphs of text using that paragraph style—and only such paragraphs—will have sequential numbering, even if other numbered lists appear between them.

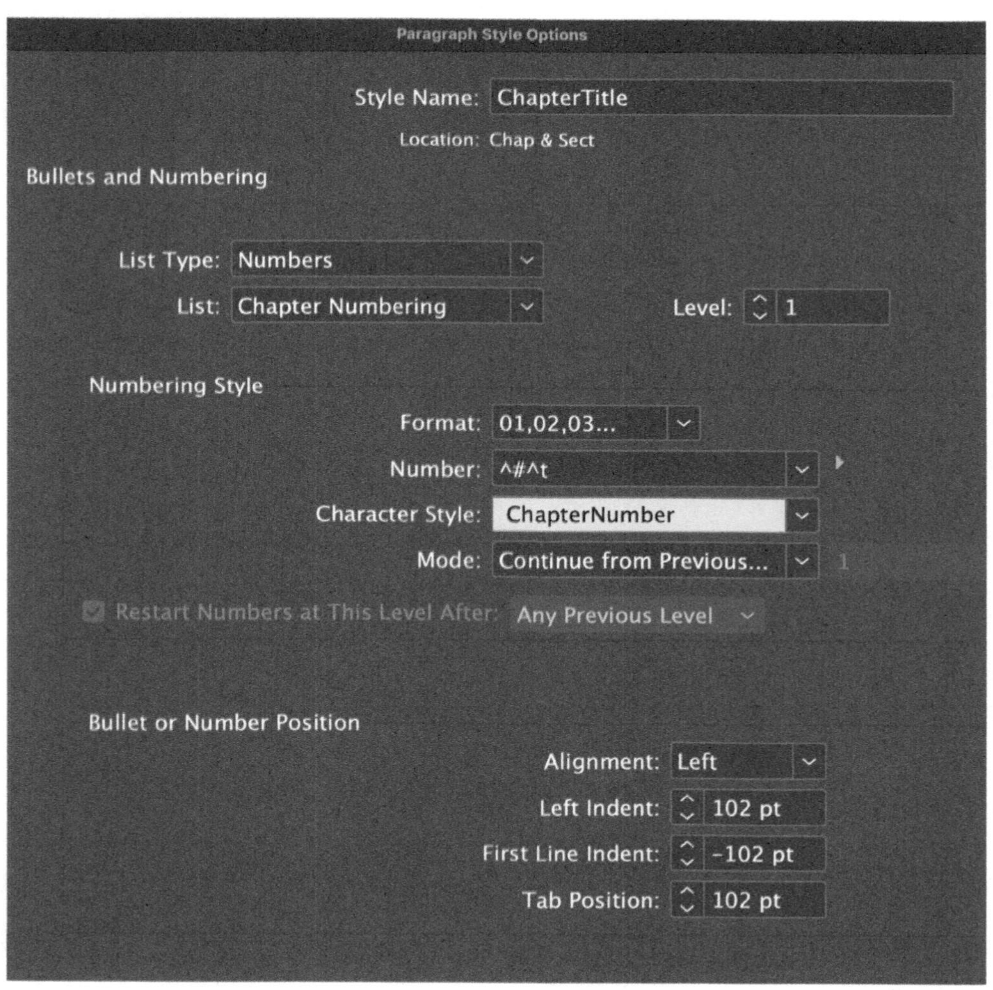

Add a Symbol Before Headings

❯ Section 2: Concerts and Events

Aborepedi doluptatur? Um doluptaspero odis sa sim cuptas endelest, imi, consequam explique quo earume poriberum, volo quas architae inihit estiis reprem

Headings are an everyday part of most documents. They're text needed to help breakup, organize, and categorize content. When coupled with PDF bookmarks, assistive technology Elements lists, and other such features, headings are an incredible navigation aid. They can also be mac-and-cheese—yummy, but boring. Here's one way to spice up that box.

1 Create the paragraph style for your headings.
2 Edit the style, and go to the Bullets and Numbering pane of the Paragraph Style Options.
3 Set the List Type field to Bullets.

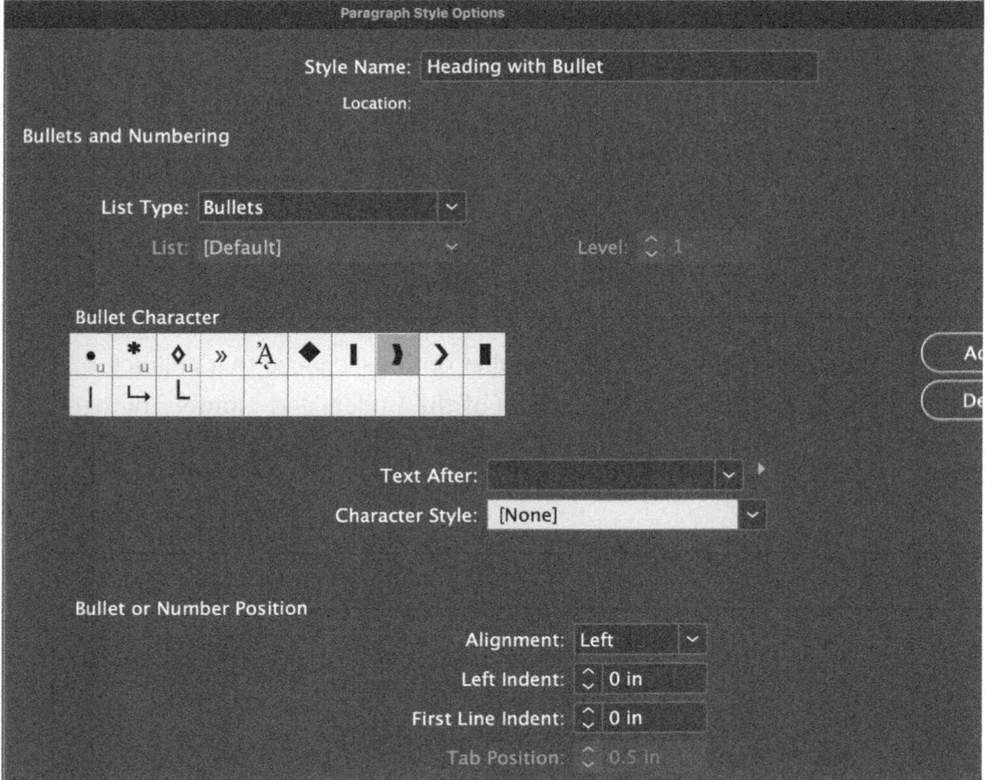

4 Odds are, the six default bullets won't thrill you, so click the Add button to the right.
5 In the Glyphs panel-like Add Bullets dialog that appears, go looking for the perfect symbol to prefix your headings. For example, try setting the Font Family to Wingdings and scrolling to the end of that font's glyph set. There are some great arrows there, as well as circles, dots, squares, boxes, and stars with three to 16 points. Try other fonts, too, especially symbol fonts. In my example I used Heavy Right-Pointing Angle Bracket Ornament from the font Zapf Dingbats.
6 Choose the character you want and click OK.
7 Then set the other options—Text After (I used a space instead of the ^t code for a tab), Bullet or Number Position, and so on.

Add a Different Color Symbol Before Headings

❱ Section 2: Concerts and Events

Aborepedi doluptatur? Um doluptaspero odis sa sim cuptas endelest, imi, consequam explique quo earume

For a little more spice in your headings, make the symbol before the headings a different color. Create a character style for the different color, then follow the steps for "Add an Arrow or Other Symbol Before Headings". When you get to the bullet options, choose that character style in the Bullet Character section of the Bullets and Numbering pane.

Create an Outline Structure from Paragraphs

Styles

└ Paragraph Styles

└ Logical Style Names

└ Cascading Styles

└ Character Styles

└ Drop Caps

└ Nested Styles

└ End Nested Style Here

I'll be frank—*hi, Frank!*—Yes, my humor includes *The Rocky Horror Picture Show*. So, I'll be frank—*hi*—*stop*. To be *candid*, the following technique is usually way more work than is worth it. However, once in a great (*Scott!*) while, it can be useful.

The figure above shows a nested list, an outline structure, created entirely using paragraph styles with bullet symbols. If I was creating fewer than a dozen of these, I'd probably do them by hand. However, if you want to be able to create a long list like that example with the ease of applying paragraph styles, follow this recipe:

1. Create paragraph styles for each of your outline levels. In my example I have three—Outline L1, Outline L2, and Outline L3.
2. Set all the formatting, Based On, and whatever else is needed in those styles.
3. Assuming Outline L1 doesn't need a symbol before it, edit Outline L2 and navigate to the Bullets and Numbering pane in its Paragraph Style Options dialog.
4. Set the List Type to Bullets.

5 Click Add.

6 In the Add Bullets dialog, set the Font Family to Arial. (Darnnit, Janet! Just trust me!)

7 In the main area, scroll down a little. Just past unaccented and then accented alphabet are symbol glyphs that can be used to create boxes and diagrams. One of those is Box Drawings Light Up and Right, which is the one I used. Select that or whatever else catches your fancy, and click OK.

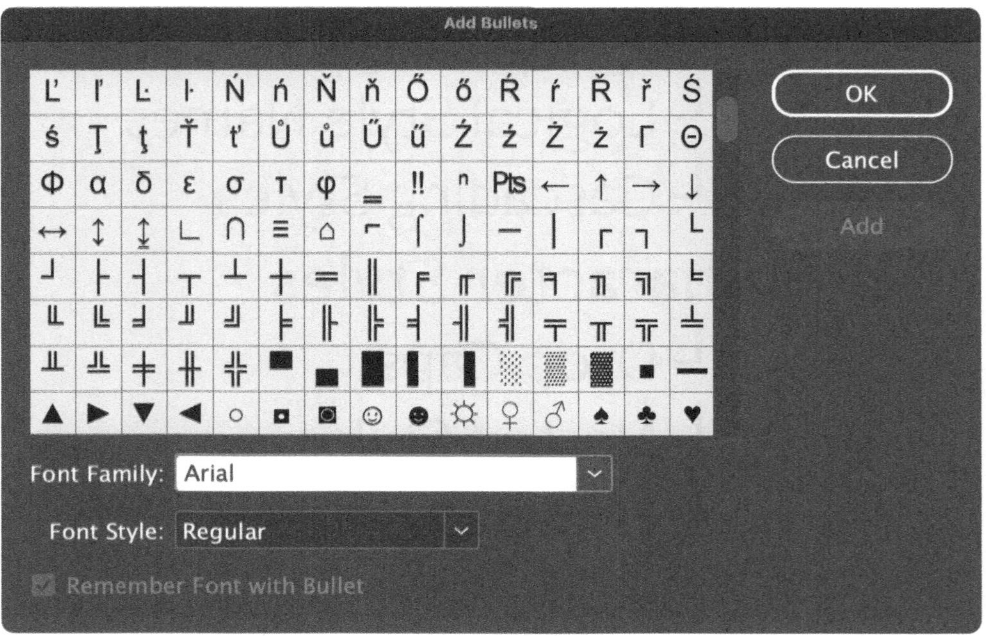

8 Back in the main Bullets and Number pane, the symbol you chose should be selected. If you have Preview enabled in the bottom-left corner of the dialog, you'll see that symbol displayed in your text.

9 Now set the Left Indent to give you the level of indenting you require of your outline, and then click OK.

10 Edit the next outline level paragraph style—Outline L3 in my case—and set the same options. This time, though, set the Left Indent to be twice as large as the previous one.

11 Repeat for every level of paragraph style in your outline.

Keep in mind that Arial has more than just the Box Drawings Light Up and Right. With a little exploration and careful glyph selection, coupled with judicious indents, you could create a much more complex outline structure, too.

Add a Placed Image Before Headings (Manually)

Flower Bed 101: Textual Contrast

Incorporate plants with different foliage textures, like smooth-leaved hostas, fuzzy-leaved lamb's ear, and wispy grasses, to add depth and visual appeal.

Want to put an icon, a multi-colored dropcap (without using OpenType-SVG), or some other image in front of headings? Here's how:

1. Create your illustration—raster or vector—either directly in InDesign or in Illustrator, Photoshop, Canva, or whatever. It can be in any format InDesign understands, including PNG, JPG, SVG, PSD, PDF, or even Adobe Illustrator AI format. (Astute observers will notice that the illustration I used is one of Illustrator's default symbols from the Symbols panel.)
2. Place that illustration into InDesign, if it's externally created. If it was created directly in InDesign, make sure you group all the components of the illustration by selecting them and pressing CMD+G/CTRL+G.
3. Select the illustration and copy it with CMD+C/CTRL+C.
4. Create (or edit) a text frame and enter the text before which you want that illustration.
5. Move your Type tool cursor to the beginning of that text and paste the illustration using good old CMD+V/CTRL+V—no special pasting required. Your illustration should appear in front of the text, though you may want to insert a tab, a full space, or another space from the Type ▸ Insert White Space menu to give the icon some separation.
6. Switch to the Selection tool and size the illustration as needed for best fit. You may have to zoom in to be able to grab the control corners.
7. Still with the Black Arrow (Selection) tool selected, click on the illustration, and then choose Object ▸ Anchored Object ▸ Options. In the Anchored Object Options dialog you're looking to insure that Inline is chosen, and, if

you need to move the illustration up or down, you do that with the Y Offset field. When it's in the right place, click OK.

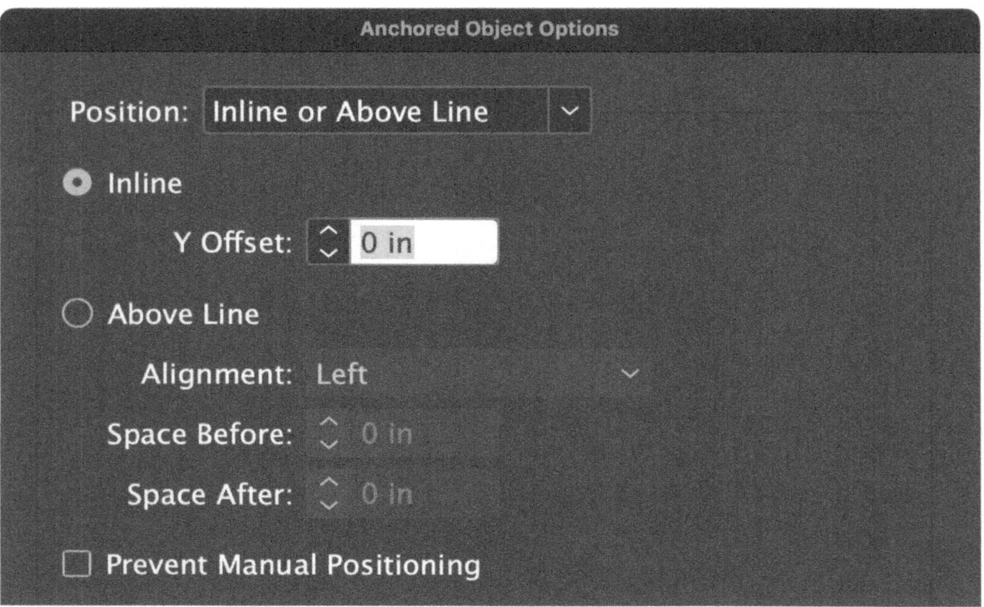

8 With the illustration still selected, open the Object Styles panel from Window ▸ Styles ▸ Object Styles.
9 Create a new object style called... something that indicates your usage of the illustration. Maybe Header Icon, Sidebar Icon, or whatever makes sense for your use of the illustration. This new object style will record the Anchored Object Options by default, but you can also edit it to automatically apply the sizing of the graphic frame and the fitting of the image to the frame, which will be important if you change illustrations per header (more on that shortly).
10 Apply the new object style to the selected object.
11 Switch to the Type tool and select the illustration and any space(s) or tab you've placed after it.
12 Copy those with CMD+C/CTRL+C.
13 Now move through the rest of your headings, one at a time, setting the cursor at the beginning and pressing CMD+V/CTRL+V to paste. The illustration, with its object style and spacing, should appear perfectly without the need to manually adjust anything, unless you need to...

Add Different Placed Images Before Headings

You can also put different illustrations before each heading, or maybe each heading level, or whatever. If that's your need, follow the instructions for "Add a Placed Image Before Headings (Manually)". Then, using the Black Arrow (Selection) tool, go to each image, one at a time, select it, and place a new image with CMD+D/CTRL+D. Alternatively, load in all your images, then click to place one at a time in those icons, replacing the original illustrations with the new ones from the loaded cursor. The use of an object style with anchoring and fitting options built in is going to make all your icons appear consistently.

Add a Placed Image Before Headings (via JavaScript)

Aspirin-Free Workflow: Live-Caption All Images at Once

If you have many images requiring captions, save yourself a headache by creating Live Caption objects on them *all* in one step. Instead of right-clicking an individual image, go to the Links panel and highlight its entries for all the images requiring captions, photo credits, or other live or static caption objects. Now right-click one of those Links panel items. On the context-sensitive menu, you'll find a Captions submenu, complete with the commands Generate Live Captions, Generate Static Captions, and Caption Setup. Executing one of the former pair of commands will generate a caption on all the highlighted objects in one fell swoop.

Before *InDesign Masterclass: Type and Tables,* I wrote many other books, including *Mastering InDesign for Print Design & Production* (Sybex, 2007 and 2010 editions). It was a few years ago, but, surprisingly, the book is still 99.86% applicable to InDesign in 2025. One of the features I created for that book was something called "The Aspirin-Free Workflow," a series of sidebar boxes that specifically focused on tips and techniques that could save you from process- and software-based headaches. Above is an image of one such "The Aspirin-Free Workflow" box, complete with my vector illustration of an aspirin tablet. Here's how we did it, but, given the changing nature of computers, I can't guarantee it will work for every version of InDesign on every version of a given operating system.

1. Create your illustration—raster or vector—either directly in InDesign or in Illustrator, Photoshop, Canva, or whatever. It can be in any format InDesign understands, including PNG, JPG, SVG, PSD, PDF, or even Adobe Illustrator AI format.
2. Place that illustration into InDesign, if it's externally created. If it was created directly in InDesign, make sure you group all the components of the illustration by selecting them and pressing CMD+G/CTRL+G.
3. Open your favorite JavaScript editor, which can even be Mac TextEdit or Windows Notepad.
4. Paste the following JavaScript (I really hope you bought the PDF or EPUB version of this book so you don't have to retype it all):

```
   // Get the clipboard contents
   var clipboardContents = app.scriptPreferences.clip-
boardContents;

   // Define the paragraph style name to target
   var targetParagraphStyle = "MyParagraphStyle";  //
Replace with the actual paragraph style name

   // Loop through all paragraphs in the active document
   var doc = app.activeDocument;
   var paragraphs = doc.stories.everyItem().paragraphs.
everyItem().getElements();

   for (var i = 0; i < paragraphs.length; i++) {
       var para = paragraphs[i];

       // Check if the paragraph uses the desired style
       if (para.appliedParagraphStyle.name == targetPara-
graphStyle) {
           // Prepend the clipboard contents
           para.contents = clipboardContents + para.con-
tents;
       }
   }
```

5 In the script, change “`MyParagraphStyle`” to the actual name of your document’s heading style. For instance, if you’re trying to add icons before the text attached to the FeatureTitleAspirin paragraph style, replace `MyParagraphStyle` with `FeatureTitleAspirin`.

6 Save the script with a name like `AddIconsBeforeStyle.jsx` in the correct folder for your operating system.

Mac: `/Users/<YourUsername>/Library/Preferences/Adobe InDesign/Version <Version>/en_US/Scripts/Scripts Panel`

Windows: `C:\Users\<YourUsername>\AppData\Roaming\Adobe\InDesign\<Version>\Scripts`

7 Back in InDesign, size the illustration to *exactly* the dimensions you want it to appear in the text.

8 Create, save, and apply an object style to the illustration’s frame (meaning: do it with the Black Arrow Selection tool selected).

9 Select that illustration with the Selection tool and copy it to the system clipboard with CMD+C/CTRL+C.

10 Open Window ▸ Utilities ▸ Scripts.

11 On the Scripts panel, expand the User section to reveal your User scripts. If you wrote and installed the JavaScript correctly, you should see AddIconsBeforeStyle as an option.

12 Double-click it and wait a moment. If everything was done correctly (and if the script still works in your current version of InDesign), the contents of your clipboard—the illustration—should appear in front of every instance of the paragraph style you specified.

If it works but the formatting is a little off, try adjusting the object style you created before undoing and starting over with the illustration.

If the script doesn’t work at all, try the following troubleshooting steps:

- Make sure the name of the style in the Paragraph Styles panel and the script are exactly the same, without space, punctuation, or capitalization differences.
- Try copying just a word or letter of text and running the script. If the script is working, it will insert that word or letter. If that works but it doesn’t work with your illustration, make sure you’re copying the illustration correctly—by selecting its frame, not the contents of the frame, with the Selection tool. Note: If you have the Content Grabber (a.k.a. the donut) turned on View ▸ Extras ▸ Show Content Grabber, you might be accidentally selected the contents rather than the frame.
- Try a simpler illustration, such as a placed icon in PNG format.

Heading Rules

Simple Rule Below

Personnel Data Changes

Please ensure that any changes to personal information, such as addresses or emergency contact details, are submitted through the HR portal. It is crucial that this information remains up-to-date to avoid

Follow these steps to create this simple and elegant separator below your headings.

1 Select the text of your title.

2 From the Paragraph panel, go to the panel flyout menu and choose Paragraph Rules.

3 Select Rule Below and turn it on with the checkbox control.

4 Set your options like mine to get the same simple, 2pt stroke floating a little below the heading text.

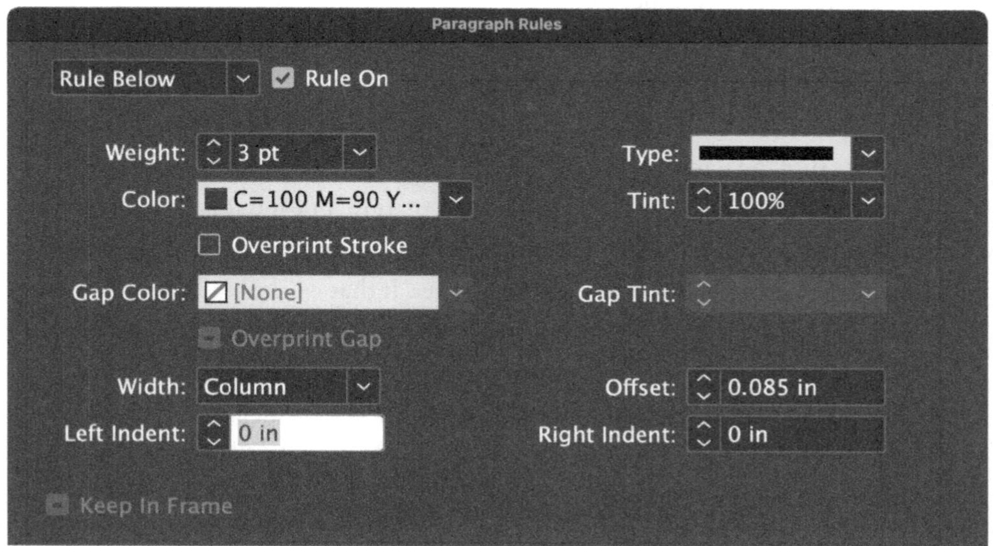

Simple Rule Above

Employee Performance Reviews

Employee performance reviews are scheduled annually to assess individual contributions and set goals for the upcoming year. Managers will provide feedback on strengths, areas for improvement, and

You can also put rules above paragraphs.

1. Follow the same procedure as above...er, as below, which is above... Hmm. How about this? Follow the same procedure as for "Simple Rule Below", which is above this text in this book. Now let's get down and get funky. Try to keep up.
2. This time, don't turn on Rule Below. Instead, choose Rule Above from the drop-down menu in Paragraph Rules, and turn that on.
3. Replicate my settings. You can see I went for a thicker weight stroke, changed its color to stand out, and set the Width field to `Text` so that the rule is automatically only as wide as the heading text itself. It will always match the width of your headings, whether they have one glyph or an entire line.

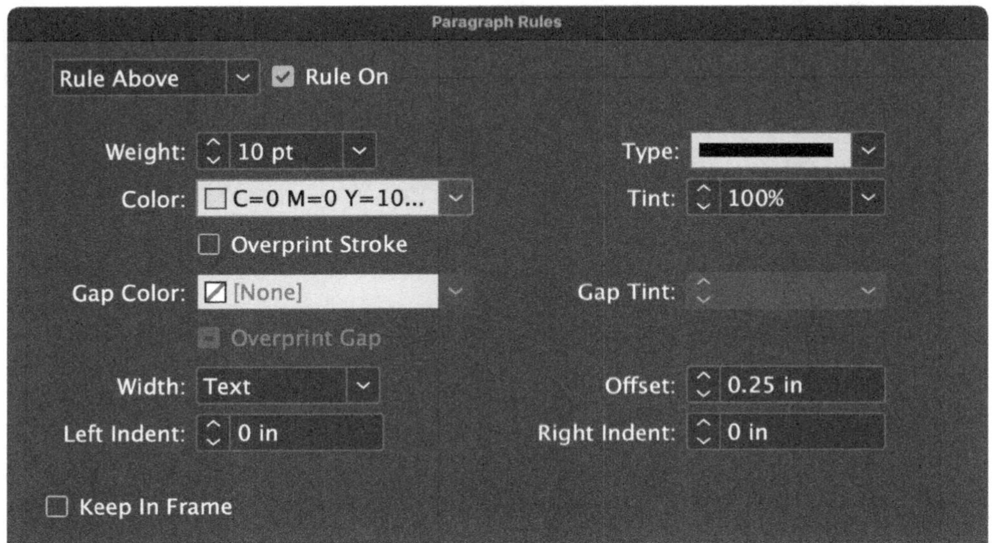

Short Rules Above

Expense Reimbursement

To submit expense reimbursements, employees must fill out the designated form and attach all relevant receipts. Approved expenses

If you want a short rule that *doesn't* automatically resize to text, follow this recipe.

1. Do everything the same as in the "Simple Rule Above" technique.
2. Select `Column` from the Width field.
3. Give the Left Indent and/or Right Indent fields positive values, increasing until you've whittled your rule down to the width you want.

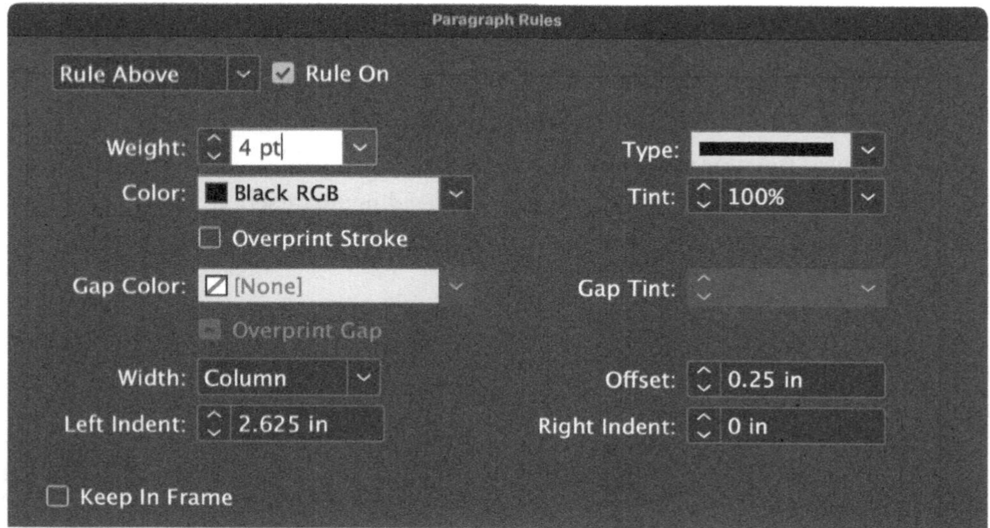

Multiple Rules Above

Attendance Policy

Employees are expected to adhere to the company's attendance policy, which allows for a set number of sick and personal days. Any

Heading rules are so fun, why stop at one?

1 Complete the "Short Rules Above" technique.
2 On the same text, highlight it again and go to Paragraph Rules.

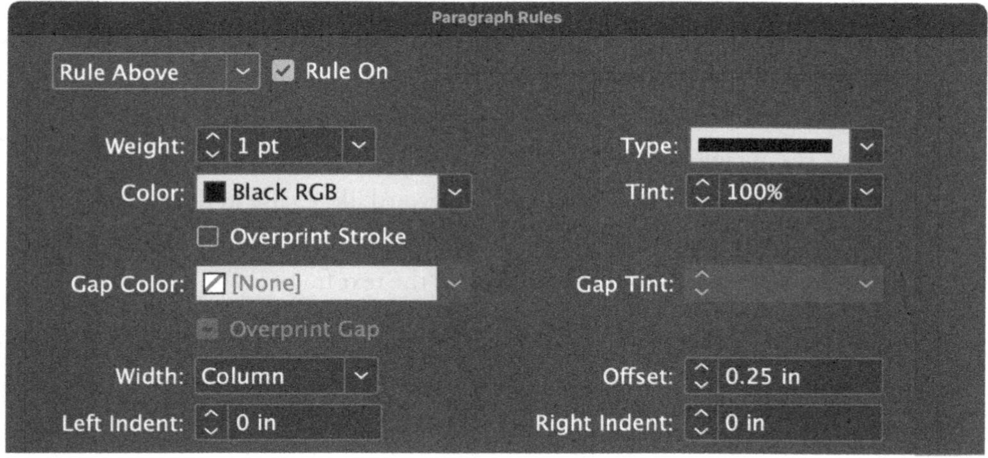

3 You should already have Rule Above turned on, so select Rule Below and turn that on, too. You'll now have a rule under your text.
4 Drop the Offset field's value down into the negative and keep clicking that down arrow button until this line meets the rule above.

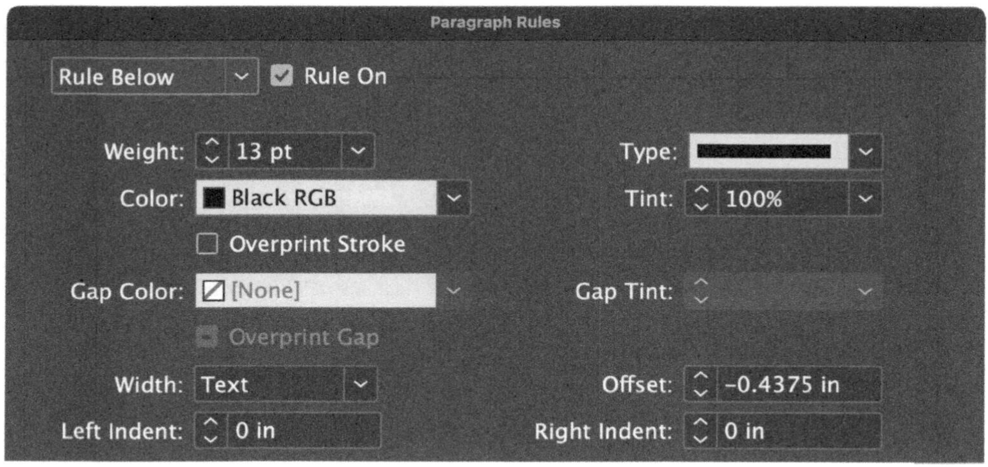

Multi-Colored Rules

Wage or Salary Increases

Wage or salary increases are reviewed on an annual basis and are based on individual performance, company budget, and market

Heading rules aren't limited to single colors. Try this effect.

1 Add the Paragraph Rule(s) you want.
2 In the Type field, choose any type of stroke other than `Solid`. I selected the fifth type in the drop-down list, `Thin - Thick`, for my Rule Above, and the third, `Thick - Thin`, for my Rule Below.
3 Adjust the Weight and Offset until you can see the details of your rule.
4 Change the Gap Color field to the color you'd like to use in the empty parts of the rule(s). Note that I also set negative Left and Right Indents to push the rules out beyond the bounds of the text frame.

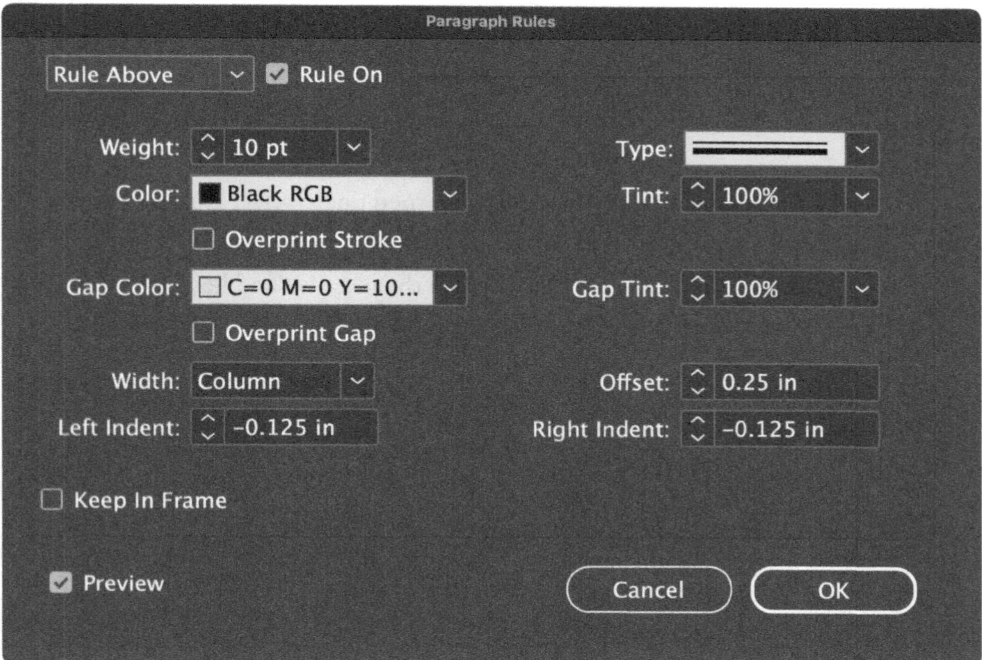

Boxed Paragraph

Ruby Key

Creating boxed paragraphs for headings, instructor-only content, and note and tip boxes used to entail some fancy footwork, but with Paragraph Borders, it's a breeze.

1. Select the heading text.
2. From the Paragraph panel's menu choose Paragraph Borders.
3. Set your borders like mine, seasoning to taste.

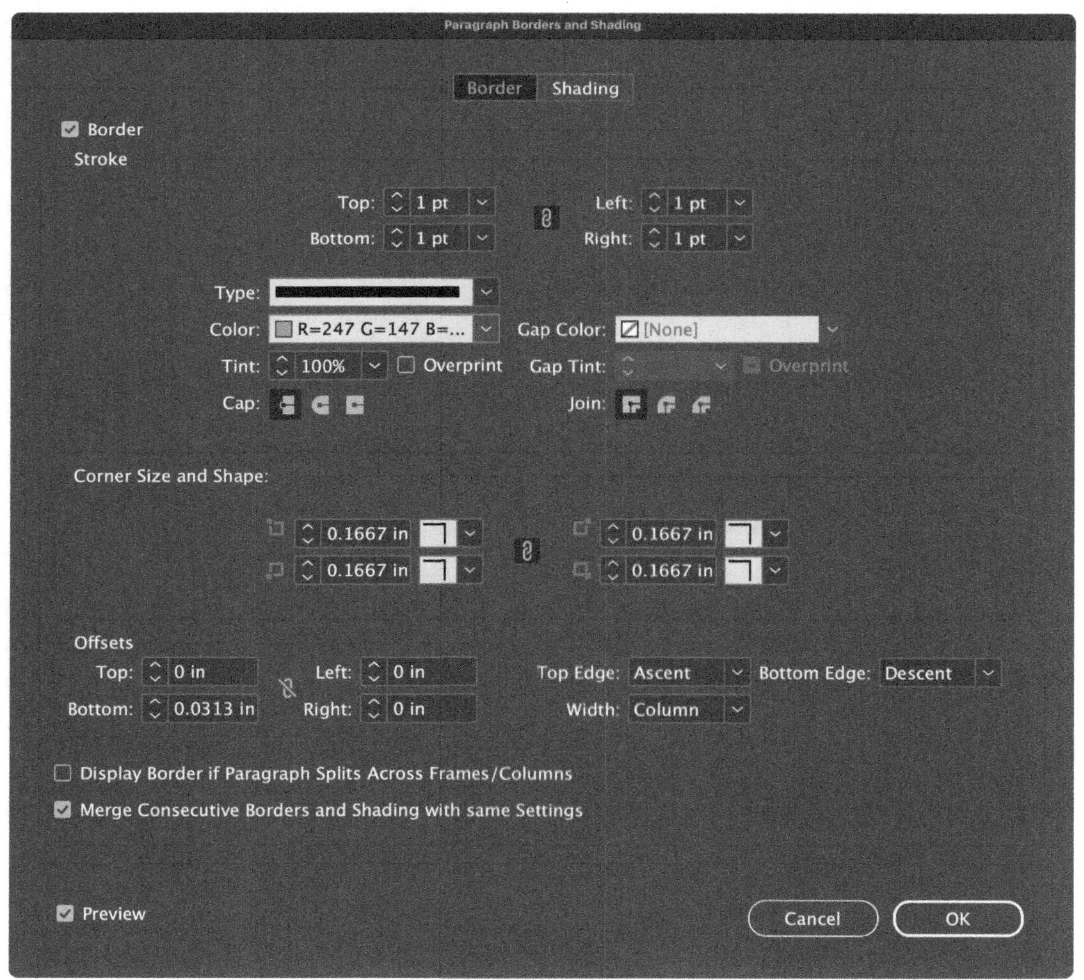

Angled Box Paragraph

Personnel Neural Interface Updates

All crew members must submit for quarterly neural interface diagnostics. Any updates to personal data, cognitive augmentations, or biometric markers should be transmitted to the ship's AI for secure integration. Fail-

Looking to put a modern twist on your boxed paragraphs? Try replicating my settings below for an angled, or mitered, box paragraph.

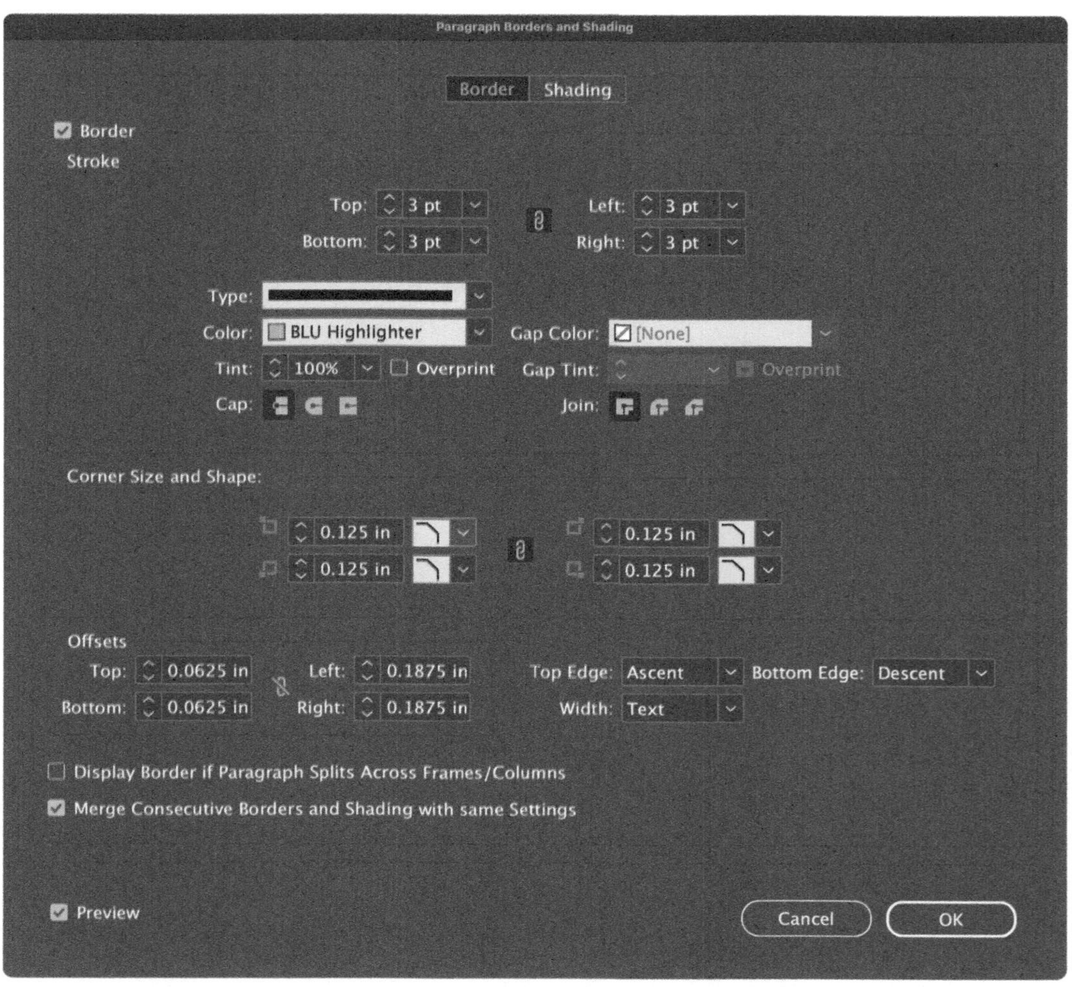

Scalloped Box Paragraph

GMs are free to use any riddle you would like of any difficulty level. GMs may ask the riddle as a group or as individuals.

This scalloped box paragraph, used to style game master hints in a Dungeons & Dragons® adventure module, incorporates the same corner shapes in the border and shading, though a subtle *partial* filling of the border is accomplished by *not* reducing the Paragraph Shading offset to account for the multi-line stroke type in the border.

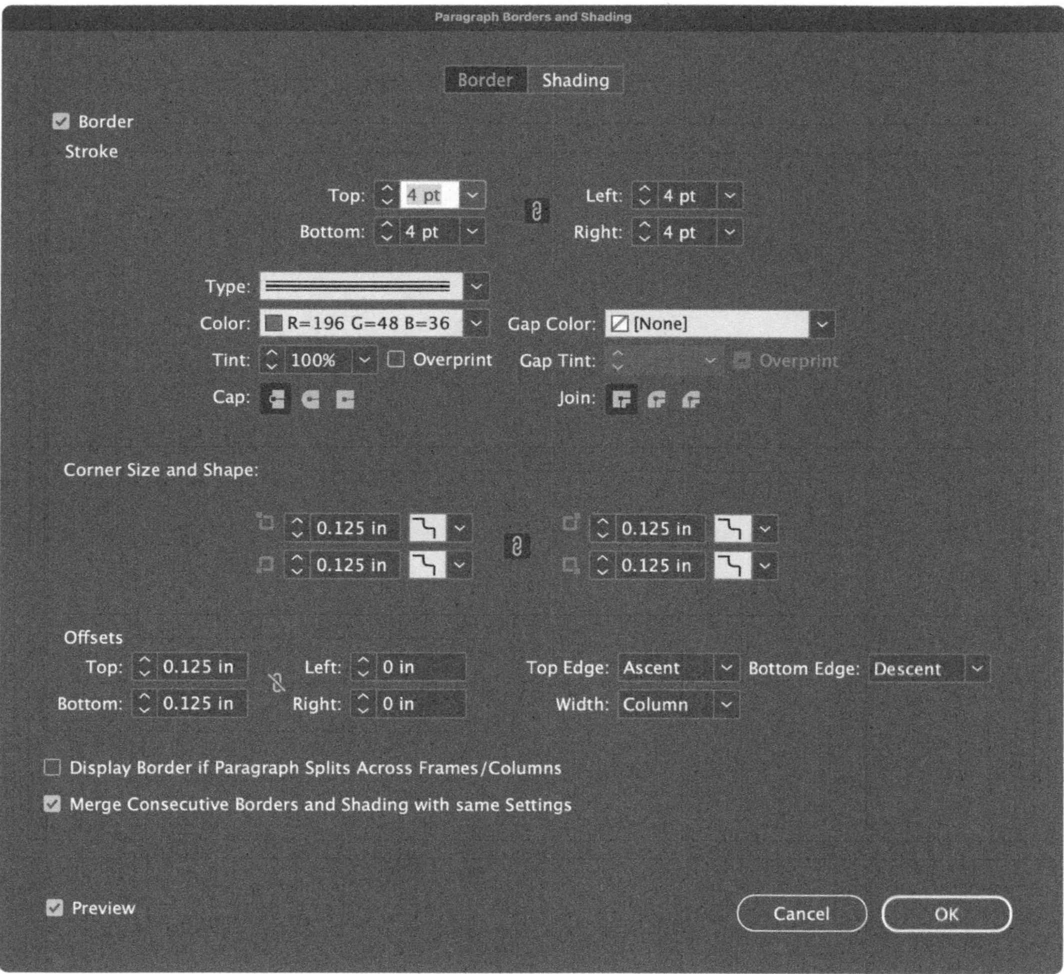

Rules on Two Sides

Quantum Performance Evaluations

Crew efficiency is evaluated through quantum entanglement feedback, ensuring alignment with mission protocols. Performance assessments include both biological output and predictive AI modeling, ensuring opti-

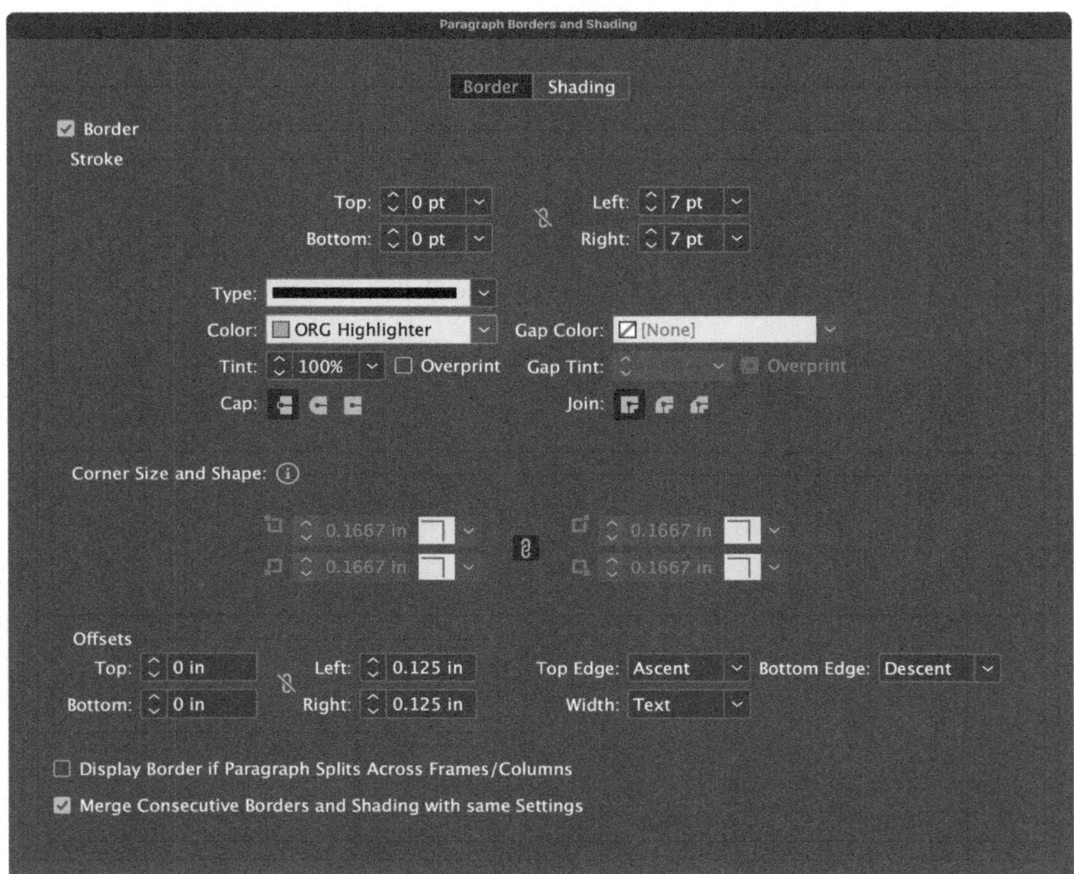

Rules Up to Headings

Cryo-Salary Adjustments

Wage recalibrations occur following each successful mission or deep space cryo-phase. Adjustments are based on individual output, system

This method has a drawback in that it isn't all that flexible. You may find yourself constantly adjusting the Right Offset field.

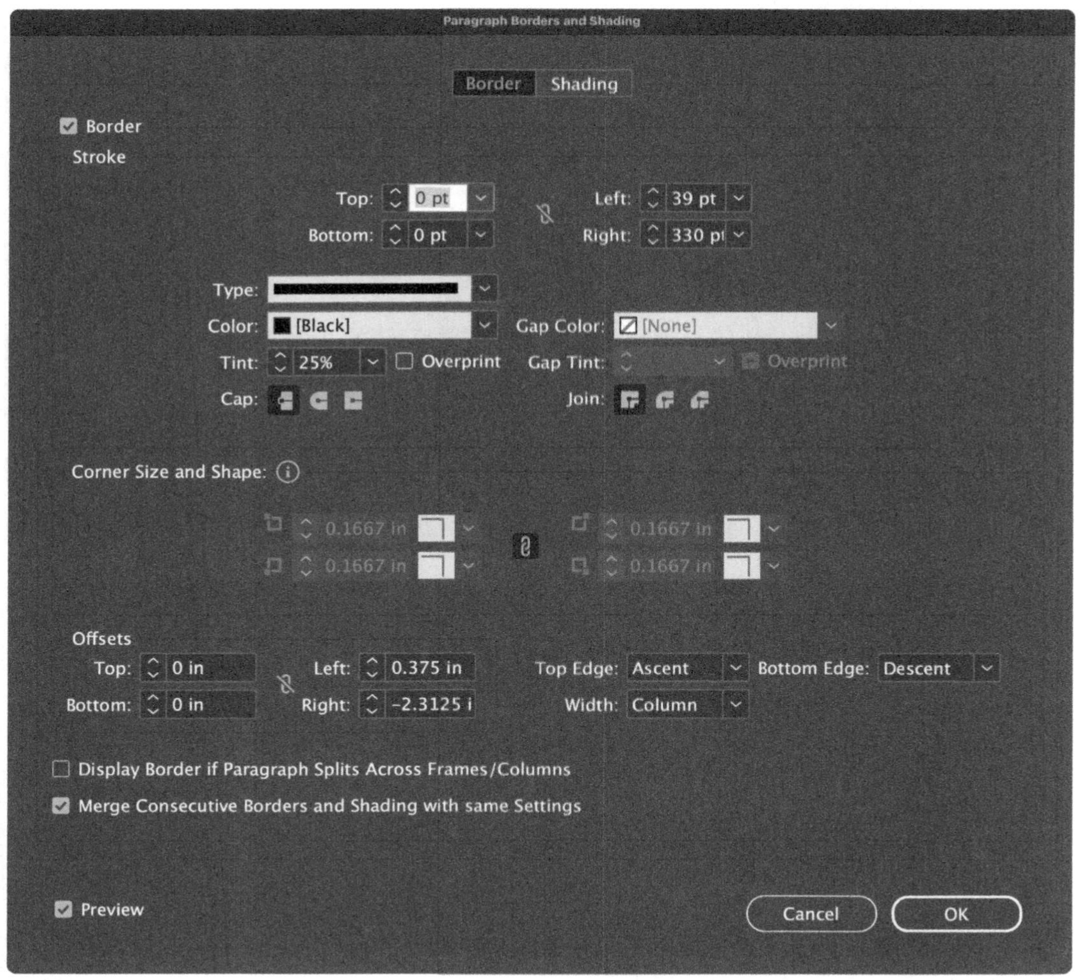

Rules Up to Headings (Better)

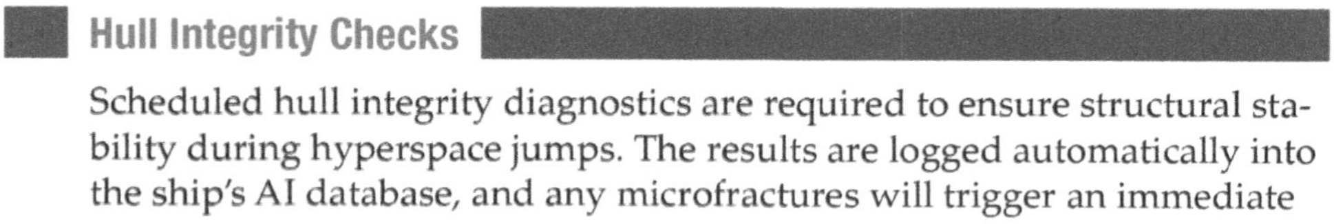

Hull Integrity Checks

Scheduled hull integrity diagnostics are required to ensure structural stability during hyperspace jumps. The results are logged automatically into the ship's AI database, and any microfractures will trigger an immediate

A more flexible method, albeit one that precludes the page or frame background being visible around the heading, is to forgo Paragraph Borders and instead combine Paragraph Shading with Paragraph Rules. The rule blots out the shading with [Paper] to create the effect of a heading magnetically floating between color bars.

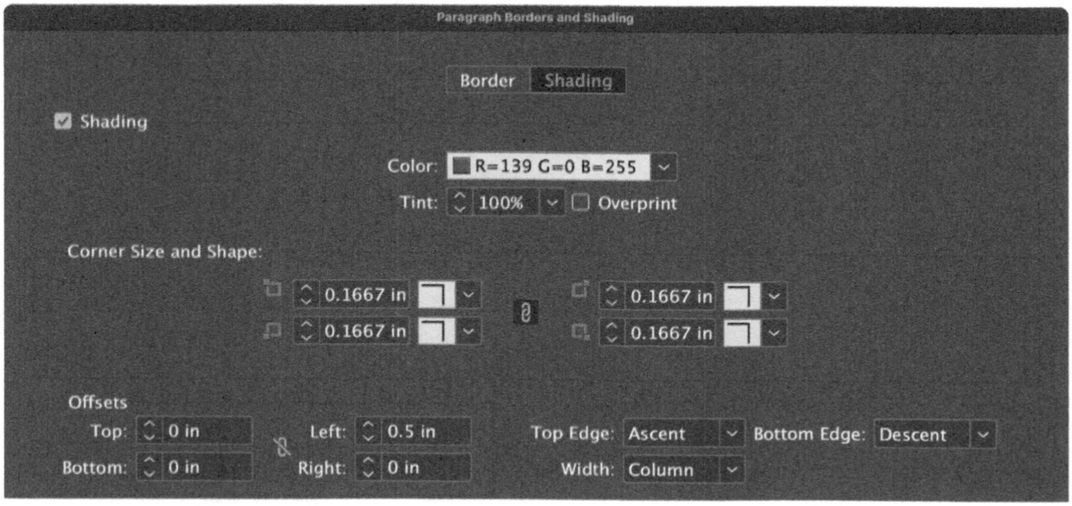

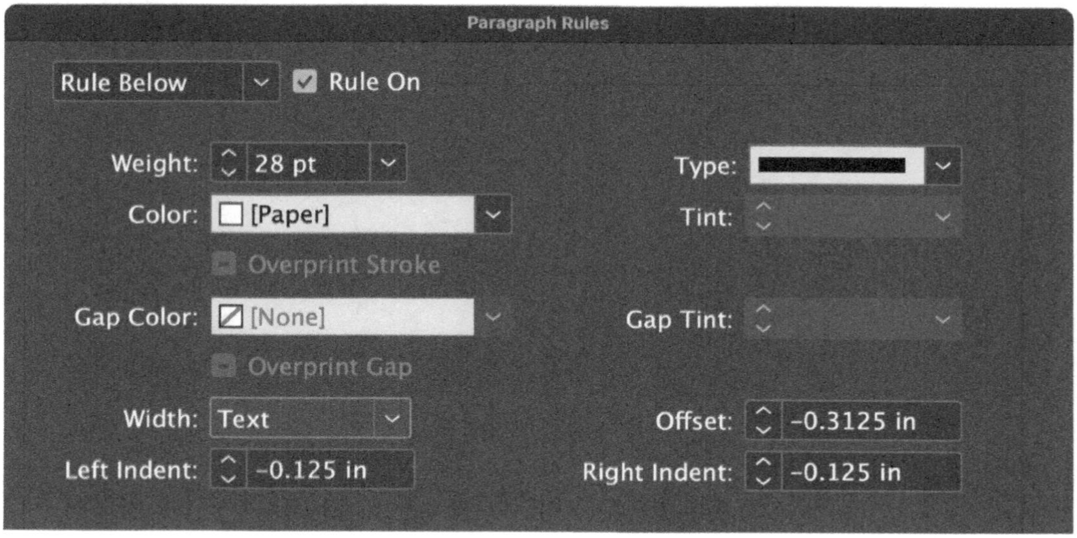

Paragraph Borders and Shading
Border Shading
Shading
Color: R=139 G=0 B=255
Tint: 100% Overprint
Corner Size and Shape:
0.1667 in 0.1667 in
0.1667 in 0.1667 in
Offsets
Top: 0 in Left: 0.5 in Top Edge: Ascent Bottom Edge: Descent
Bottom: 0 in Right: 0 in Width: Column

Paragraph Rules
Rule Below Rule On
Weight: 28 pt Type:
Color: [Paper] Tint:
Overprint Stroke
Gap Color: [None] Gap Tint:
Overprint Gap
Width: Text Offset: -0.3125 in
Left Indent: -0.125 in Right Indent: -0.125 in

File Tab Headings

Zero-Gravity Resource Reimbursement

Reimbursement for off-world resource allocation requires submission of holo-receipts within one solar cycle of procurement. The Fleet Quarter-

File tab headings are sleek and attention-grabbing. They can be created using both Paragraph Border and Paragraph Rules options, with the Rule Below hiding part of the Rule Above, as in the following settings.

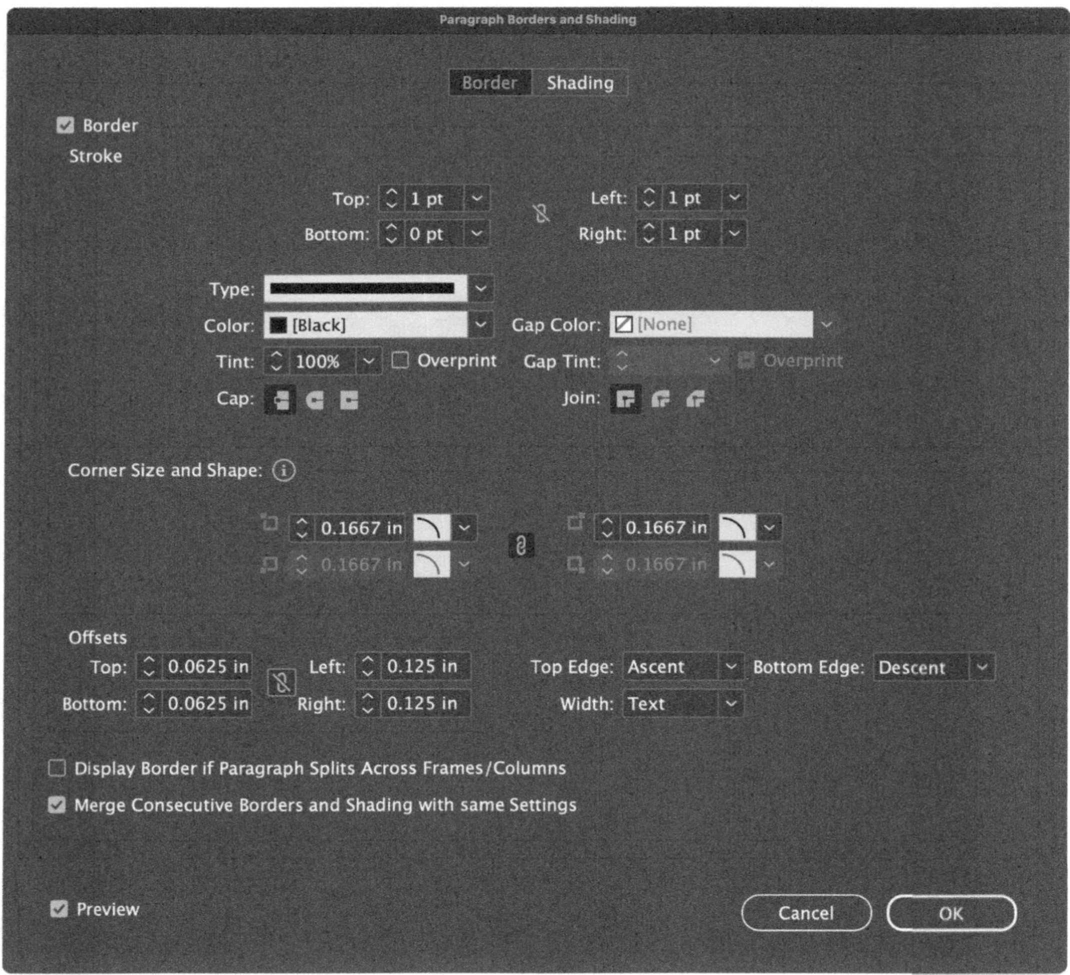

(Settings continue on next page.)

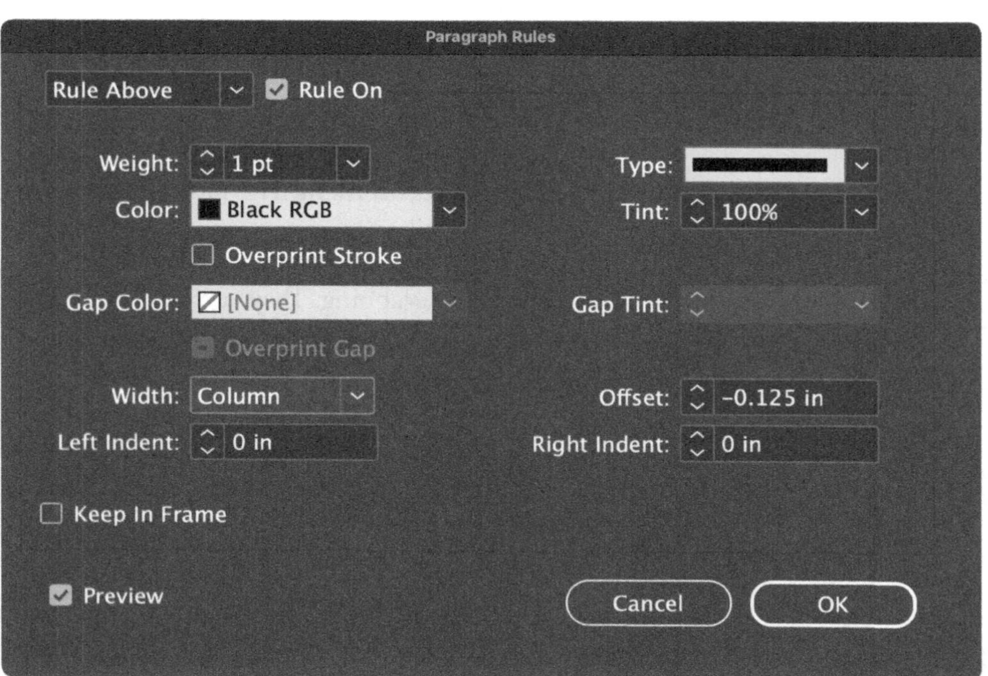
Paragraph Rules
Rule Above
Rule On
Weight: 1 pt
Color: Black RGB
Overprint Stroke
Gap Color: [None]
Overprint Gap
Width: Column
Left Indent: 0 in
Type:
Tint: 100%
Gap Tint:
Offset: -0.125 in
Right Indent: 0 in
Keep In Frame
Preview
Cancel
OK

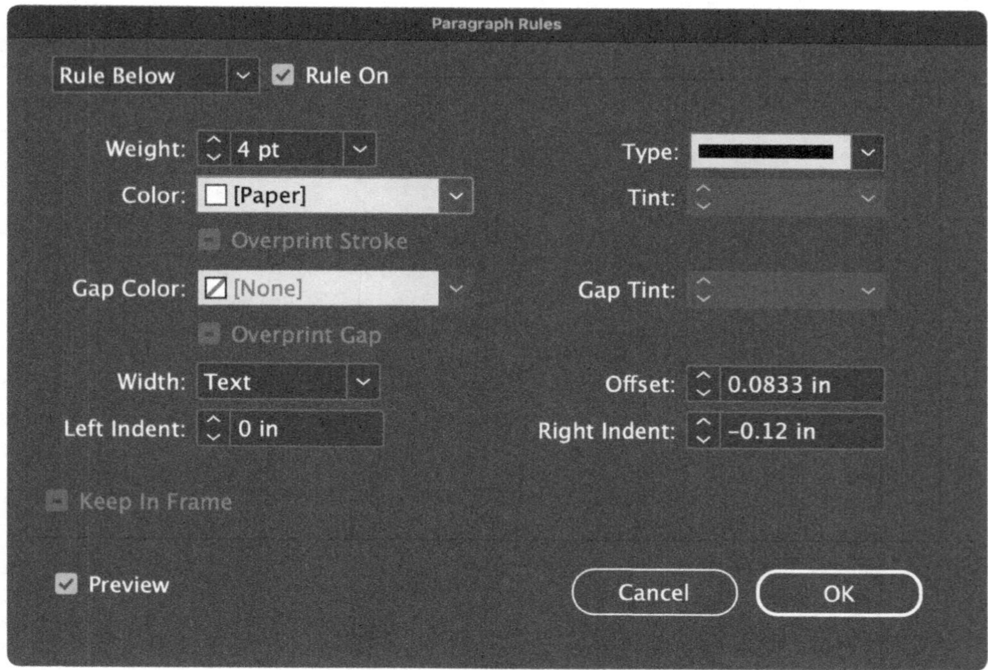
Paragraph Rules
Rule Below
Rule On
Weight: 4 pt
Color: [Paper]
Overprint Stroke
Gap Color: [None]
Overprint Gap
Width: Text
Left Indent: 0 in
Type:
Tint:
Gap Tint:
Offset: 0.0833 in
Right Indent: -0.12 in
Keep In Frame
Preview
Cancel
OK

File Tab Headings (Filled)

Human Crew

Human crew members require oxygenated environments and routine physiological maintenance, including hydration, nutrition, and sleep cy-

Methane-Breathing Crew

Methane-breathing crew members require environments with pressurized methane atmospheres for optimal function and longevity. All maintenance

Android Crew

All android crew members are equipped with adaptive learning processors and autonomous repair protocols. In the event of malfunction, core

Filling file tab headings is also simple with paragraph shading and a rule below. Moreover, they can have any horizontal alignment. In my examples I merely set the paragraph alignment to left, center, and right, respectively, but a tab system that needs more than three tabs could use the paragraph's Left Indent field to move tabs.

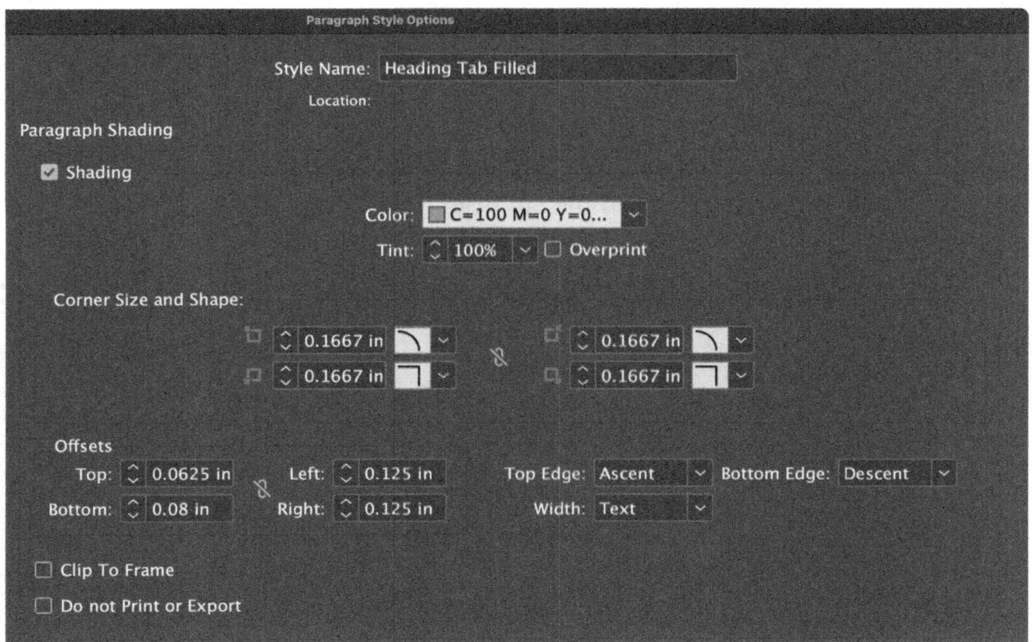

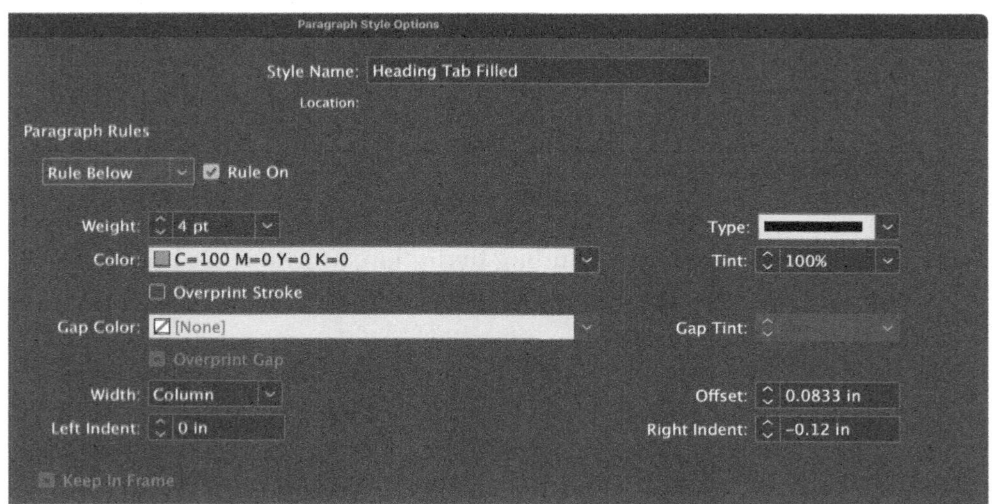

File Tab Headings (Filled & Outlined)

Power Core Status

Periodic scans of the ship's power core ensure stable output levels and efficiency. Any fluctuations in energy readings should be reported imme-

Add Paragraph Shading for the trifecta of Rules, Border, and Shading, and you can create filled file tab headings.

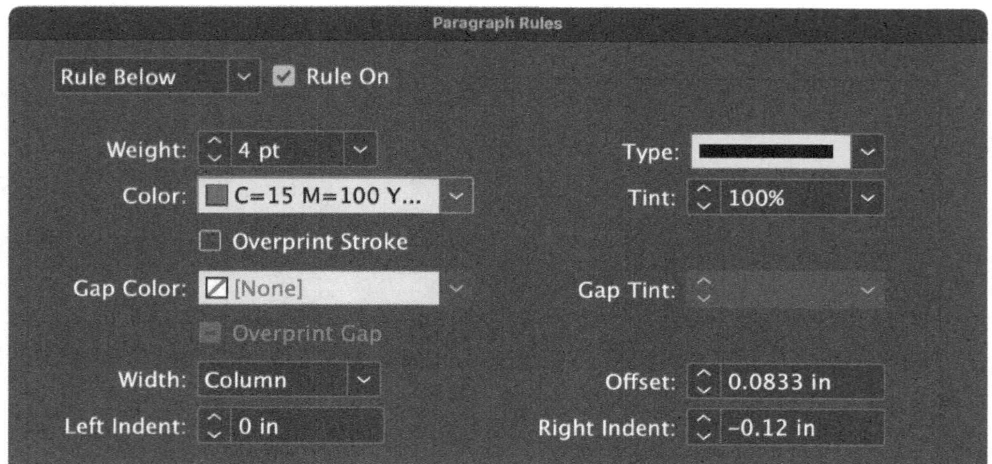

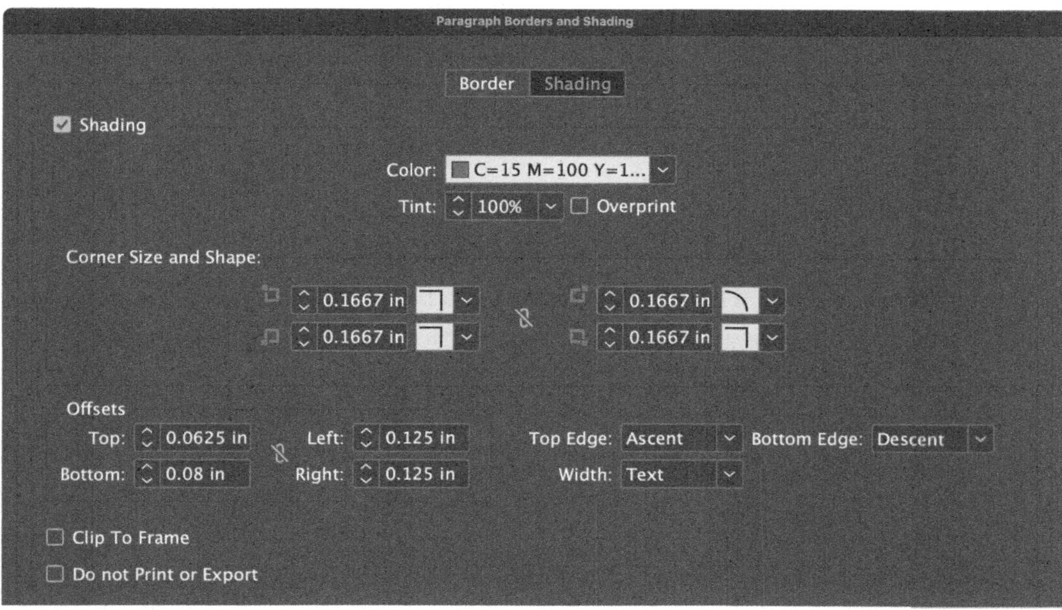
Paragraph Borders and Shading
Border
Shading
Shading
Color: C=15 M=100 Y=1...
Tint: 100%
Overprint
Corner Size and Shape:
0.1667 in
0.1667 in
0.1667 in
0.1667 in
Offsets
Top: 0.0625 in
Bottom: 0.08 in
Left: 0.125 in
Right: 0.125 in
Top Edge: Ascent
Bottom Edge: Descent
Width: Text
Clip To Frame
Do not Print or Export

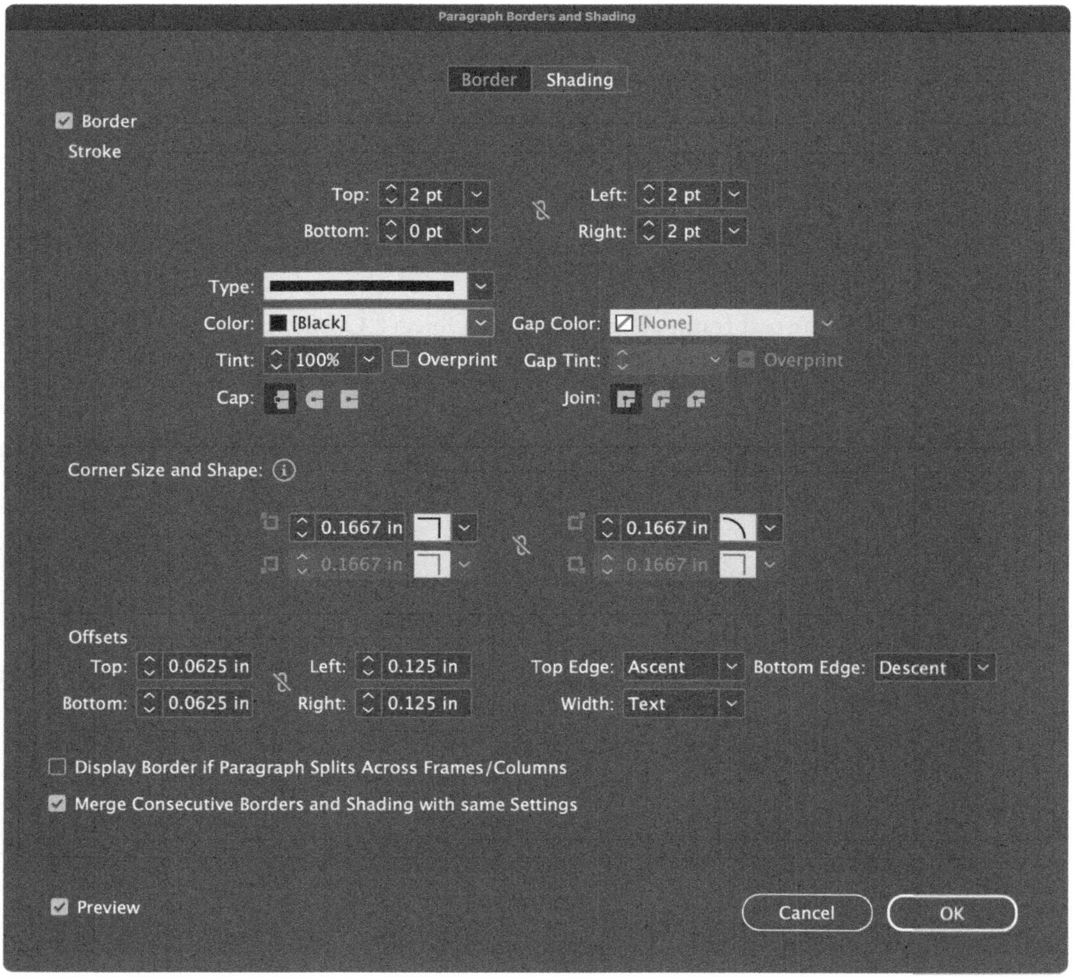

Paragraph Borders and Shading
Border
Shading
Border
Stroke
Top: 2 pt
Bottom: 0 pt
Left: 2 pt
Right: 2 pt
Type:
Color: [Black]
Gap Color: [None]
Tint: 100%
Overprint
Gap Tint:
Overprint
Cap:
Join:
Corner Size and Shape:
0.1667 in
0.1667 in
0.1667 in
0.1667 in
Offsets
Top: 0.0625 in
Bottom: 0.0625 in
Left: 0.125 in
Right: 0.125 in
Top Edge: Ascent
Bottom Edge: Descent
Width: Text
Display Border if Paragraph Splits Across Frames/Columns
Merge Consecutive Borders and Shading with same Settings
Preview
Cancel
OK

Filled Box with Floating Title 1

Note

Remember: If InDesign crashes while your document has unsaved changes, **do not re-open it by double-clicking the document file!** Always launch InDesign (and any Adobe or Microsoft application) **from the application icon or executible.** That will have the application try to recover your file, including unsaved changes. If you re-open from the file itself, you're telling the application to discard its backup of your unsaved changes.

There are several ways to create the look of this Note box. I'll walk you through two different methods with their own advantages and disadvantages.

This first method requires the Note box be its own text frame, though it can be anchored to other text.

1. Fill the text frame with your desired background color. In my example, from my *ePublishing with InDesign* book, I used a 20% tint of a Tyrian purple.
2. Give the text frame same padding by using the Inset Spacing controls on the General tab of Text Frame Options (Object ▸ Text Frame Options). I used 0.125 in all around.
3. With the text frame selected, choose Object ▸ Corner Options and set the options similar to mine and click OK.

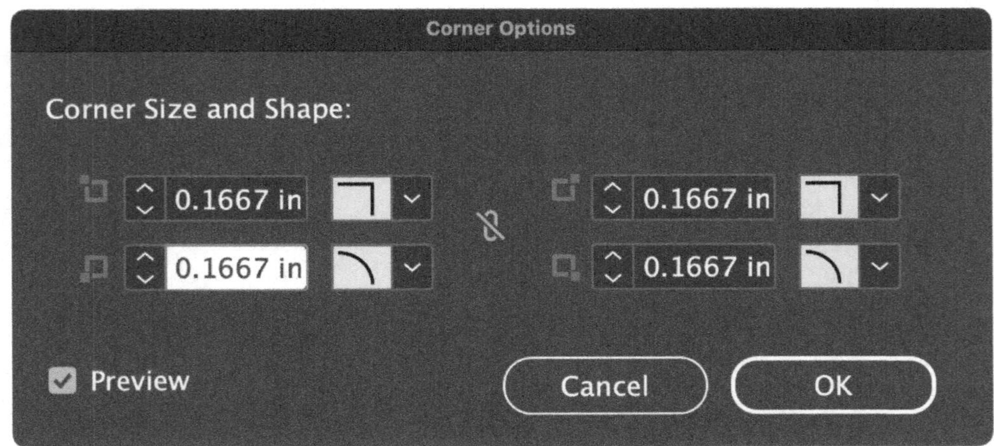

4. Select the title paragraph with the Type tool.
5. On the Paragraph panel, select Paragraph Rules from the panel flyout menu.
6. Select Rule Below from the drop-down menu at the top of the dialog, and then check the box beside the drop-down to turn on the Rule Below.
7. Set your Rule Below options like mine, using the [Paper] color, and click the OK button.

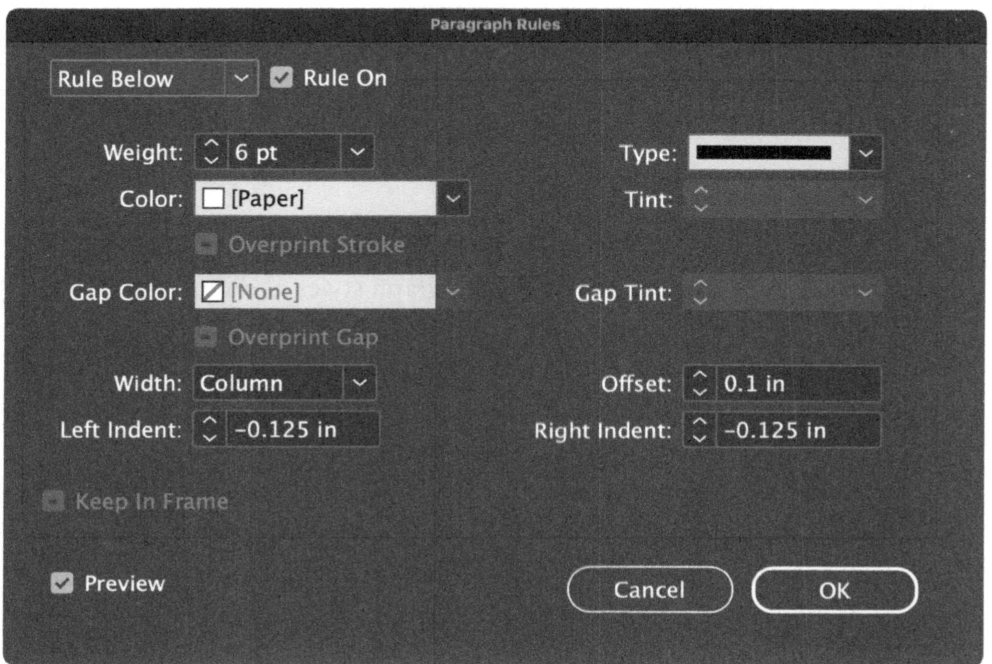

Now you have a text frame with a floating title. Obviously, the title isn't *really* floating; it's an opaque rule the color of paper blotting out some of the background fill. An advantage to this method is that the bulk of the formatting—the background fill, tint, and rounded corners—can be saved into, and applied from, an object style. The paragraph rule under the title can be part of the title's paragraph style.

One obvious drawback to this method is that, should you place the block on top of something like a watermark, rules, a gradient, or other non-solid color background, that background won't properly shine through that horizontal separator no matter what stroke color you choose. If that's an issue for your design, try the second "Filled Box with Floating Title" method.

Filled Box with Floating Title 2

Note

Remember: If InDesign crashes while your document has unsaved changes, **do not re-open it by double-clicking the document file!** Always launch InDesign (and any Adobe or Microsoft application) **from the application icon or executible.** That will have the application try to recover your file, including unsaved changes. If you re-open from the file itself, you're telling the application to discard its backup of your unsaved changes.

This second technique achieves the same floating-title effect using only text formatting that can be saved in paragraph styles *and* allow colors and objects behind the floating box to peak through that gap between title and body. Additionally, this technique allows for a filled box within a story rather than as a separate text frame that has to be created, anchored, and positioned.

1. Leave the text frame fill and stroke empty. Also, leave (or make) all the corners standard right angles, and don't use inset spacing on the text frame. We're not going to modify the frame itself in any way from it's default; all the formatting is done on the text.
2. With the Type tool, select *all* the text in the box, title and body paragraph(s).
3. On the Paragraph panel, select Paragraph Borders and Shading from the panel flyout menu.
4. Switch to the Shading tab at the top, activate the checkbox to turn on Shading, and then make your settings like mine (see the next page) before clicking OK . Note that there is no corner rounding at this point.
5. Select the last paragraph in the floating box and return to Paragraph Borders and Shading.
6. Break the chain link in the Corner Size and Shape area by clicking on it, and then make the two bottom corners rounded in a radius that suits you. Leave all other settings unchanged, and click OK..

   Like the previous one, this method has pros and cons, too.

   On the pro side, the effects are entirely text decoration and can be set in paragraph styles. This method will work whether the Note box is in its own text frame or in the middle of a story with unshaded paragraphs above and below. Also, the gap between the title and the body text is in-

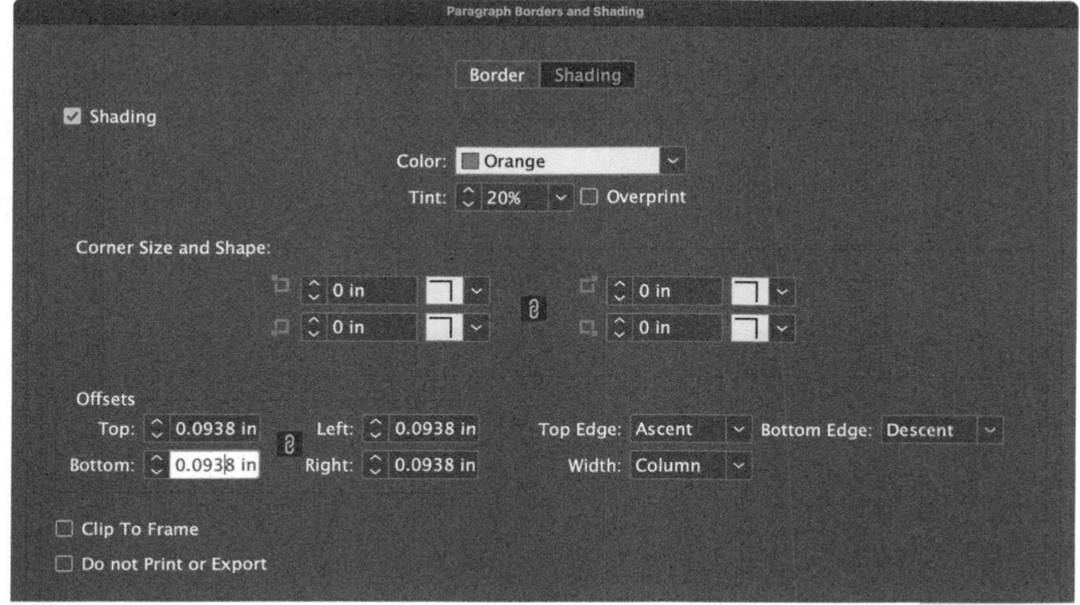

deed a gap, not a white overprint, so background colors and objects will be visible through that gap.

The cons list is pretty short, but it's a big one: it doesn't work as well as the filled frame method when there are multiple paragraphs below the title. Shading is a paragraph-level effect; when a paragraph ends, there will be rounded corners and potentially a gap before the new paragraph begins to repeat the shading. There a couple of ways to handle that problem, however. You could no round corners, or you could make sure the Top and Bottom offsets of the shading are big enough to cause the shading of consecutive paragraphs to overlap and cover up the rounded corners. This would mean tweaking either or both the offsets and the paragraph Space Before or Space After.

I also want to point out that, because of the offsets, the shading was put outward beyond the bounds of the text frame. If that doesn't work for your design, reduce the offsets values and use Left Indent, Right Indent, and/or Baseline Shift to push the text inward from where the shading will fall. You could also leave the offsets on the shading but put matching insets on the text frame itself.

Sci-Fi Code Display

```
// Decrypt binary feed and activate subroutine
while (signalIntegrity < 99.9) {
      phaseShift(quantumKey(42));
      if (trace_detected) {
            initiateFallback(ghostMode);
      }
}

// Initiate hyperspace jump countdown
secure_protocols.lockAllNodes();
executeJumpSequence(override_safety: true);
```

Life support is failing. You have minutes left. If you can't get the hyperdrive online in time to get your meteor-damaged ship to Sigma-9 Station, you and your cargo bay brimful with intergalactic refugees will suffocate in the lonely dark void beyond Sol's heliosphere…

Teenage wunderkinds are hacking the CIA's mainframe, digging for any remnant of the crucial file deleted by the treasonous Director of Unit Ultra-Black. Even as our group of young heroes desperately works to circumvent the firewalls, traps, and dead ends of the pinnacle intelligence agency's most secure system, all around the world ICBMs are warming up in their silos. If our youthful cypherpunks can't get the proof they need in front of the President in time, it will be World War III…

You abruptly realize that you haven't received a spam email in months. Spam folder? Empty. Not a single "Your Society Security Suspended Has" message, not even a bogus "Receipt for your $474.00 purchase" letter. You haven't received a single unsolicited email since… Since that vacation you can barely remember taking and coming back from. *Huh. When* did *you come back?* For that matter, *where did you vacation?* Suddenly your computer screen glitches, flashing—just for a second—vertical green text on a dark background falling like rain in strange languages and symbols. Instantly you realize: *this isn't the real world! I'm* inside *a too-perfect computer simulation…*

For a variety of reasons, you may want to create science fiction-inspired code or code-like gobbledygook text in InDesign. Choose a suitable monospace typeface, and then use the following recipe, which combines paragraph shading and borders with a greenish-black-filled, rounded corner text frame as a starting point for your sci-fi code display.

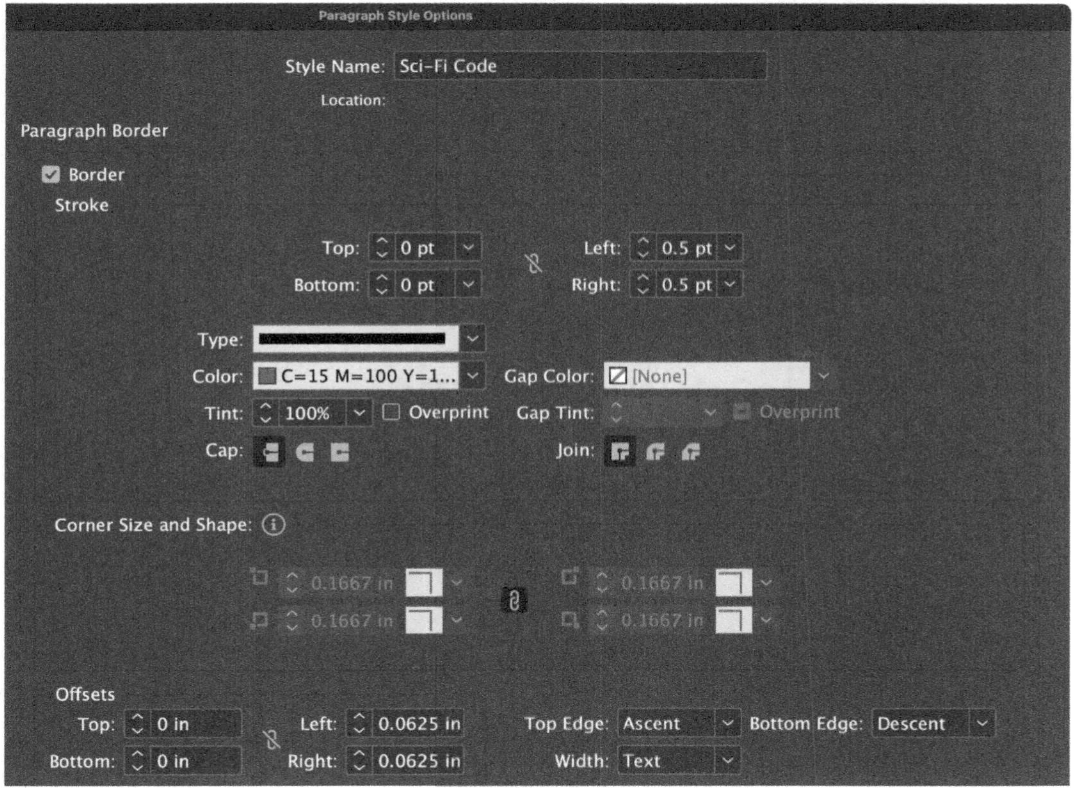

(Figures continue on next page.)

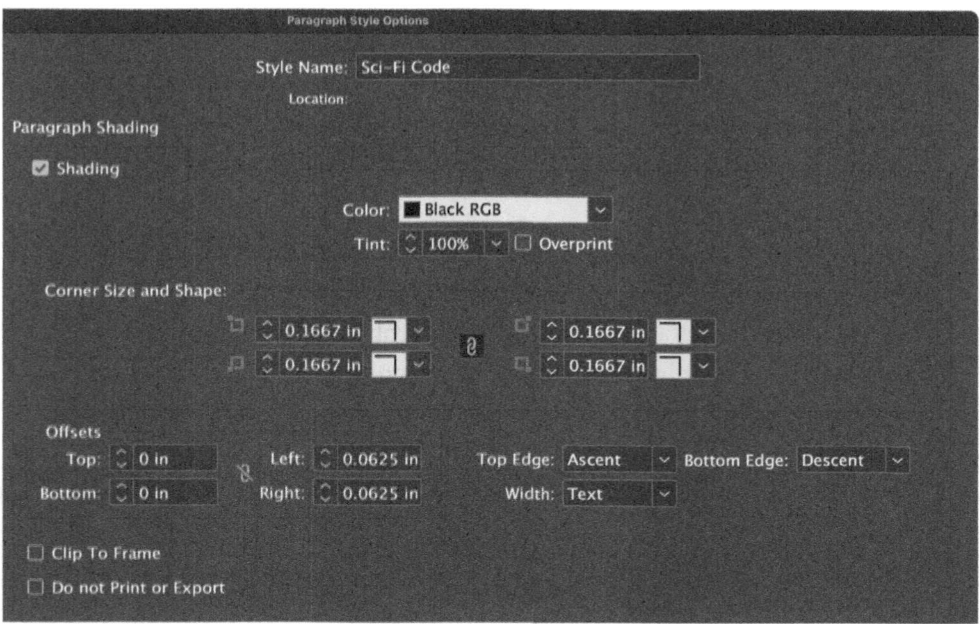

Outdent Headings 1 (a.k.a. Hanging Heads)

Want to have headings that are wider than the body text in your document—like this book, this very paragraph? It's a clever technique that will be so obvious once you learn how, which you can by following these steps:

1. Edit the paragraph style for your body copy or select the text that should be narrower than your headings.
2. Go to the Left Indent field in the Indents and Spacings pane of the Paragraph Style Options or just on the Paragraph, Control, or Properties panels.
3. Give the Left Indent field a positive value, pushing the entire paragraph in from the left.

4 Duplicate the setting in the Right Indent field.

5 Click OK, if in the Paragraph Style Options dialog.

Your headings and other paragraphs will now outdent or hang out, seemingly beyond the borders of columns and text frames. That's the trick: the headings don't really *outdent*, everything else *indents*. Make the difference as much as you desire.

Note that, if your heading paragraph styles were based on your body copy, they, too, will suddenly indent. Just edit the heading styles to set both Left Indent and Right Indent fields to `0`.

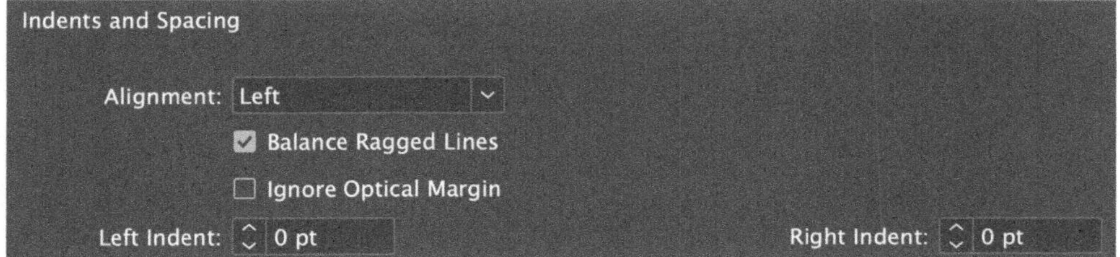

Outdent Headings 2

The "Outdent Headings 1" technique is by far the easier, more flexible, and more controllable method. The headers never leave their place in the flow of the story, and they aren't structured using anything more complex than a paragraph style. Still, sometimes you decide late in the game that you want hanging heads, and indenting all the other text would require an HGTV-style teardown and renovation of the entire publication (and Joanna Gaines is nowhere to be found). That's where the second and third techniques can be helpful.

Heres' the second:

1 Make sure hidden characters are visible by selecting Type ▸ Show Hidden Characters.

Section 2: Concerts and Events¶

Aborepedi doluptatur? Um do-
luptaspero odis sa sim cuptas

2 With the Type tool, select your first heading, *excluding* its normally invisible paragraph mark.
3 Go to Table ▸ Convert Text to Table.

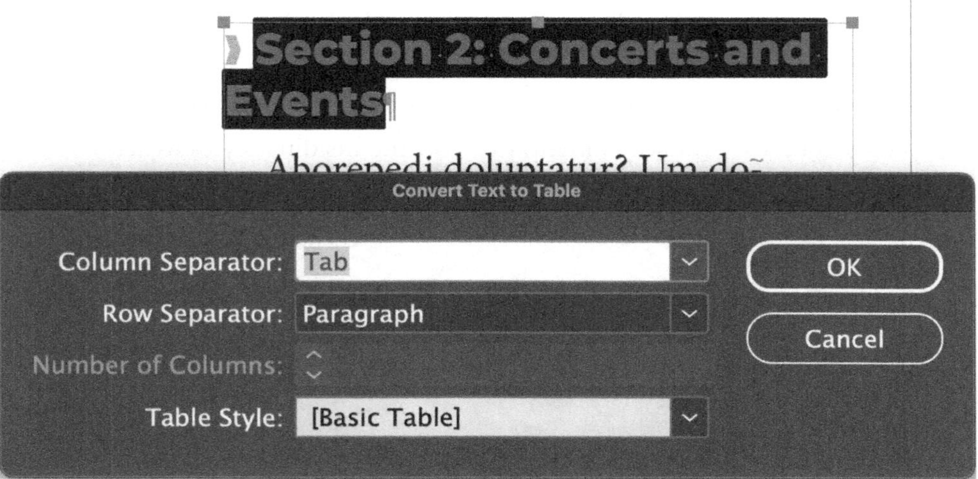

4 When the Convert Text to Table dialog box appears, make sure it Column Separator set to Tab while Row Separator is set to Paragraph. Click OK, and you're heading will become a single-celled table.
5 Tables, as you know, can be wider than their containing text frames (which still blows my mind after all these years). However, with left-aligned text, you can't actually drag the left side of the table to make it wider. You can, however, work around that, so, drag the *right* side of that table cell outward to widen the table to the desired with for your heading.

Section 2: Concerts and Events
Aborepedi doluptatur? Um doluptaspero odis sa sim cuptas

6 Move your type cursor outside the table, between the table and the paragraph mark, and change the paragraph's alignment to Right Aligned. The table should then snap its right edge to the right side of the frame or column, with the left side now jutting out , hanging the head.

Section 2: Concerts and Events#

Aborepedi doluptatur? Um doluptaspero odis sa sim cuptas

7 Tweak the heading as needed, including, probably, removing the visible strokes of the table.
8 Repeat for all other headings.

As I alluded to, this is a much more labor-intensive method of hanging indents because you have to convert, resize, and realign each heading individually. Even table and cell styles can only help so much. Also, from an accessibility standpoint, these tables will not be WCAG-compliant, but that only matters if you're distributing the document electronically instead of only in print. The up side to this method is that you hang your heads without messing with styles of other text.

Outdent Headings 3

The third method of outdenting or hanging headings is to remove the the headings from the flow of text to their own text frames, and then anchor frames back into the text. You can then position the headings wherever you want them. Anchored Object Options can be set to move headings that appear on left-read pages differently than those that appear on right-reads. Plus, with the Anchored Object Options and Paragraph Style included as controls within any given object style, you can easily style (and later modify, if needed) all your headings with ease.

If you'd like to use this anchored object outdenting method, just follow the instructions in "Vertical Side Heads without Tables" but don't rotate the heading frames.

Hanging Drop Caps 1

If you want your drop cap to hang farther left than the text it's a part of, there are two methods.

In the first, put a positive left indent on all text and a negative first line indent just on the paragraph with the drop cap, just like the "Outdent Headings 1 (a.k.a. Hanging Heads)" technique. This is the easier method to accomplish, but it requires more compromises.

Hanging Drop Caps 2

The other method, which takes a little more initial effort, is more flexible and involves fewer long-term consequences to worry about six pages later.

Do this:

1. *Before* the drop cap, insert a hair space.
2. Set the Drop Cap One or More Characters to *two* characters to account for the space and the actual cap.
3. Insert your cursor between the hair space and the drop cap, and kern the two together with large negative numbers. As you do, you'll be pulling your drop cap out to the left and past the edge of the text wrapping around the cap. The cap will overlap and eventually surpass the thin space.

Layering Drop Caps, Nested Style, and Nested Line Style

ONE THING **WAS CERTAIN, THAT THE *WHITE*** kitten had had nothing to do with it:—it was the black kitten's fault entirely. For the white kitten had been having its face washed by the old cat for the last quarter of an hour (and bearing it pretty well, considering); so you see that it *couldn't* have had any hand in the mischief.

The way Dinah washed her children's faces was this: first she held the poor thing down by its ear with one paw, and then with the other paw she rubbed its face all over, the wrong way, begin-

With the exception of paragraph borders and character styles for each, this styling of the opening lines to Lewis Carrol's *Through the Looking Glass* was done entirely on the Drop Caps and Nested Styles pane of a paragraph style. To build something like this yourself, follow these steps:

1. Create three character styles--First Line, First Words, and Drop Cap.
2. In the First Line character style, set the type family and style, size, and other options for the *entire* first line of text, from "ne thing" through "the white" in my example. Below are my First Line character style settings.

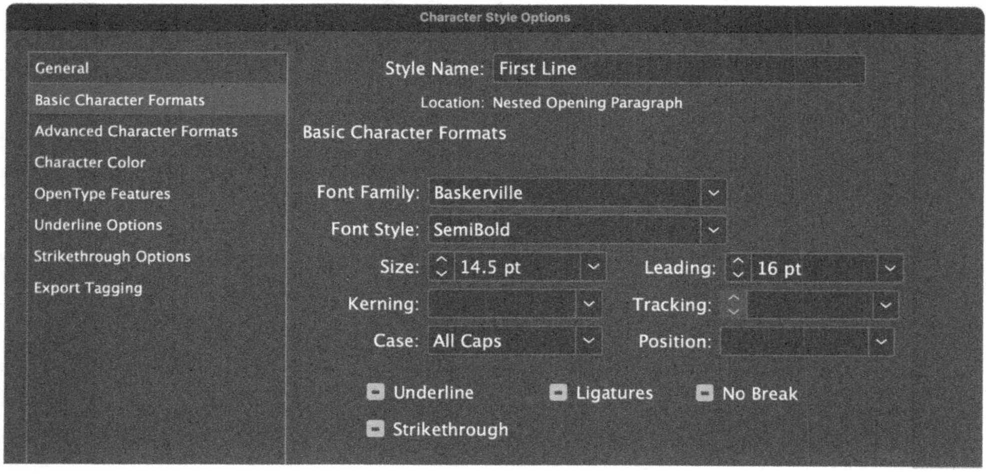

3 Once you've finalized those, create and edit the First Words character style. In my case, I changed the color to red and gave the text a subtle underline. All the other options were left empty.

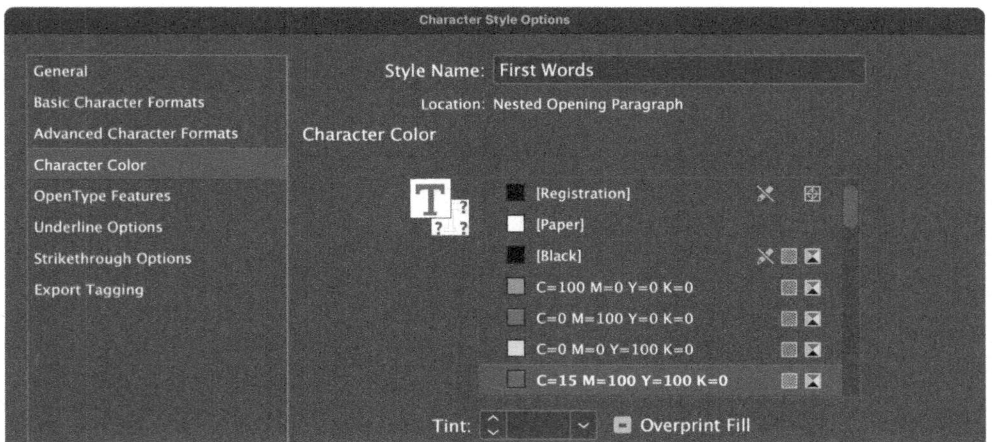

4 In the Drop Cap character style, set the options to apply only to the drop cap character itself. Don't change the size; the paragraph style will do that. Note that you may also have to tweak this style after actually creating the drop cap. Things like kerning and baseline shift, in particular, are best done while looking at the effect on the final design.

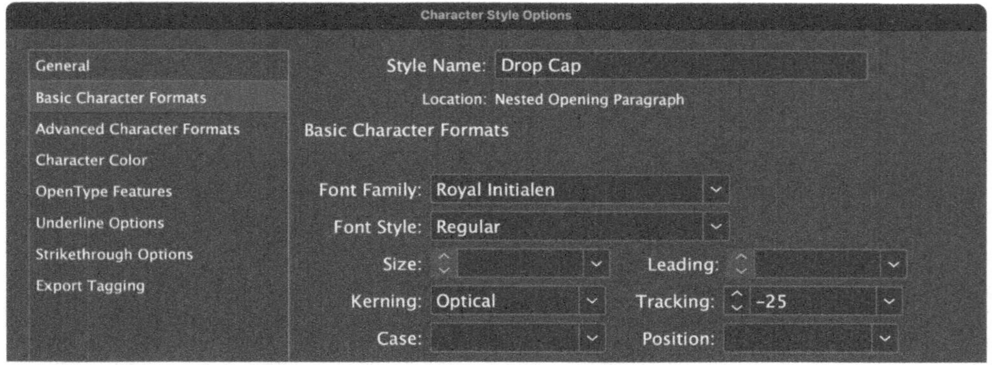

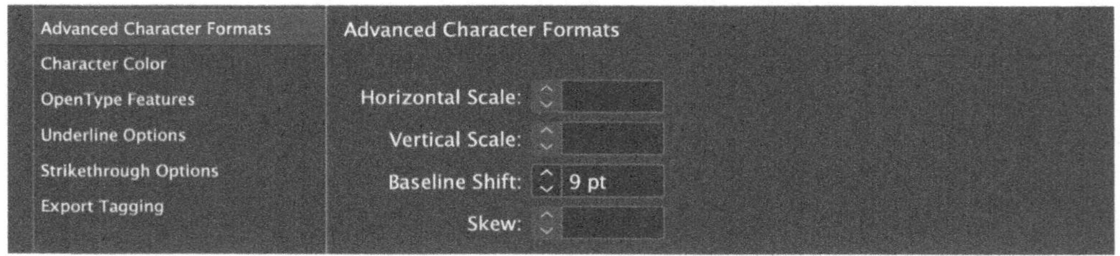

5 Now create the paragraph style for the passage that will host those character styles. Set everything else the way you want it, but on the Drop Caps and Nested Styles Pane, configure the three sections with these settings:

Drop Cap
Lines: 3
Characters: 1
Character Style: Drop Cap
Align Left Edge: Active

Nested Styles
Character Style: First Words
Scope: up to
Count: 2
Stop Character: Words

Nested Line Styles
Character Style: First Line
Scope: for
Count: 1 lines

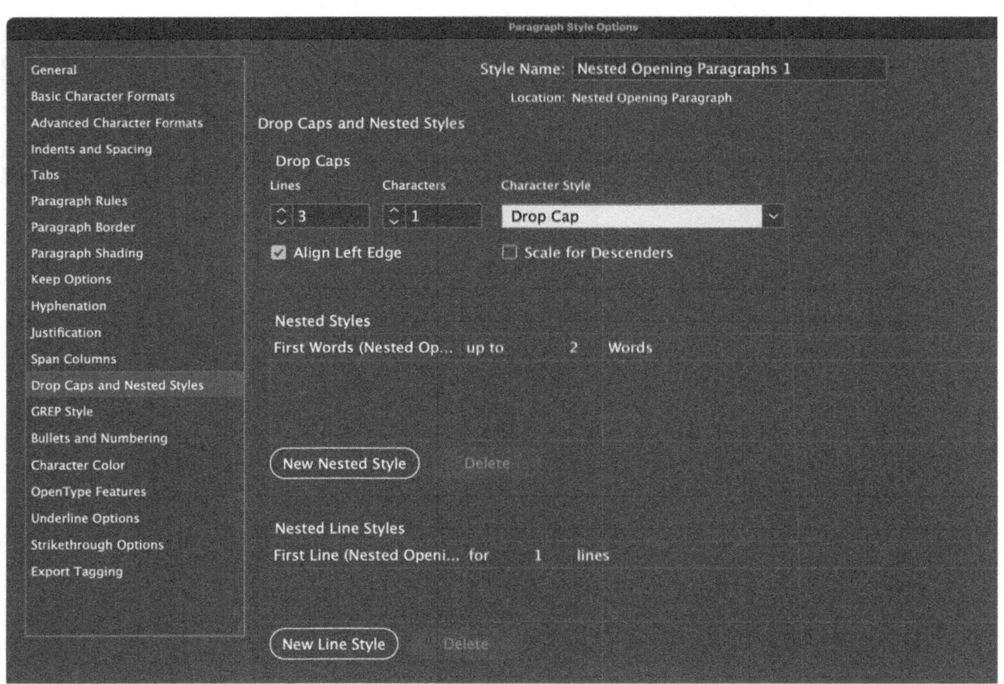

6 Click OK, check your work, and go back and adjust any of the three character styles that need it.

7 To add a border like mine, create a gradient swatch, and then, in the Paragraph Style Options dialog, replicate my settings from the Paragraph Border pane.

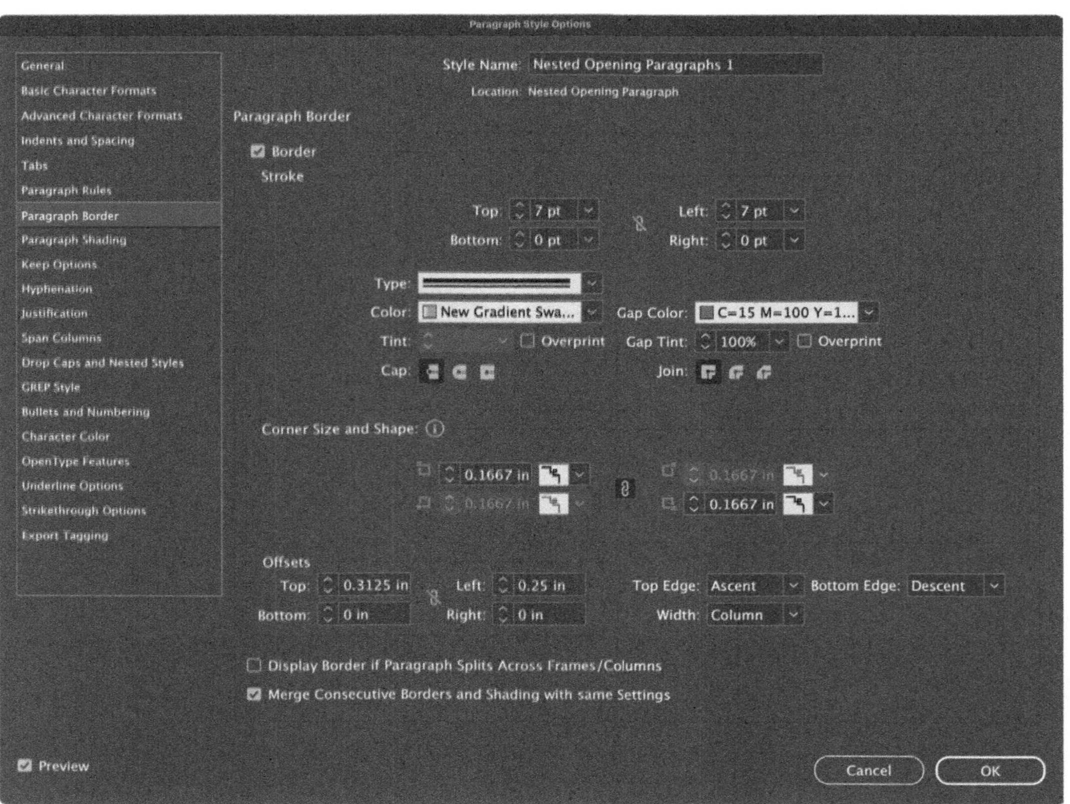

Alternating Paragraph Formatting

Enter the following JavaScript code:

```
var doc = app.activeDocument;var textVar = doc.
if (textVar.isValid) {
    var sel = app.selection[0];
    if (sel && sel.constructor.name == 'TextFra
        sel.contents = textVar.variableOptions.
    }
}
```

Striping tables to have alternating fills is easy, but can you do the same with paragraphs that aren't tables? Absolutely! Of course, there are different methods for alternating by paragraph (every hard return) or alternating *within* a paragraph, every line without the need for a hard return

First, follow the below steps to get formatting that changes with every hard return. This can make it easy to get spreadsheet-style lists without having to convert them to tables. It's also helpful for code display.

1 Format your text and create a paragraph style from it. Call this paragraph style Alt Graphs A or something else that will help you keep track of it.
2 On the Paragraph Shading pane in its Paragraph Style Options, set your paragraph shading options. Below you can see what I used.

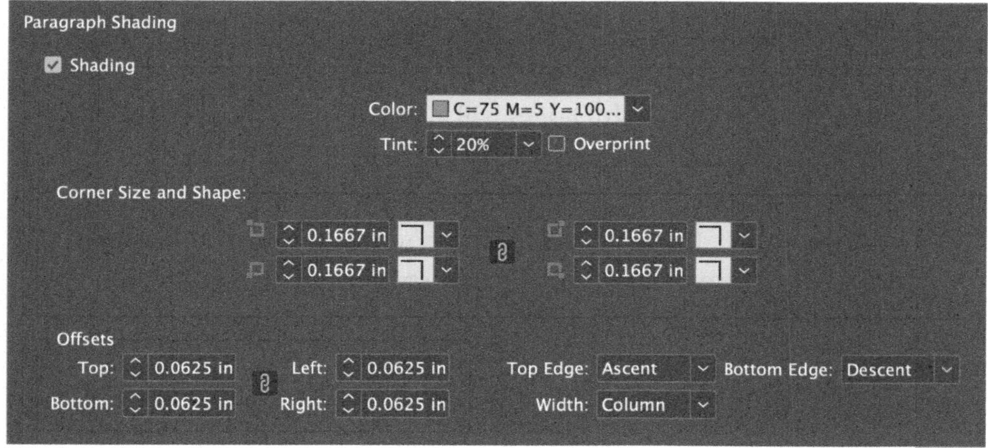

3 Click OK to save the style.
4 With the same text selected, create a new paragraph style and open its options.
5 On the General pane of Paragraph Style Options, name this new style Alt Graphs B, make sure Based on says Alt Graphs A, and set Next Style to Alt Graphs A also.

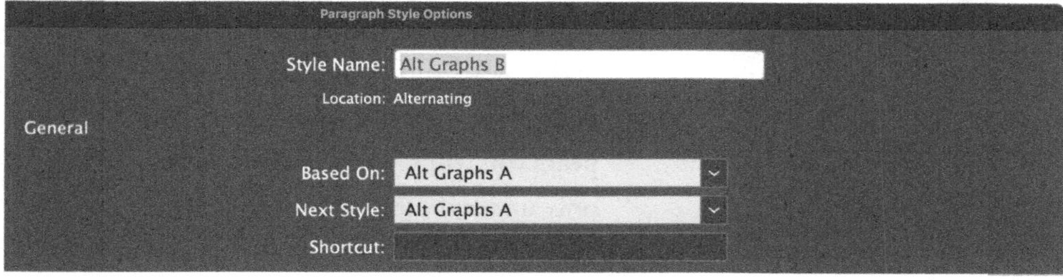

6 Change the Paragraph Shading options for this style. All I did was change the color of mine to [Paper]. Click OK to commit the change.
7 Open A for editing again, and on its General pane, set the Next Style drop-down to be Alt Graphs B. Click OK, and your styles will be set up to alternate.

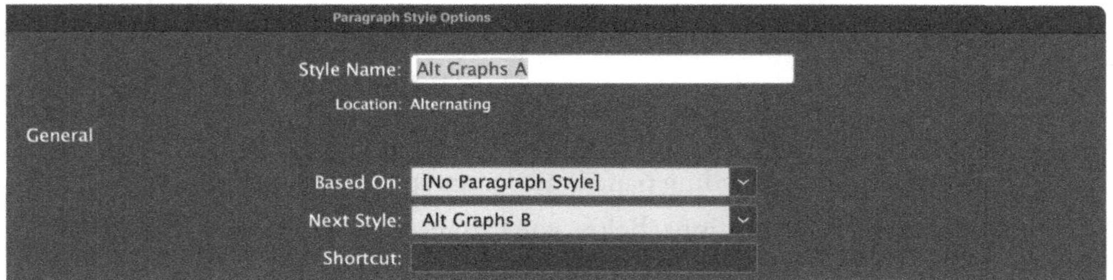

The way it works is like this: when you're typing text, starting with the A paragraph style, InDesign will automatically switch the B style when you insert a carriage return by pressing Return/Enter on your keyboard. Type your line of B-styled text, press Return/Enter again, and you're back to typing in A. That's how the Next Style attribute works. It tells InDesign what the next style will be every time you insert a hard return. Because both styles list the other as their Next Style attribute, you get a cycle of A to B, B to A, A to B, and so on.

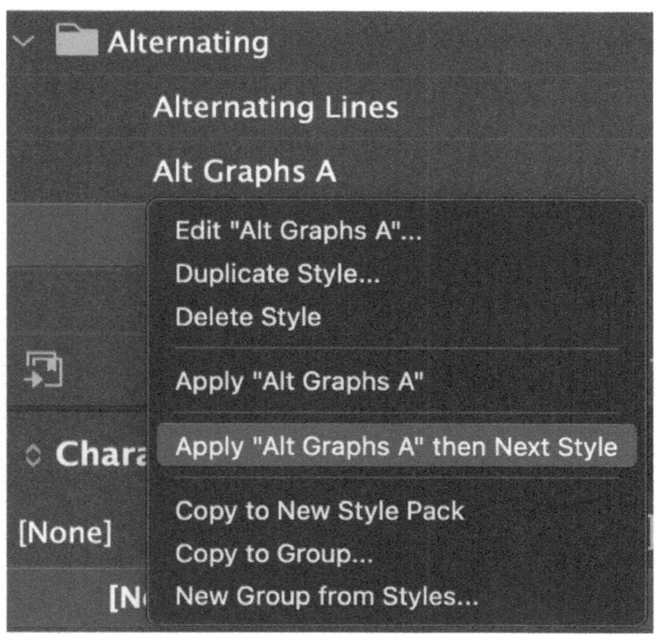

And, if you're typing new content from scratch, that's all you need to do for this recipe. If, however, you *already had text* and wanted to give that alternating paragraph formatting, you can do that, too—with one more action to activate a super secret, hidden feature of InDesign known only to the wisest of InDesign masters.

8 Select all the text, every paragraph, to which you want to apply the alternating formatting.
9 With that text select, go to the Paragraph Styles panel and right-click on Alt Graphs A. In the context-sensitive menu that appears you will see a one command available only under these rarest of circumstances--Apply "Alt Graphs A" then Next Style.

10 Activate that command and your entire selected text will suddenly look like my example, every paragraph having A/B alternating formatting.

Paragraph Alternating Line Formatting

I had a solemn time travelling north that day. It was fine May weather, with the hawthorn flowering on every hedge, and I asked myself why, when I was still a free man, I had stayed on in London and not got the good of this heavenly country. I didn't dare face the restaurant car, but I got a luncheon-basket at Leeds and shared it with the fat woman. Also I got the morning's papers, with news about starters for the Derby and the beginning of the cricket season, and some paragraphs about how Balkan affairs were settling down and a British squadron was going to Kiel.

The "Paragraph Alternating Line Formatting" technique will format every *line* of a paragraph differently, without the need to insert hard returns that break up those lines.

Here's how:

1 Set up two character style. We'll call these Style A and Style B, and we'll format them very similarly, with some noticeable difference. In my character styles I made Style A blue and Style B red. Set whatever difference you want for your lines.
2 Create or edit a paragraph style for your paragraph to stripe, and open that style's Paragraph Style Options.
3 Go to the Drop Caps and Nested Styles pane.
4 In Nested Style Lines, click New Line Style.
5 If your first line will be shaded or otherwise formatted, choose from the drop-down field Style A. If you want your first line unshaded, leave the drop-down at [None].
6 Click New Line Style again and set the opposite option—[None] or Style B.

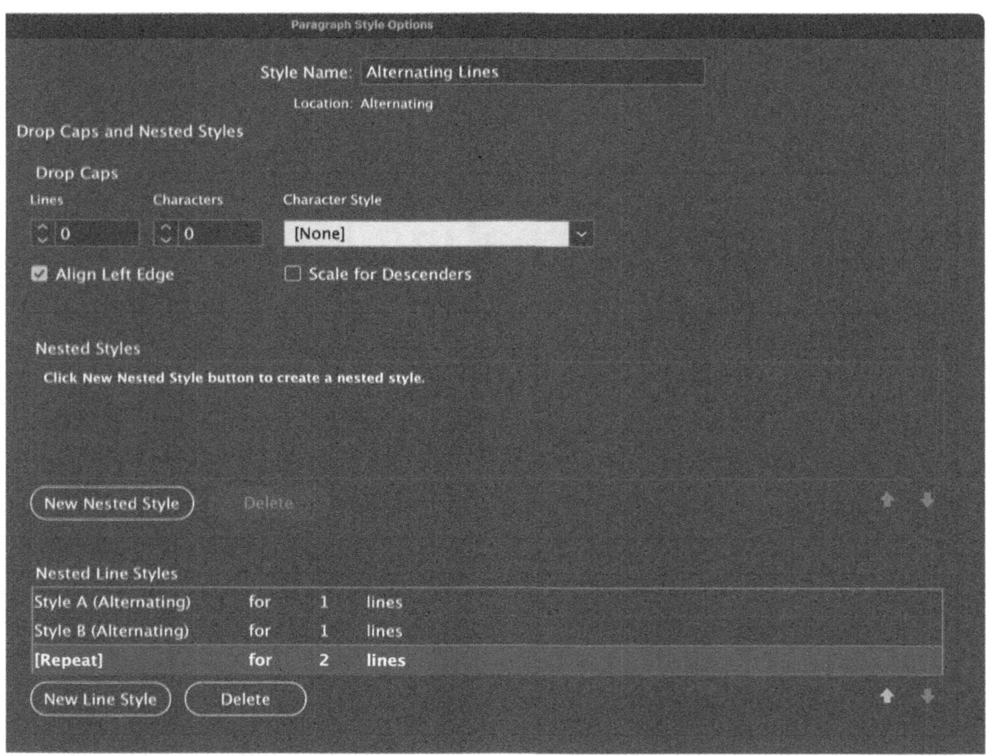

7 Add a third line style, but set this one to [Repeat] and for 2 lines instead of 1. When you're finished, your Drop Caps and Nested Styles pane should look like mine (next page).

The result will be alternating line formatting throughout the entire paragraph.

If you want three styles, create three nested line styles (and matching character styles), and set the [Repeat] row to 3. That [Repeat] command says, effectively, after *x* number of lines, go back to the beginning and apply the nested line styles in order again. Therefore you get, just like with paragraph Next Style, A, B, A, B, and so on, through the end of the paragraph.

Locate Used Paragraph Styles

Longer InDesign documents like a book typically employ quite a few paragraph styles, and you may not know at a glance where they're used—especially if you inherited the document from someone else. Who knows what they were up to! Importing Word documents with their own styles can compound the problem.

Dragging a style that *seems* unused to the trash bucket at the bottom of the Paragraph Styles panel will delete the style if it is, in fact, not used anywhere. If it *is* applied to text, InDesign will prompt you for a replacement style, but it won't give you a Find First button like you get when using Find/Replace Fonts.

Because of this, many designers go through the tedium of using Find/Change to locate where paragraph styles are used, leaving the Find What and Change To fields blank, and choosing the Attributes to Find button to select and locate the suspect paragraph style… one style at a time.

Here's a trick I learned long ago as a hired gun designer who spends way more time than he should deciphering what someone else did. This handy, dandy ploy can significantly speed up the process of identifying style usage.

1. Edit the paragraph style in question.
2. On the Paragraph Shading pane, turn on shading and set its color to the default process magenta swatch, either RGB Magenta or C=0 M=100 Y=0 K=0.
3. Click OK to save the settings, and then flip through the publication spread-by-spread. You can't miss that neon magenta paragraph shading.

GREP Recipes

Format Figure and Table References

This one you may have already learned by its inclusion in InDesign Masterclass: Type & Tables, Chapter 5, "Styles", but just in case, here's a quick GREP expression to format figure and table references in text.

```
(?i)(Figure|Table)\s\d+
```

Remember: replace "Figure|Table" if your document uses something other than "Figure" and "Table" to start a reference to an image and table, respectively. The pipette (|) is used as a separator between multiple terms, telling InDesign to find either "Figure" or "Table."

(Subtly) Callout Out a Brand Name Automatically

Want to subtly call out brand names or any other piece of information without having to hunt it down in your stories and manually apply character styles? That's easy. Just follow this recipe:

1. Create a character style for the thing you want to highlight. Maybe that character style changes the Font Style field to Semi-Bold or Medium, or maybe you employ a tip I gave in *InDesign Masterclass: Type & Tables*, Chapter 2, "Characters" and ever so slightly increase the vertical scaling (on the Advanced Character Formats pane of the Character Style Options).
2. Create or edit your paragraph style and open its Paragraph Style Options dialog.
3. Go to the GREP Style pane and click the New GREP Style button.

4 Choose the character style you just made from the Apply Style drop-down menu.

5 In the To Text field is where we'll put the GREP formula to search for, and apply that character style to, our brand name or phrase. So, replace the default `\d+` formula with nothing like the exact word or phrase you're searching for.

For instance, if I was calling out the title of this book in italic, my To Text would read simply, without quotation or mother marks, `InDesign Masterclass: Type & Tables`.

GREP Style

Apply Style: Italic

To Text: InDesign Masterclass: Type & Tables

Apply Style: Italic

To Text: InDesign Masterclass: Text Techniques

6 Click OK and verify that it worked. If it didn't, make sure your character style actually shows a visible effect, that the paragraph style is actually applied to the desired text, that there are no overrides on that text, and that you didn't have a typo in the GREP style's To Text field.

The result should be a subtle stylistic change for every instance of your search term, anywhere it appears in any paragraph to which that paragraph style, or a child of that style via Based On, is assigned.

Call Out Many Names & Terms

After that recipe, the next logical question is: *how do I apply that subtle emphasis to more than a single search term or phrase?* The answer is simple: follow all the same steps, except, use a different formula in the To Text field, one that looks for multiple distinct terms or phrases in the same GREP style.

Let's say I was searching for these terms to apply a bolding character style to them: "Widget", "Gadget", and "Gizmo". My formula would need to say, effectively, find any of these whole words, not if they appear as parts of other words, and then apply the chosen character style. That would be the following formula.

```
\b(Widget|Gadget|Gizmo)\b
```

`\b` at the start of a GREP formulas tells InDesign to look for words that begin with the selected word—"Widget, Gadget, or Gizmo".

Then the search terms themselves are listed, separated by pipettes (|), which are the symbol for the `OR` operator—e.g. *find this* or *that*. You can also search for phrases; anything between the pipette is considered the search term, whether that's one word or more.

Finally, another `\b`, for word boundary, tells InDesign not to include any instances of text where the word does not end the way the search terms end. For example, if I searched for `\b(the)\b`, the `\b` instances tell InDesign not to include words like "breathe" or "theatre" where "the" is a part but is not itself a self-contained word. Also, because the GREP search is case-sensitive, my search for `Widget|Gadget|Gizmo` will not find and apply the style to "widget," "gadget," or "gizmo".

Creating a Case-Insensitive GREP Style

In the previous recipe, `\b(Widget|Gadget|Gizmo)\b` is case-sensitive, meaning "Widget" will be matched but "widget" won't. To create a case-insensitive GREP formula, prefix your search with `(?i)`, as in the same search below that will match "widget" as well as "Widget."

```
(?i)\b(widget|gadget|gizmo)\b
```

Automatically Small Cap Acronyms & Abbreviations

One thing you may have noted throughout this book[1] is that I used small caps on my acronyms and abbreviations, like JPG, CMYK, and even GREP. I absolutely did not manually do that. Instead, I made a character style with a singular setting—Case is OpenType All Small Caps—and then a GREP style to apply it everywhere any common acronym or abbreviation appeared. You can see my settings in the screenshots below, but here's my GREP formula, as it's used in the main body copy paragraph style for this very book:

```
\b(JPEG|JPG|PNG|TIFF|EPS|PSD|AI|INDD|INDT|PDF|TTF|OT-
F|SKU|ITC|CMYK|RGB|GREP|BCE|XML|QWERTY|EULA|US-
B|SQL|BAT|ASCII|HTML|EPUB|RAM|SVG)\b
```

Apply Highlight or Redaction Automatically

GREP styles can be used to apply any character style to any piece of text anywhere within the story. Therefore, if you find yourself needing to highlight or apply a redaction effect on the same words or phrases everywhere they appear in a story, employ a GREP style.

1. Create the character style for your highlight, redaction, or faux redaction, as we did earlier in this chapter.
2. Create or edit your paragraph style and open its Paragraph Style Options dialog.
3. On the GREP Style pane, create a new GREP style.
4. Set the Apply Style to your chosen character style.
5. In the To Text, enter the following, where "this," "that," and "the other thing" are the words or phrases you want to highlight or redact throughout the en-

---

1 Only in the print and PDF editions of this book. Ebook versions (EPUB, Kindle, and Fixed-Layout EPUB) do not yet support OpenType Small Caps.

tire document. Add more terms by typing the term separated by pipettes (|). Remember that the last term should not be followed by a pipette.

```
\b(this|that|the other thing)\b
```

Every instance of those words assigned to the current paragraph style, as well as to any paragraph style based on this one, will instantly be highlighted or redacted.

Apply OpenType Fractions to All Typed Fractions

Using a GREP style and the OpenType Fractions attribute, typing text such as `1/2`, `5/8`, or even `99/100` will instantly be converted to proper fractions, assuming the font in use is an OpenType with real fraction glyphs inside.

1. Create a character style that includes the OpenType Fractions attribute on the OpenType Features pane of the Character Style Options.
2. Edit the paragraph style in use and go to the GREP Style pane.
3. Create a new GREP style.
4. In the Apply Style field, select the character style you just created.
5. In the To Text field, enter this code: `\d+/\d+`
6. Click OK to save the paragraph style.

All instances of text where numeric digits surround a forward slash will be converted to OpenType fractions, in existing text or as they're typed.

Ignore Everything Before

Quick tips are often the most useful, and this is one of them. The GREP command of `\K` means ignore everything before, well, whatever comes after the `\K`. This makes it great for finding some text anywhere in a paragraph without having to worry about the text that comes before it.

Styling Words That May Have Diacritics

What do all of the following words have in common? Cafe, resume, naive, and fiancee. If you said, *they're all properly written with diacritics but often written without*, you'd be absolutely correct. Cafe, often written as such in English, should be café in French and Spanish. Naive should be naïve. But, for a variety of reasons, including the fact that the modern computer keyboard layout is anything but (it was finalized in 1873), some people don't always write words that should have diacritics with their diacritical marks. That means, when running a GREP search for cafe, it won't match café, and vice versa. Here's a formula to find both forms of the word in one search.

```
caf[[=e=]]
```

The trick is the `[[=e=]]`. Whatever letter(s) may or may not be written with diacriticals, wrap each of those letters with double brackets on the outside and equals signs on the inside. InDesign will then find both forms of the word, with and without accented variants.

Removing Runts and Short Ends of Paragraphs

Almost as bad as widows and orphans is runts, short bits of text left hanging out at the ends of paragraphs. There is no hard rule of how many characters or words makes an undesirable, short end of a paragraph. Most designers have differing numbers. Whatever your limit for what you'll accept, a GREP style can prevent runts automatically.

1. Create a character style that includes the No Break attribute on the Basic Character Formats pane of the Character Style Options.
2. Edit the paragraph style in use and go to the GREP Style pane.
3. Create a new GREP style.

4 In the Apply Style field, select the character style you just created.
5 Set the To Text field to be this code: `.{9}$`
6 Click OK to save the paragraph style.

The GREP formula looks for any text at the end of a paragraph or story (the `$` means both) that is shorter than nine characters, and then applies the No Break attribute via the character style. With Paragraph Composer active, as it is by default, InDesign will typically rework a larger portion of the paragraph beyond just that last line such that the No Break portion looks much better than it would otherwise. The result of this GREP style is that you should never again have a runt in your paragraphs.

Adjust the number of characters (`9` between the curly braces in my code) if you want a different minimum length of word you'll allow alone on a line at the end of a paragraph.

Highlighting Consecutive Paragraph Returns

I'm not going to tell you why multiple hard returns in a row is bad. I think I probably did that back in InDesign Masterclass: Type & Tables, Chapter 3, "Paragraphs". Which is why I know *you'd* never use them, but with inherited documents, or documents that include placed textual assets, it's always a risk. The GREP tab of Find/Change can automatically remove them for you, but if you just want to *see* multiple returns before removing them, there's a way GREP Styles can help.

1 Create a character style that uses a bright highlight effect (see "Highlight Text at the Character Level"). Try to avoid making the type huge or some other alteration that could explode the page geometry accomplished by the multiple, consecutive hard returns.
2 Edit the main or base paragraph style and create a GREP style that applies you highlighting character style to matches to this expression: `(\r\r)+`
3 Click OK, and then cruise through your document looking for highlighted returns. (This works best when hidden characters are showing.) Then fix them with paragraph spacing, break characters, or whatever else might fit the situation.

Automatically Formatting Quotation Marks

you to begin, you see nobody would ever say anything, so that—"

"Five times as warm, and five times as cold—just as I'm five times as rich as you are, and five times as clever!"

"Ridiculous!" cried the Queen. "Why, don't you see, child—" here she broke off with a frown, and, after thinking

Let's say you have a would-be pullquote like the bland paragraph I have highlighted below. You'd like to format that so it grabs attention (which is the whole purpose of a pullquote), and you'd like to format the starting and ending quotations without having to manually highlight them and apply character styles. GREP styles to the rescue!

always ready for a little argument," and if you only spoke when you were spoken to, and the other person always waited for _you_ to begin, you see nobody would ever say anything, so that—"¶

"Five times as warm, and five times as cold—just as I'm five times as rich as you are, and five times as clever!"¶

"Ridiculous!" cried the Queen. "Why, don't you see, child—" here she broke off with a frown, and, after thinking for a minute, suddenly changed the subject of the conversation.

1. Create a paragraph style for the body of the pullquote, and a character each for the opening and closing quotes. Make these look however you desire. I created a paragraph style called unironically, Pullquote. My character styles are Pullquote Open and Pullquote Close.
2. Edit your paragraph style.
3. On the GREP Style pane of Paragraph Style Options, create a GREP Style.
4. Set the Apply Style filed to Pullquote Open (or whatever you named yours), and the To Text field to ~{ , which is the GREP code for an opening quotation mark. If you forget the code, you can insert it by clicking on that @ symbol special character menu and choosing Quotation Marks > Double Left Quotation Mark.
5. Create a second GREP Style configured to show Pullquote Close and using this code: ~} . Your quotation marks should now style independently of the pullquote itself. Tweak your character styles as needed.

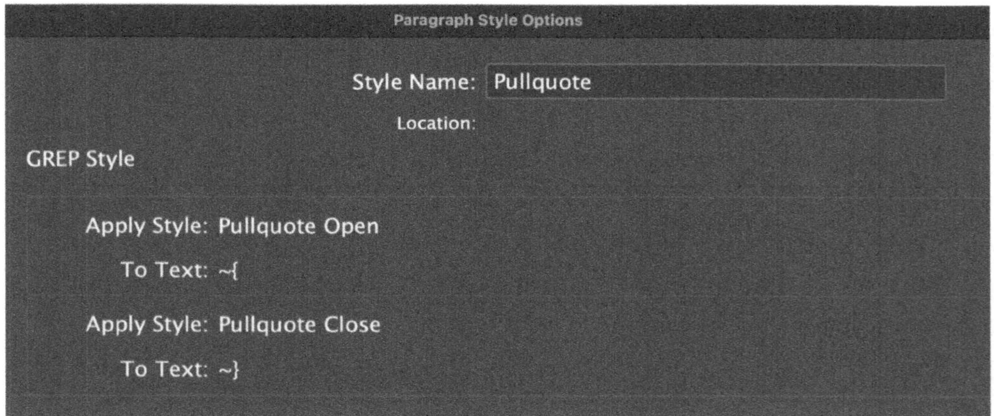

Formatting Email Addresses

This won't actually turn them into hyperlinks, but creating a GREP Style to search for the following (admittedly long) expression will find and apply a character style to *format* email addresses.

```
[a-zA-Z0-9._%+-]+@[a-zA-Z0-9.-]+\.[a-zA-Z]{2,}
```

Formatting Web URLs

Here's another potentially handy GREP Style expression, one that can target all your website URLs, with or without *https*, *www*, and other optional bits. Again, this won't actually make hyperlinks of your URLs, but the Hyperlinks panel has a built-in feature for that. Note that this is all a single line of code.

```
(https?:\/\/)?(www\.)?[a-zA-Z0-9._-]+\.[a-zA-Z]{2,}
(\.[a-zA-Z]{2,})?(/[a-zA-Z0-9._-]*)*
```

Formatting Dates and Times

If I had a dollar for every time I had to format dates differently than their surrounding text, especially in course catalogs, journals, and technical publications, I'd be writing this book from my own private hut on a Fijian beach. Fortunately, thanks to GREP, I can at least save myself the long hours of doing it by hand. Use the below expressions in GREP styles to find and format dates in a variety of formats.

4-digit years `\b\d{4}\b`

YYYY-MM-DD dates `\b\d{4}-\d{2}-\d{2}\b`

MM/DD/YYYY `\b\d{2}/\d{2}/\d{4}\b`

DD/MM/YYYY `\b\d{2}/\d{2}/\d{4}\b`

Month DD, YYYY `\b[A-Za-z]+ \d{1,2}, \d{4}\b`

HH (24-hour format) `\b\d{2}:\d{2}\b`

hh AM/PM (12-hour format) `\b\d{1,2}:\d{2}\s?[APap][Mm]\b`

24-hour format with seconds `\b\d{2}:\d{2}:\d{2}\b`

12-hour format with seconds `\b\d{1,2}:\d{2}:\d{2}\s?[APap][Mm]\b`

Tab Recipes

Equal Width Spacing without Tabs

Music Submission Form

Are you a(n) ◉ Artist ◉ Plugger ◉ Label
Genre
◉ Ready to Air ◉ Embargoed (until below date)
Embargoed Until

Music Submission Form

Are you a(n) ◉ Artist ◉ Plugger ◉ Label
Genre
◉ Ready to Air ◉ Embargoed (until below c
Embargoed Until

Compare the two images above. See how the upper version has equally spaced radio button options while the lower doesn't? The reason is because the lower version uses tabs, and the upper doesn't.

Tabbing to make a line of text equally spaced is a common and great technique—when it works. The issue is that, if the words being tabbed are different widths, they'll occupy different amounts of space while the tabs remain frozen at their locations. The result is inconsistent space between the words instead of clean, equal-width gaps. You can carefully nudge the tab stops in the Tab palette, but that can be difficult and time-consuming as you adjust this one, then tweak all the others, then readjust to make it all fit. Here's another method, the one I used to get the upper set of text in the example.

1. Replace all tabs in the tab-separated list with single spaces. You can do that manually, or use Find/Change to replace a tab (`^t` code on the Text tab of Find/Change) with a standard space.
2. The replacement done, select one of the spaces.
3. On the Character, Control, or Properties panel, set the Horizontal Scale field to `500%`.
4. Open the Character Styles panel and create a new style for the space.
5. Apply that style to all the spaces between the items that should space out across the line. Again, Find/Change can be helpful here.
6. Adjust the Horizontal Scale in the character style's Advanced Character Formats pane as needed to get the perfect fit.

The Horizontal Scale field accepts values up to 1,000%. If you need more space, replace the, uh, spacing spaces with two spaces or a wider space from the Type ▸ Insert White Space menu, and then adjust the Horizontal Scale of both via the character style. (You can compare the size of InDesign's different spaces in "Special Characters" in *InDesign Masterclass: Type & Tables*, Chapter 2, "Characters")

By using the Horizontal Scale field on a single space, we can precisely control the width of the gap between text. It can even be easily changed with one tweak to the character style if the column width changes.

The biggest drawback to this method is that it only really works on a single line of text at a time. If you try it on multiple lines where the space-separated text is different lengths, the columns won't line up. In such cases, you'll have to go back to the tab stop method.

Create Many Tab Stops in Two Clicks

All Tracks by Length

Title	**Artist**	**Album**	**Track No.**	**Length**
Louder Than Hell	Motley Crue	Theatre of Pain	3	2:32
Blame It On You	Poison	Look What the Cat Dragged In	8	2:34
You Really Got Me	Van Halen	Van Halen I	3	2:38
Crawl Space	Warrant	Ultraphobic	6	2:38
Big Balls	AC/DC	Dirty Deeds Done Dirt Cheap	6	2:38
Riot Act	Skid Row	Slave to the Grind	10	2:40

In two shakes of a lamb's tail, er, I mean, in two clicks of your mouse, you can make as many tab stops as you need. It's more a tip than a recipe, but this section is the best place for this handy dandy trick, so here we go.

1. With the Type tool, select the tab-separated text you need to straighten out.
2. Open the Tab ruler either by choosing Type ▸ Tabs or by pressing CMD+Shift+T/CTRL+Shift+T.
3. Make your first tab stop as usual, positioning it precisely—that's important.
4. With that tab stop still selected, go to the tiny, easy-to-miss menu button at the right end of the palette, and choose Repeat Tab. *Voila!* Your tab stop will be repeated through the remain space in the column or frame, equally distant from each other as your first, manually created tab stop is from the left.

Just think about all the times you manually created tab stops, and how useful this can be going forward.

If you don't need equidistant tab stops but ones with varying distances, you've still saved yourself time and effort in their initial creation. Now, just move them one at a time until they're in position.

Striped Tab-Separated Lists

All Tracks by Length

Title	**Artist**	**Album**	**Track No.**	**Length**
Louder Than Hell	Motley Crue	Theatre of Pain	3	2:32
Blame It On You	Poison	Look What the Cat Dragged In	8	2:34
You Really Got Me	Van Halen	Van Halen I	3	2:38
Crawl Space	Warrant	Ultraphobic	6	2:38
Big Balls	AC/DC	Dirty Deeds Done Dirt Cheap	6	2:38
Riot Act	Skid Row	Slave to the Grind	10	2:40

Tables easily allow you to create alternating fills for striping rows (see the "Create Alternating Row Fills" technique), but sometimes you need a list instead of a table. Should you therefore lose out on the benefits of horizontal striping for general readability and accessibility for people with disabilities? Not with this technique you won't.

The answer is actually in a previous recipe earlier in the chapter. All you have to do is follow the steps for "Alternating Paragraph Formatting" creating two paragraph styles with different shading settings (or one with paragraph shading, one with out), and apply them to your list with the slick master-level Apply Then Next command I showed you in that recipe. That can format your entire list, whether it's five rows or more than 55,000, like my actual list of songs to play on the *Hard, Heavy & Hair Show*.

Align On Decimals, Even When They're Missing

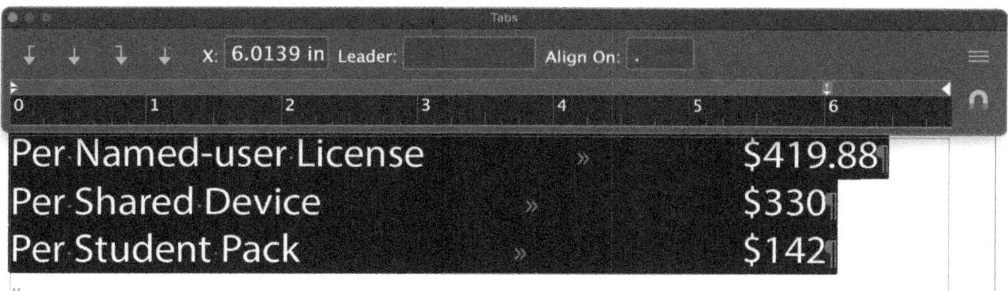

Hopefully, while reading about "Tab Basics" in *InDesign Masterclass: Type & Tables*, Chapter 3, "Paragraphs" you took note of the fact that you could use the Tab palette's Align On field to align columns of numbers, dates, or other data on specific characters that appear within the text of that tab stop. For example, in a list of prices containing dollar and cent values, you can align on the decimal between the dollar and cent amounts. You can also align on the decimal, even if there is no decimal.

InDesign infers the presence of a decimal after a whole number value, so, if you have mixed values of whole numbers and wholes with decimal places, InDesign will still align them all to the decimal—visible or not. Just set the Align On field for your tab stop to include a period (.), press Enter/Return, and you're done.

Loose Tab Dot Leaders

Character Recipes. 404
Highlight Text at the Character Level. 404
Highlighter Colors 405
Round End Text Highlighter 407

Dot leaders on tabs can sometimes feel too dense, with the dots (periods) too close together. Here's a simple technique to loosen them up.

1 Select the paragraph(s) containing one or more tabs that have, or should have, leaders.

Character Recipes.. 404
Highlight Text at the Character Level............................404
Highlighter Colors...405
Round End Text Highlighter..407

2 Open the Tabs palette from the Type menu or by pressing CMD+Shift+T/CTRL+Shift+T, or edit the Tabs pane in the Paragraph Style Options of the relevant paragraph style.
3 Select or create the desired tab stop.
4 In the Leader field, instead of entering the customary singular period (.), type a period and then a space (.).
5 Press Return/Enter or Tab on your keyboard to commit the change and see the result. It should be a dot leader with looser dots.

Looser Tab Dot Leaders

To make your dot leaders even looser, enter *two* spaces after the period in the tab stop's Leader field, or space-period-space. Of course, that could get *too* loose, and full space characters are definitely harder to control than with the next technique.

Better Loose Tab Dot Leaders

Character Recipes 404

Sometimes the period-space loosening method is exactly what's called for, though that isn't *my* preferred method of loosening the periods in a dot leader. This is:

1 Create tab stops as needed in the Tabs palette.
2 In the Leader field enter a single period without spaces anywhere.
3 Using the Type tool, select just the tab with dot leader in the actual text within the text frame.
4 On the Character, Control, or Properties panel, find the Tracking field and begin adding a positive tracking value. The dots in the leader will begin to loosen. Keep going until you're happy with their spacing.

Tab characters are singular characters, which shouldn't really display much change when adjusting Tracking beyond extreme changes, but the *leaders within tabs* have to treated as multiple characters. Therefore, applying character-level formatting like tracking, while not obvious on the tab itself, apply to the leaders inside as they would any text. Thus, unlike the period-space technique, this Tracking-adjusted technique gives you easy, absolute control over how loose or tight your dot leader dots appear. The tracking can be added to a character style, which can be manually or automatically applied to tab leaders (more on the automatic way shortly).

Smaller Tab Dot Leader Dots

Character Recipes 404
Highlight Text at the Character Level 404
Highlighter Colors 405
50%
50%
407

If you've read the "Better Loose Tab Dot Leaders" recipe, you can skip the following steps except for this: replace Tracking with the Scale fields. If you haven't read it yet, follow these steps:

1. Create tab stops as needed in the Tabs palette.
2. In the Leader field enter a single period without spaces anywhere.
3. Using the Type tool, select just the tab with dot leader in the actual text within the text frame.
4. On the Character, Control, or Properties panel, find the Vertical Scale and Horizontal Scale fields and begin scaling down from 100% in both until your leader dots are the size you want them.

This can give you more demure or delicate dot leaders without needing to change typefaces. You could change the Font Size field for the dot leader, but that can mess with your spacing; the Scale fields offer greater control. Either change to the dots is character-level formatting, which can be saved into, and applied from, character styles, which be applied manually or via automated means.

Non-Round Tab Dot Leader Dots

To create non-round dot leaders, follow the steps for the "Smaller Tab Dot Leader Dots" but set the Vertical Scale and Horizontal Scale to noticeably different values—maybe `50%` for Horizontal Scale but `150%` for Vertical Scale.

Automatically Format Tabs

To automatically format all tabs in your text (which I personally find totally awesome for tables of contents) use a GREP style like so:

1. Create a character style with the appropriate options to format the tab, with or without a leader.
2. Edit the paragraph style in effect on the text.
3. On the GREP Styles pane of the Paragraph Style Options, create a new GREP style.
4. Set the Apply Style field to your tab character style, and in the To Text field enter `\t`, the GREP code for a tab character. All tabs in that paragraph style will now instantly and automatically format themselves according to the character style.

Make Underscores with Tabs 1

Name Wile E. Coyote
Occupation Super Genius
Location American Southwest

THIS CONTRACT is made and entered into on 17 September 1949 by and between Acme, Inc. and Wile E. Coyote (Customer), whose principal offices or cave dwelling is at 900 foot Mesa Bluff, American Southwest

Dot leaders are dots separating text on either side of a tab. Line leaders are—you guessed it—are lines, usually underlines, between text on either side of a tab. Creating a line leader is as simple as placing an underscore

(_) in the Tab palette's Leader field instead of a period. In the first example above, that works, but in the second… not so much. Underscores as line leaders can complicate uneven areas because of the need to set absolute tab stop positions. Moreover, given that some typefaces' underscores aren't the full width of the space the character is allowed, creates gaps on the end or divots where the end of one underline glyph meets the beginning of the next. For those cases there's a better way to make underscores—which, coincidentally, is also great for even the first use case of lines that go all the way across a column or area.

Make Underscores with Tabs 2

THIS CONTRACT is made and entered into on 17 September 1949 by and between Acme, Inc. and Wile E. Coyote (Customer), whose principal offices or cave dwelling is at 900 foot Mesa Bluff American Southwest.

A better way to make line leaders, which is also a great way to make underscores for non-interactive ("flat") forms, is to do it this way.

1. Create your text—in this case, I'm creating a flat form contract with blanks to be filled in by hand—and use tabs to create the blank spaces someone will eventually write over. You can leave these at their default lengths and never open the Tabs palette, or you could adjust the width of the spaces with custom tab stops. Either way, *do not* enter *anything* in the Leader field.
2. Select one of your tabs with the Type tool.

3 Open the Character panel and select Underline Options from the panel menu.

4 Turn on Underline and set the options to create the perfect fill-in line for your form.

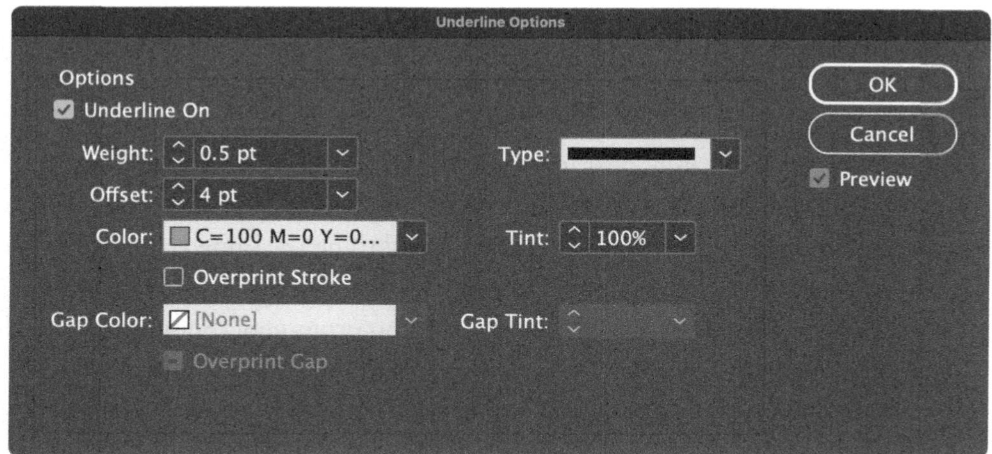

5 Create a characters style from that one tab, and then apply it to all the other tabs—either manually or via a GREP style (see “Automatically Format Tabs”.”

Dash Leaders the Right Way

Dash -------------------------------- Leader (Bad)

Dash————————————Leader (Good)

Dash leaders aren’t common, but they are out there. They’re often made by using hyphens in the Tab palette’s Leader field, and they just as often have the telltale gapping between hyphens. If you want a dash leader that is a series of short lines with gaps, then, by all means, do it that way. However, if what you’re really after is simply a horizontal line connecting one side of a tab to the other at x-height, then use strikethrough on the tab character instead of anything in the Leader field. The result will be much cleaner, and decidedly much easier to get just right.

Colored Leaders

HALESTORM .... "I MISS THE MISERY"
RIVAL SONS .... "PRESSURE AND TIME"
GRETA VAN FLEET .... "HIGHWAY TUNE"
DOROTHY .... "RAISE HELL"

After extensive research, peer interviews, and decades of experience in several areas of graphic and publication design, I have concluded the following: there is no rule that your leaders need to be the same color as the text they separate. So, why not take advantage of that missing limitation?

Leaders are nice, but sometimes they're too prominent. Sometimes they detract from their main purpose of connecting two pieces of text by themselves becoming noticeable. So why not lower the tint percentage or change the color entirely? Remember: leaders are wholly contained within tab characters, and tab characters can be colored or tinted just like any other character. Just select the tab character and change the tint or color on the Swatches panel, Color panel, or other place.

Faded Leaders

HAWKWIND .... "SILVER MACHINE"
BLACK SABBATH .... "PARANOID"
BAD COMPANY .... "FEEL LIKE MAKIN' LOVE"
LED ZEPPELIN .... "STAIRWAY TO HEAVEN"

No, I'm not talking about presidents, premieres, or supreme chancellors slipping into that mellow blur or nodding off of old age at their desks. I'm talking about dot (or whatever) leaders that fade from one color to another, creating a gradient leader that, like all gradients, can lead the reader's eye from one place to another without being overpowering.

Gradient leaders are extremely rare. I suspect that fact is honestly because so few people realize they *can* use gradients on tab leaders, not because people don't like it. Gradients lead the reader's eye from one place to another, which is also the exact definition of a tab leader. Why not combine them? Just be careful to follow basic color rules and psychology—for example, and at the risk of being accused of oversimplification, evolution has programmed human beings to "seek the light," meaning we are enticed to follow a path from a darker color to a lighter color, or a cooler color to a warmer one, both of which come from humans being diurnal creatures drawn to the safety of light over dark and specifically that skyward massive sphere of glowing plasma powered by nuclear fusion.

Don't be afraid to apply a gradient to your dot leaders by selecting the tab character and giving it a gradient via the Gradient panel, and, after that, a character style. The only practical problem with applying gradients to leaders is when leaders are different lengths, which is common. In such cases, linear gradients will often need to be adjusted for each instance to achieve the actual this-to-that color transition without losing some portion of one end or the other.

Radial Gradient Leaders

GODSMACK.."I STAND ALONE"
SKILLET.."MONSTER"
SHINEDOWN.."SECOND CHANCE"
10 YEARS.."WASTELAND"

Radial gradients used on leaders create the one-two-one color fading. This challenges the "seek the light" programming for humans without completely breaking it, but variable-width objects like tab leaders handle it better than linear gradients. So there's a design cost *and* benefit. Often—by no means always—flicking that Gradient panel Type dropdown to Radial can immediately improve the appearance and eye-leading effectiveness of your tab leaders. Sometimes, the change to Radial is to the detriment of leaders. In this case, all I can do is tell you *how* to do it, not *when* or *why*. Which is greater, what is the balance between the two, is your subjective opinion for your specific content.

Here's the how: select your tab character with a Linear gradient leader, and, on the Gradient panel, change the Type drop-down to Radial.

The real benefit to radial gradients in tab leaders is as a shortcut to the one-two-one color transition. Instead of creating a linear gradient with three color stops, you can just switch the Type to Radial to achieve the same effect.

Double-Up Gradient Leaders

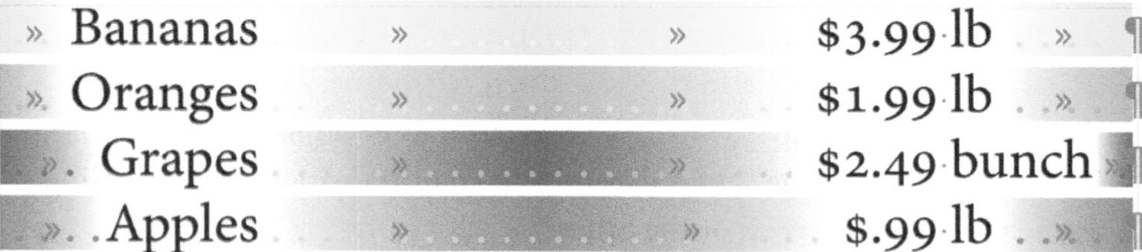

Here's another way to use gradient effects on leaders: two tabs are better than one. Well, not usually, but for this recipe, sure.

1. Set your text and where you would normally put one tab, put two instead.
2. Select the tab character on the left of the split and give it a linear gradient from color 1 to color 2.
3. Now select the next tab character, the one on the right side of the split, and give it the same but opposite gradient—color 2 to color 1—which is easy to achieve with that Reverse button the Gradients panel.

To get the gradients to and from the left and right columns, make sure you have a tab before the left column and a tab after the right. Then give them, respectively, color 1-to-color 2 and color 2-to-color 1 gradients.

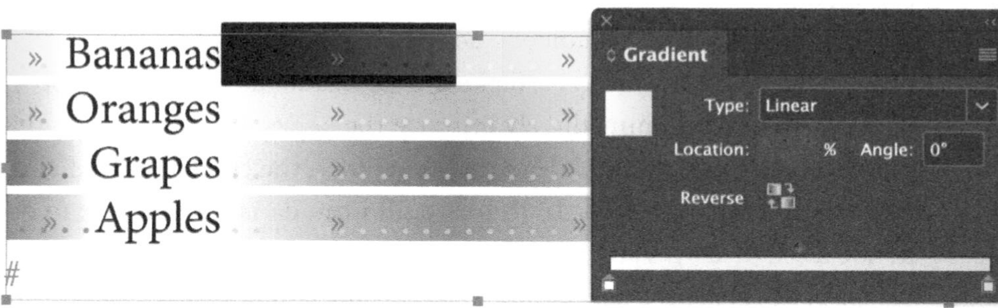

Want Perfect Right-Aligned Tabs? Then Don't Use Tabs

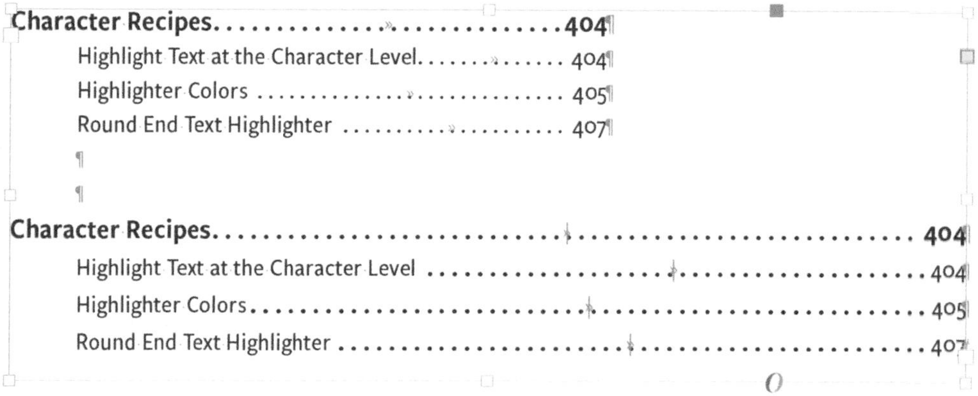

Character Recipes.......................404
Highlight Text at the Character Level............ 404
Highlighter Colors 405
Round End Text Highlighter 407

Character Recipes...404
Highlight Text at the Character Level 404
Highlighter Colors..405
Round End Text Highlighter 407

How many times did you read that title trying to make sense of it before you concluded that I must have a chemical imbalance that slipped past all my editors? (For what it's worth, I had to explain that heading to no less than three different editors via inline comments in Word and InDesign, Discord messages, private text message, and two "uh"- and "um"-laden conference calls because, as talented as they are, as freaking awesome as they are at their respective jobs, only my tech editor truly understood what I meant by that heading after a single explanation [shout out to my tech editor Michael Taylor!]).

Here's the tea: if you have two columns of text you want to separate by a tab—something like a table of contents, for example—your first instinct is to (usually) separate the left text from the right text with a tab. Amiright? If so, do not follow that instinct. You'll (usually, not always) have a much easier time of separating those tab-separated columns *if you don't use tabs.* Go head: read that statement a few more times. I'll wait.

If you use tabs you're locked into the rigid structure of the tab stop's position and whether and how it fits into the column and/or frame. That means your two columns—heading and page number in the image below—are as far apart as you make the tab stop in the Tabs palette. To change that horizontal relationship you need to move past tabs like moving past a lover who can't grow with you.

With me so far? (Need a moment to cry over that last hard breakup? Take your time. I gotchu, fam. *All* the time in the world.) Now, imagine the space for that TOC text frame expands (you meet "The One"), giving you more horizontal space and requiring that the page number needs to move further to the right. How do you flex with that? Right: you edit the paragraph style, going to the Tabs pane of the Paragraph Style Options dialog, and moving that right-aligned tab stop to the edge of the—*Darnit!* I moved it too far. Rip! Now I have to hit the Cancel button, then come back and edit the paragraph style again, and... *F in the chat!* I did it again. I moved the right-aligned tab stop too far for the Tabs pane ruler, and now I need to start all over. *What a pain in the...* uh, neck.

Instead of dealing with all that crap, there's a way easier way. Let's rewind.

1 Create, type, paste, or import your list of text. In my case, I'm using the partial table of contents for this chapter, as shown in that first image under the most perplexing H2 heading.

2 Instead of using a tab between the subject and the page number, choose Type ▸ Insert Special Character ▸ Other ▸ Right Indent Tab (master tip: use Shift+Tab if you do it often, as I do), and...

   Heh, *done.* The text to the right—the page number in my case—immediately jumps to be right-aligned to the right edge of the column or frame (see the original image in this section).

   Seriously, it's a two-step how-to.

What happened? The Right Indent Tab command inserts a marker of the same name. That Right Indent Tab marker takes whatever text is to the right of itself and aligns it to the right of the paragraph, column, or frame. No muss. No fuss. All chill. The text to the right of the Right Indent Tab marker will *always* be aligned to the right edge of the space alloted to the line, even if you resize the frame. If you make it wider, the text will move further from its left-aligned mates, including filling in a leader if you have one. If the frame has to narrow, then the Right Indent Tab will shrink, keeping its following text on the same line (as long as it all fits) without the need to futz with tab stops. Honestly, Right Indent Tab is *the* way to do right-aligned text after a tab. Don't bother with an actual tab. That's like going back to a toxic ex: it feels good for a minute, but quickly you realize why you moved on from such a limited partner.

Table Recipes

Format an Entire Table in One Click

I would be remiss if I didn't point out right at the start that cell styles include an option to automatically apply a paragraph style. In its simplest terms, that means: Gug apply cell style, paragraph style follow. Gug walk into the sunset, throw fist into sky god realm like Judd Nelson in *Breakfast Club*. Gug is badass.

In slightly less simplistic terms: when you create a cell style, you can choose a paragraph style for the text inside the cell. That means that, when you apply a cell style to a cell or range of them, you can also automatically apply paragraph styles to the text within that cell(s). And, because table styles can automatically apply multiple cell styles at once, you can format an entire table in one click. You just have to connect your paragraph, cell, and table styles properly.

Seriously, if you want that action-hero-unflinchingly-walking-away-from-an-explosion moment, *this* is the way to get it. Click a table style, swirl out of your swivel chair, and strut in slo-mo like a baller out of the conference room. (Just make sure it's the client's laptop you leave blazing in your rearview, not your own beloved MacBook Pro.)

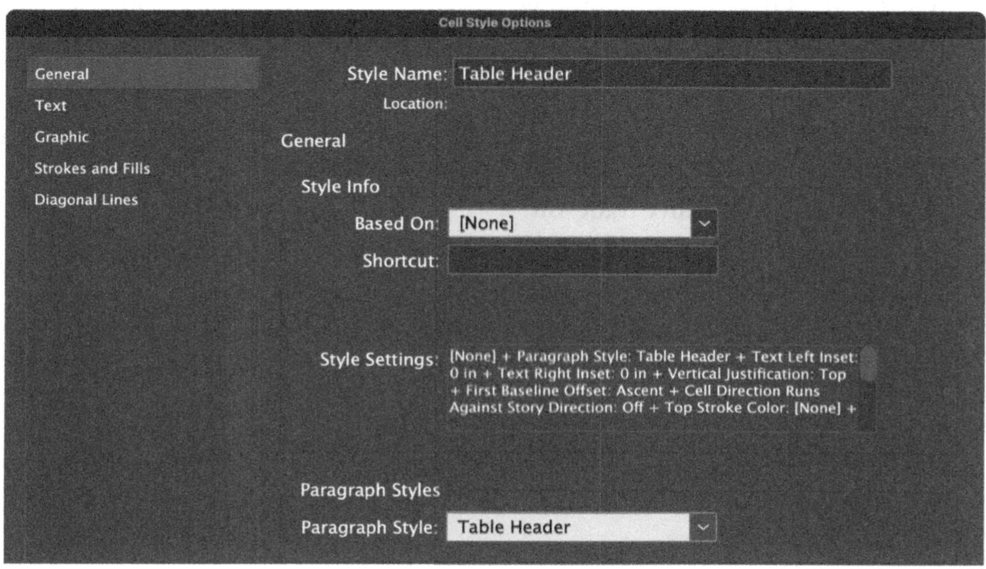

Different Header Row(s) on the First Page of a Table

Table 4.1—OUTLAYS BY AGENCY: 2011-2021							
(in millions of dollars)							
2011	2012	2013	2014	2015	2016	2017	2018
4,582	4,440	4,316	4,164	4,330	4,728	4,880	5,019
7.293	7.227	7.063	6.893	7.137	7.729	7.749	7.902

Table 4.1—OUTLAYS BY AGENCY: 2011-2021 (Cont'd)							
(in millions of dollars)							
2011	2012	2013	2014	2015	2016	2017	2018
678,074	650,867	607,800	577,898	562,499	576,328	586,834	568,600

As you read in *InDesign Masterclass: Type & Tables*, Chapter 4, "Tables", InDesign tables can include one or more header rows with the ability to automatically repeat those rows at the top of any continuation of a table into subsequent columns, frames, or pages. What it does not have, at least in the Table Options dialog, is a way to show one header on the first instance of the table, and a different header on continuations. If you look at the images above, the first is the start of a multi-page table while the second image is the header rows of continuations of that table on subsequent pages. The difference between them is that the designer set the continuations to include "Cont'd)" in the title row. That qualifier doesn't appear on the first page. Getting that difference between first set of header rows and all the repeating header rows is not a setting in InDesign. It's not difficult, but it does take a little manual preparation within the table itself as well as a conscious accessibility trade-off.

For longer tables to have different headers on the first page, frame, or column than on subsequent instances, follow these steps:

1. Build and style your table as desired, but hold off on converting any body rows to header rows.
2. At the top of the table, on its first page, frame, or column, where there table actually begins rather than any continuation, create and style your header rows as you would like them to appear at the top of that first instance only.

Note that you *can* use cell styles for this technique as long as you don't convert the rows themselves to header rows via Table ▸ Convert To ▸ Header Rows. We'll call this set of header row or rows your "First Header Rows."

3. Decide how many header rows the continuations of your table will need. Will it be the same headers with something "Cont'd" or "Continuation" added, or will you be using a slimmer set of headers for table continuations? Choose your approach and think of that row or rows as the "Continuation Header."
4. Select the Type tool and place your cursor into the highest row, first column of your First Header Rows.
5. Choose ▸ Table ▸ Insert Row.
6. In the Insert Row(s) dialog box, choose the radio button beside Above, and then set the Number field to be the number of header rows for your Continuation Header, not for the First Header Rows. Click OK.
7. In this new row or rows, the Continuation Header , enter the title, column header(s), and other information you've decided to include atop continuations of your table. Copy and paste from First Header Rows, and then customizing, is probably the easiest way to go.
8. Style the Continuation Header, including filling, stroking, merging, splitting, and whatever other formatting you want for those not-the-first-page-of-the-table headers.
9. Select *only* the Continuation Header rows, and choose Table ▸ Convert To ▸ Header Rows.
10. From the Table menu, choose Table Options ▸ Headers and Footers.
11. The correct number for only the Continuation Header rows should already be in the Header Rows field. Set the Repeat Header drop-down to how often you'd like that continuation header to appear.
12. Activate Skip First and press OK.

On the page, your Continuation Header should disappear from the top of the table, leaving only the First Header Rows. The First Header Rows will only appear on that first page, while the Continuation Header will re-appear at the top of each continuation of the table, at every column, frame, or page, as you choose in the Repeat Header field.

Header Rows	Table 4.1—OUTLAYS BY AGENCY: 2011-2021 (Cont'd) (in millions of dollars)						
Department or other unit	2011	2012	2013	2014	2015	2016	2017
Body Rows	**Table 4.1—OUTLAYS BY AGENCY: 2011-2021 (in millions of dollars)**						
Department or other unit	2011	2012	2013	2014	2015	2016	2017
Legislative Branch	4,582	4,440	4,316	4,164	4,330	4,728	4,880
Judicial Branch	7,293	7,227	7,063	6,893	7,137	7,729	7,749
Department of Agriculture	139,397	139,717	155,895	141,808	139,115	153,773	151,485
Department of Commerce	9,930	10,273	9,140	7,895	8,958	10,527	10,546

How does it work? Here's the trick, secret, and catch to this technique, plus a pair of tips:

The Trick What makes the technique work is that Skip First field; it tells InDesign to show all header rows—currently, just the Continuation Header—in every instance *except* the first.

The Secret The secret to making it work is that we never turned the First Header Rows into actual header rows; they're still *body* rows. Thus, Repeat Header will never repeat them, but also won't hide them because of the Skip First setting.

The Catch There's a mild catch to this technique, a drawback, that will require you to adjust a few tags within Acrobat for any PDFs you create from a table using this technique. By not converting First Header Rows to actual header rows, they won't be tagged properly for accessibility. If that's important to you, which I hope it is, you'll need to edit the TD tags for all the cells in the First Header Rows to convert them to TH tags. That has to be done inside Adobe Acrobat, either using the Reader Order tool's Table Editor mode and Cell Properties, or the easier way of directly editing the tags in the Tags panel.

Tip #1 You can't select, much less change, the Continuation Header when it appears on subsequent parts of the table, but you can edit it with a little-known command. Select Edit Header from the Table menu, and suddenly the first instance of the Continuation Header will become selected and editable.

Tip #2 This technique also works with footer rows. Just follow the same steps, but wherever I say "header" go feet-over-head.

Create Alternating Row Fills

Table 4.1—OUTLAYS BY AGENCY: 2011-2021 (in millions of dollars)										
Department or other unit	2011	2012	2013	2014	2015	2016	2017	2018	2019	20
Legislative Branch	4,582	4,440	4,316	4,164	4,330	4,728	4,880	5,019	5,135	5,2
Judicial Branch	7,293	7,227	7,063	6,893	7,137	7,729	7,749	7,902	8,055	8,2
Department of Agriculture	139,397	139,717	155,895	141,808	139,115	153,773	151,485	153,011	149,038	146,8
Department of Commerce	9,930	10,273	9,140	7,895	8,958	10,527	10,546	11,074	13,120	16,9
Department of Defense--Military Programs	678,074	650,867	607,800	577,898	562,499	576,328	586,834	568,600	569,886	575,2
Department of Education	65,484	57,249	40,910	59,610	90,029	79,098	68,438	75,866	84,765	91,2

Especially in wider tables, alternating row fills can be very helpful in allowing readers to track a single row or record across columns. Creating alternating fills in InDesign is simple, just make your Table Options Fills tab settings the same as mine.

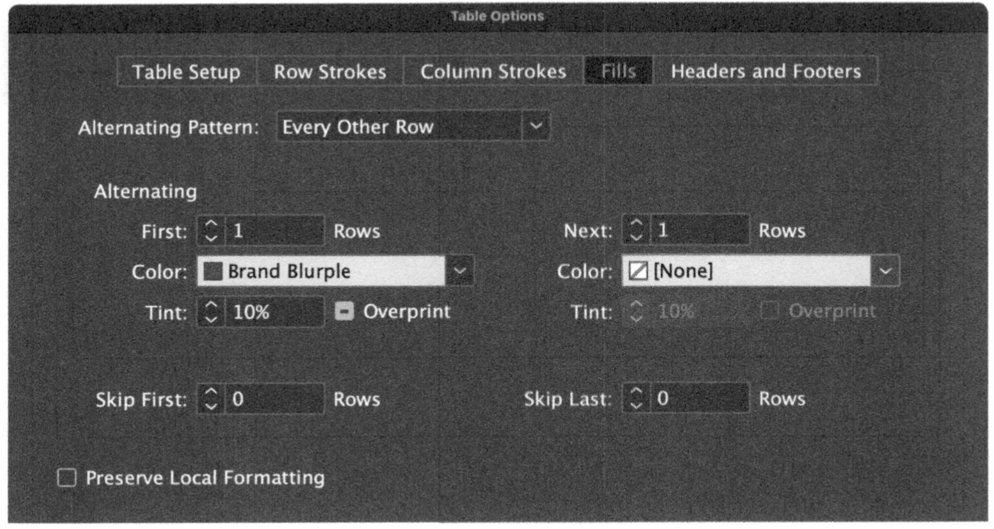

Starting Alternating Row Fills with an Empty Fill

Shading the first row beneath a shaded header is sometimes not as nice looking as leaving that first row unshaded. To get that unshaded first row, match my Fills settings, which gives the first row a [None] fill (or [Paper], if you prefer) and picks up the shading with the next row thanks to putting it in the right column of settings.

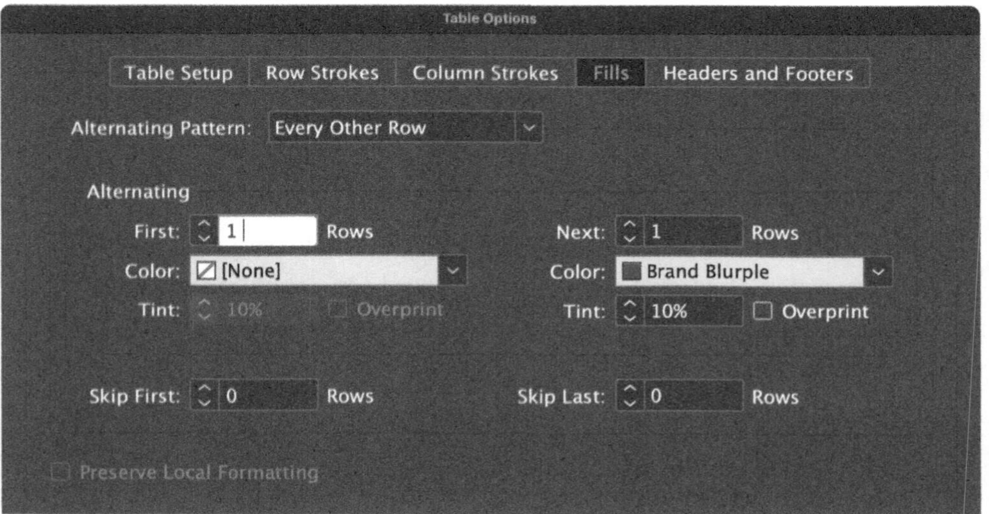

Stroking or Filling All Rows, Columns, or Cells

2011	2012	2013	2014	2015	2016	2017
4,582	4,440	4,316	4,164	4,330	4,728	4,880
7,293	7,227	7,063	6,893	7,137	7,729	7,749
139,397	139,717	155,895	141,808	139,115	153,773	151,485
9,930	10,273	9,140	7,895	8,958	10,527	10,546
678,074	650,867	607,800	577,898	562,499	576,328	586,834

When looking at Table Options, what may not be obvious is how to stroke or fill all selected columns, rows, or cells. Indeed, having an All option on the Alternating Pattern menus would have been nice. Alas, the option isn't as obvious as that, though it's exceedingly simple to do. Choose Custom Row or Custom Column, then set the First alternating field to `1` and the Next alternating field to `0`. That's it. Now every selected column, row, or cell will be stroked or filled with whatever color and style you choose.

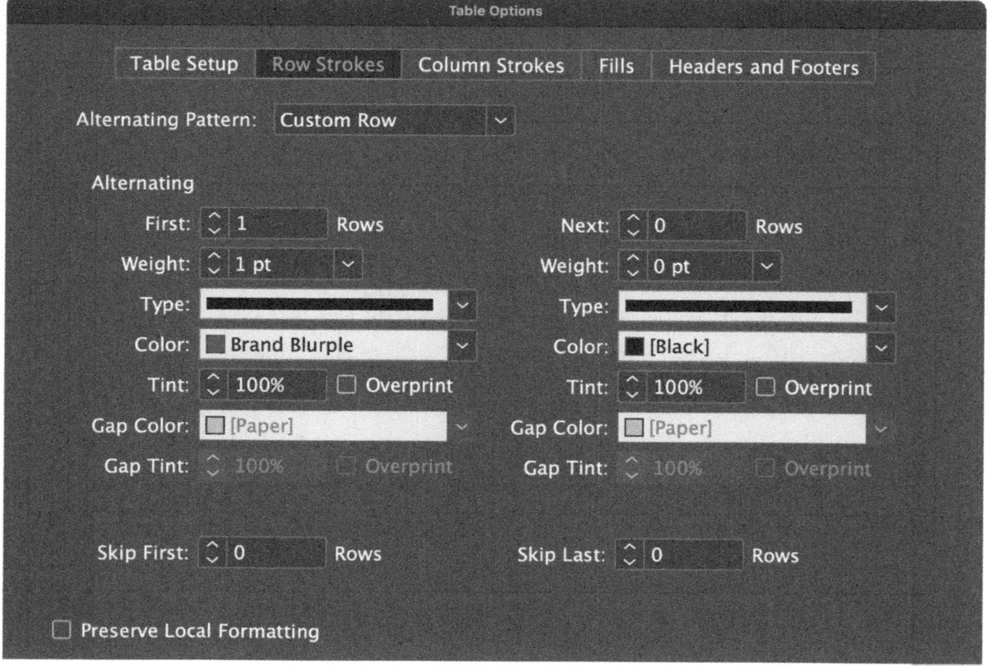

Add Row Headers

Table 4.1—OUTLAYS BY AGENCY: 2011-2021 (in millions of dollars)						
Department or other unit	**2011**	**2012**	**2013**	**2014**	**2015**	**2016**
Legislative Branch	4,582	4,440	4,316	4,164	4,330	4,728
Judicial Branch	7,293	7,227	7,063	6,893	7,137	7,729
Department of Agriculture	139,397	139,717	155,895	141,808	139,115	153,773
Department of Commerce	9,930	10,273	9,140	7,895	8,958	10,527
Department of Defense--Military Programs	678,074	650,867	607,800	577,898	562,499	576,328
Department of Education	65,484	57,249	40,910	59,610	90,029	79,098
Department of Energy	31,371	32,484	24,731	23,638	25,424	27,416
Department of Health and Human Services	891,247	848,056	886,291	936,012	1,027,507	1,110,428

When it comes to tables, table design, and tables accessibility, InDesign beats Microsoft Word over and over again… except in one thing: row headers.

Let's do a quick review of terms. They can get confusing, at least to me, so I'm going to set all the terms in title case, which I hope will make them less murky. (*Who's on first? Yes.*) Data Cells, what InDesign calls Body Cells, contain the actual data of a table, the content we or our readers are meant to read and evaluate. Column Headers, which are contained within Header Rows in InDesign, are the labels that classify or categorize the data beneath them. Headers aren't data unto themselves; they're pieces of information that give context to Data Cells. Row Headers are the same, but horizontally. A Row Header, usually in the first column, maybe also in the last, classifies and provides context to the data in the same row. Many tables include both Column Headers (within rows) and Row Headers (within a column), especially those tables with complex data sets such as medical, pharmaceutical, engineering, construction, and financial tables. Either or both Column Headers and Row Headers can make it easier for someone to visually understand the Data Cells. Because of advanced tagging and association possible within Adobe Acrobat, they're also extremely helpful to people using assistive technology to read the table within a PDF. HTML, EPUB, and other XML-based formats have similar tagging options for accessibility.

So, Row Headers are good and something many table designers use frequently. The problem is, InDesign doesn't have Row Headers. It has Header Rows, which, somewhat confusingly, actually contain *Column Headers*, but it can't make the first cell on a Body Row into a Row Header. Word can—it's a simple matter of activating a checkbox control on the Ribbon—but InDesign can't. Moreover, even if Row Headers are added in Word and then placed into InDesign, the latter ignores them, converting them to standard Body Row Data Cells. You will always need to fix the tagging, turning TDs into THs, in Acrobat for Row Headers created in InDesign and exported to PDF.

All that said, you *can* make Row Headers, at least visually. You'll still have to fix the tagging for assistive technology, but for visual accessibility, you'll have created obvious classifiers for data across the table's width.

Here's how:

1. Pick your first Row Header and style it to be visually different from data cells on the same row. You can fill the cell, change the typeface or style, change the text color, or whatever other formatting you want to do to make the Row Header visually distinctive.
2. Select the text in the Row Header and create a paragraph style called Row Header.
3. Keep the cell selected and, on the Cell Styles panel, create a new cell style called Row Header. On the General pane of the Cell Style Options, choose the paragraph style you just made from the drop-down at the bottom.
4. Now, create or edit your table style on the Table Styles panel.
5. At the bottom of the Table Style Options, on the General pane, set the Left Column drop-down to be your Row Header cell style. Now, every time you apply that table style, you'll automatically have Row Headers in the left column.

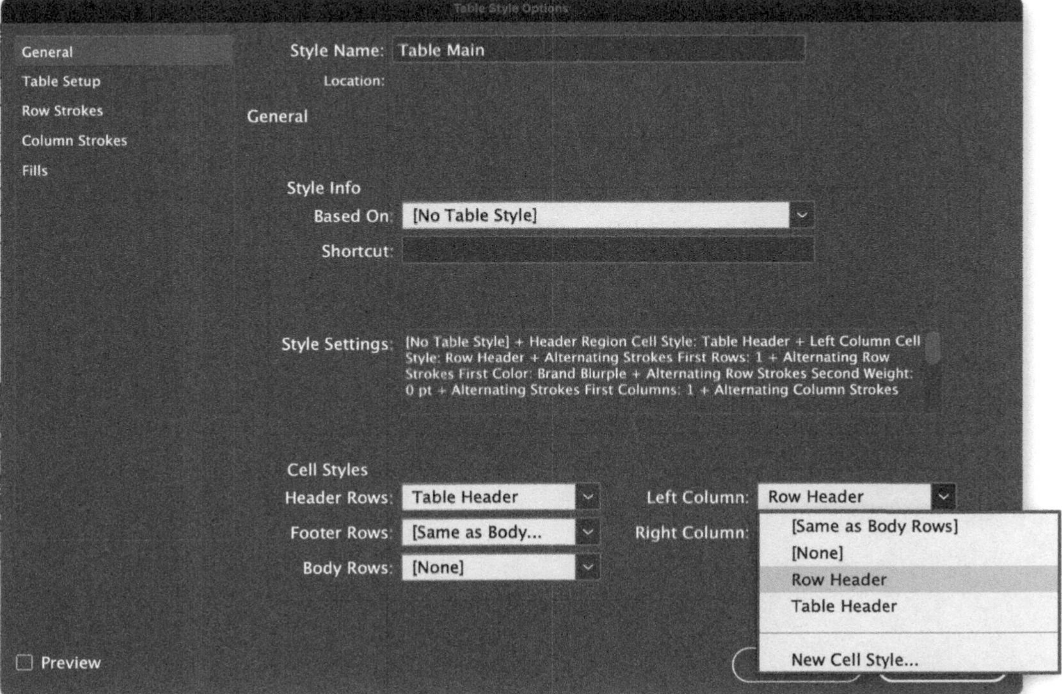

For wider tables, you may want repeat the first column's Row Headers in the last column of the table, allowing people to see the categorization at whichever end is closer to where they're reading. This is especially helpful when people have to zoom on your table, like when reading it on a phone or other small screen device. If you have Row Headers on the right as well as the left, set the Right Column drop-down to also be the Row Header cell style.

Add a Total Column

NCY: 2011-2021							
llars)							
2015	2016	2017	2018	2019	2020	2021	Total
4,330	4,728	4,880	5,019	5,135	5,229	5,309	$52,132
7,137	7,729	7,749	7,902	8,055	8,242	8,421	$83,711
139,115	153,773	151,485	153,011	149,038	146,833	150,987	$1,621,059
8,958	10,527	10,546	11,074	13,120	16,948	13,134	$121,545
562,499	576,328	586,834	568,600	569,886	575,255	582,025	$6,536,066
90,029	79,098	68,438	75,866	84,765	91,220	95,794	$808,463
25,424	27,416	30,373	30,194	31,194	33,163	33,516	$323,504
1,027,507	1,110,428	1,144,690	1,170,257	1,250,522	1,304,623	1,378,718	$11,948,351

Creating a Total column is the same process as creating a Row Headers, just usually on the right side where Row Headers are typically on the left. Follow the "Add Row Headers" tutorial to create and style your Total column. Note that, for accessibility, you should not tag a Total column with THs; leave them as TDs in the PDF you output.

Elegant Monochrome Tables

Table 4.1—OUTLAYS BY AGENCY: 2011-2021 (in millions of dollars)							
Department or other unit	2011	2012	2013	2014	2015	2016	2017
Legislative Branch	4,582	4,440	4,316	4,164	4,330	4,728	4,880
Judicial Branch	7,293	7,227	7,063	6,893	7,137	7,729	7,749
Department of Agriculture	139,397	139,717	155,895	141,808	139,115	153,773	151,485
Department of Commerce	9,930	10,273	9,140	7,895	8,958	10,527	10,546

Monochromatic color palettes, different tints or shades of the same color, is one of those design trends that never goes out of style. They can bring an elegance and sophistication to almost any element of a design, and many people think that's truest when a monochromatic color palette is applied to a table.

If you find yourself staring at a table, unable to decide how to design it or what colors to use, give a monochrome set of colors a try. Pick a color, something dark enough to allow for varying tints (mixing in white) or shades (mixing in black). Then, use the Color panel or Swatch Options in HSB mode to build shade swatches by lowering the Brightness slider, or use the built-in Tint fields just about everywhere you deal with color in InDesign to create lighter variants of the color. On the Table Options ▸ Fills pane, for example, choose an alternating pattern, and then set the same color in both columns. Change the tint field beneath each Color drop-down to create lighter variations within a monochrome table.

Transparency in Table Row Fills 1

Hard, Heavy & Hair Show with Pariah Burke Run Sheet			
Show Number:	0477	Air Date:	2024-08-23
Cover Song of the Week:	"Working Man" Sebastian Bach (cover) Rush (original)		
Rock Queen of the Week:	Lita Ford "Kiss Me Deadly"		
Triple-Shot:	Working Class Rockers: Rush "Tom Sawyer", Bon Jovi "Livin' on a Prayer", Five Finger Death Punch "Wrong Side of Heaven"		
Segment 3 Feature:	Summer of Love (Semi-Finals): Warrant "Heaven" vs. Great White "Save Your Love"		
Top of Show Anthem:	AC/DC "For Those About to Rock (We Salute You)"		
Playout Track:	GodSmack "No Rest for the Wicked"		

Alas, you can't *actually* make table fills less than 100% opaque, but with these recipes, you can make your table *look like* it has transparency, as I did with the cue sheet (loose running script) for my weekly syndicated radio show. This technique works with single- and multi-frame tables, if the colors are compatible.

1. Create and style your table. Give it some fills, in some rows or all of them, as you prefer.
2. Add your watermark, background image, or whatever it is you want to peek through the table, and send it to the back with Object ▸ Arrange ▸ Send to Back or any of the six other methods of accomplishing the same thing.
3. With the Selection tool, select the text frame containing the table.
4. Open the Effects panel from Window ▸ Effects.
5. In the top-left corner is the Blending Mode field, probably showing Normal. If your table's colors are dark, select Multiply from that menu. Choose Screen if your table's colors are lighter than the background image.

This method takes your table and blends it with what's behind it, resulting in the appearance of transparency within the table row fills. It won't work with every combination of colors and background, which is why there's an alternative technique below. Before you resort to that, though, try different Blending Modes to see if your table and background color combination works better with one of them. Typically, this technique works best with tables whose colors are all around the same tonal range—dark or light.

Transparency in Table Row Fills 2

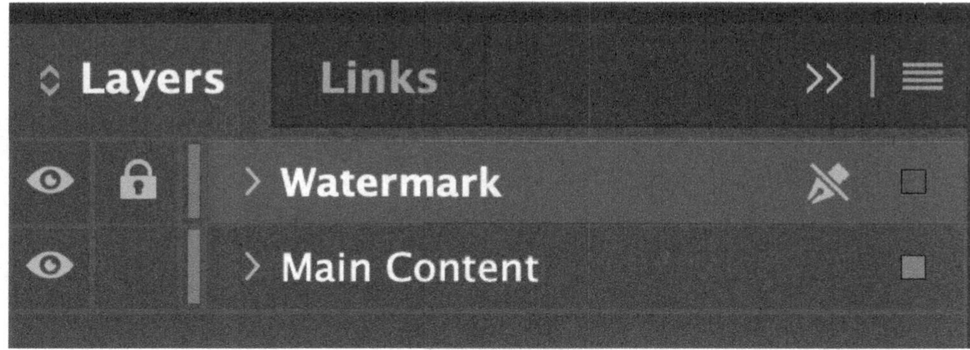

An alternative to making the table blend is to make the image you want to peek through the table blend.

1. Create and style your table.
2. Go to the Layers panel and create a new layer *above* the layer containing the table.
3. Place your logo, watermark, background image, or whatever onto the new layer and position it over the table.
4. Select the image, and on the Effects panel, choose either or both a less than 100% opacity and a blending mode from the Blending Mode drop-down menu.
5. When you're satisfied with the interaction of image and table, lock the image's layer by clicking in the second column on the Layers panel. Locking the layer allows you to click on the table for editing without the image getting in the way.

If this doesn't work, there is a third technique that isolates the composition of row fills, table content, and imagery into three separate objects.

Transparency in Table Row Fills 3

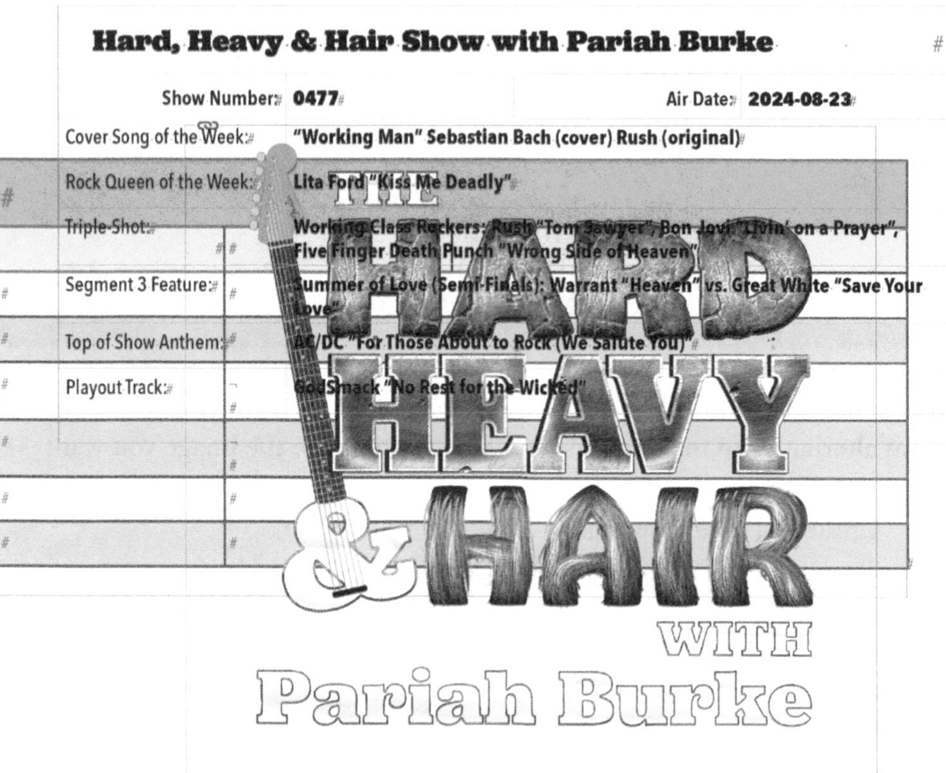

As you might expect, the technique of separating table fills from table text, and then throwing in the watermark, background image, or whatever else you want to see blending with the row fills, is the most labor-intensive of the three recipes for effecting transparency in table row fills. I highly recommend you only use this method when the other two don't produce the results you want, for instance, if the row fills blend nicely but the text doesn't. Also, you should probably only attempt this on tables that can be contained within a single frame.

1. Create and style your table, including the row fills you want.
2. If your table is part of a longer story, cut it out and paste it into its own text frame. You want to be able to work with the table as its own, self-contained story without other text. You can always anchor the table's frames back into the main story at the end if needed.
3. Select the table frame with the Selection tool choose Edit ▸ Duplicate twice to make two copies of the table.

4 Set aside the original—on the pasteboard or somewhere else out of your way. That original will be a safety net in case you want to go back and undo this technique.
5 In the first copy of your table, delete all the text and imagery. Leave only an empty table with row fills, column fills, strokes, and whatever else you might have configured in the Table Options dialog.
6 Select the second copy of the table, the one with text (and maybe images) still in it. Move your cursor to the top-left corner until you get that big black arrow, and then select the entire table. Go to Table ▸ Table Options ▸ Table Setup... to open the Table Options dialog.
7 Now move through each of the tabs in Table Options removing all row and column fills, all table, row, and column strokes. You want to see nothing but the invisible blue lines around every cell. Click OK.
8 Place the image.
9 Using the Selection tool and the Object ▸ Arrange commands, line up you two table copies atop each other, the no-text-filled version at the back, the text-no-adornment version in the front of the stack, with the image sandwiched between them.
10 Open the Effects panel, and, using the Layers panel to select the individual stacked objects, set the transparency and blending mode options for the image, the no-text-filled table, or both, until you're happy with the interaction of the colors. Note that you may choose to move the image all the way to the back depending in whether that gives you better results.

    At all times, though, the table data in that front object will be completely opaque, which should solve the most common problem with the other two techniques.
11 If you need to anchor the table into the main story flow, select all three objects and group them with CMD+G/CTRL+G, and then anchor the group as one.

For accessibility, I also recommend you artifact the no-text-filled table and, depending on its content, maybe the image as well. Assistive technology will still perceive the content of the text table as tabular text, even if it's part of a group.

Gradient-Filled Table

	Personal	Pro	Business	Enterprise
Storage Space	100 GB	500 GB	2 TB	10 TB
Bandwidth	50 GB	500 GB	1 TB	Unlimited
MySQL Databases	Unlimited	Unlimited	Unlimited	Unlimited
Email Accounts	100	Unlimited	Unlimited	Unlimited
Price Per Month	$3.95	$12.95	$19.95	$49.95

If you're reading this you fall into one of two camps. First, you already know how to do it, but you're curious if I have a different method, or, second, you don't know how to create a gradient-filled table, and you're going to slap yourself on the forehead when you see how easy it is. So, let's get to it!

1. Create your table in its own text frame. If it's already in a text frame, cut the table out and paste it in its own text frame.
2. Make sure your table doesn't have any fills or borders that connect with the outside corners of the table.
3. With the Selection tool, select the text frame.
4. Open the Gradient panel (Window ▸ Color ▸ Gradient) and create a gradient. If anything weird happens, check your Tools, Properties, Control, or Swatches panel and make sure you've targeted the fill color swatch of the frame rather than its stroke swatch, text formatting, or whatever.

Rounded Corner Table

	Personal	Pro	Business	Enterprise
Storage Space	100 GB	500 GB	2 TB	10 TB
Bandwidth	50 GB	500 GB	1 TB	Unlimited
MySQL Databases	Unlimited	Unlimited	Unlimited	Unlimited
Email Accounts	100	Unlimited	Unlimited	Unlimited
Price Per Month	$3.95	$12.95	$19.95	$49.95

Creating a rounded corner table is as elementary as creating a gradient-filled one. It's so simple, in fact, I'm not even going to give you numbered steps to follow. Instead, I'll say this: select the text frame containing the table with the Selection tool, and then use Object ▸ Corner Options to create rounded, scalloped, or whatever corners on the text frame. If needed, adjust the width and/or height of the text frame (because tables can escape their containing text frames).

Rounded Corner Table Cells

	PERSONAL	PRO	BUSINESS	ENTERPRISE
Storage Space	100 GB	500 GB	2 TB	10 TB
Bandwidth	50 GB	500 GB	1 TB	Unlimited
MySQL Databases	Unlimited	Unlimited	Unlimited	Unlimited
Email Accounts	100	Unlimited	Unlimited	Unlimited
Price Per Month	$3.95	$12.95	$19.95	$49.95

Before I show you the technique I would like to acknowledge that the following was not always possible. Up until InDesign 2015… Which, yes, I realize was 10 years ago, but a *lot* of tips, tricks, and techniques were published by me and people like me between 1999 and 2015, and so we taught you how to do rounded corner table cells with what was possible in those 26 years.

Usually those tutorials involved creating corner-like vector paths in InDesign or Illustrator, pasting four of them into the text of a cell, and adjusting the Anchored Object Options such that each one became a corner of a table cell. My colleague Diane Burns first brought that method to my attention way back at the very first InDesign Conference, where we both had conference sessions. Since 2015, however, InDesign has had a renaissance of table cells, and you no longer have to resort to what is, frankly, a seriously cludgy process of drawing and then anchoring four different corners. Now, it's so, so much easier.

1. Create and format your table.
2. Grab the Type tool and create a new text frame to hold your first rounded-corner piece of data.
3. Type the data into the text frame. In my case, that first piece of data was Personal. (I don't mean I won't tell you; it was the word "Personal".)
4. Fill and/or stroke the text frame as needed, with a solid color or a gradient.
5. With the frame selected with the Selection tool, go to Object ▸ Corner Options and setup your corners. Below are the settings I used. Click OK when you're satisfied.

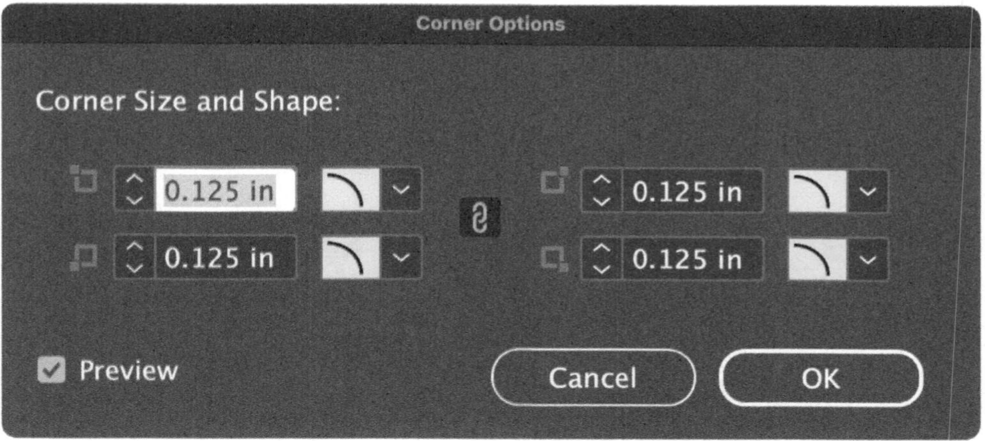

6. Resize the frame if needed, and then copy and paste it for each of your other non-rectangular table cells.
7. Edit each of those to display the text they should.

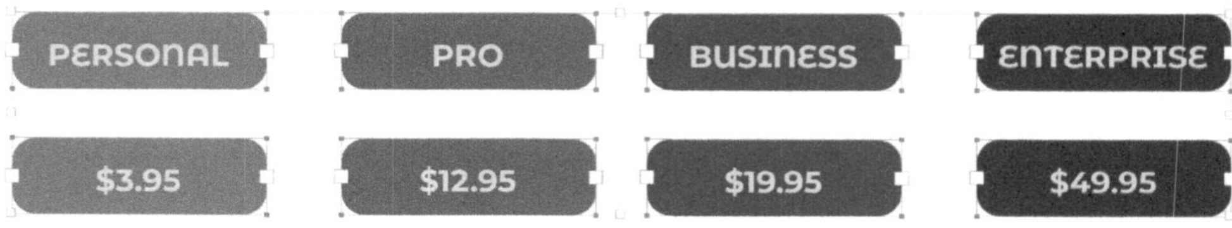

8 Switch to the Selection tool and select the first frame.
9 Copy it with CMD+C/CTRL+C (or you can cut it if you're feeling confident).
10 With the Type tool active, go into the table and select the contents of the cell where that frame you just copied (or cut) belongs.
11 Paste. Boom! Non-rectangular content in a table cell.
12 Repeat the last few steps for every other non-rectangular table cell.

You can still edit the contents of those non-rectangular table cells at any time. Just double-click them with the Type tool. They're still text, just inside text frames that are embedded inside a table. Like Sammy Hagar sang with Van Halen, with this technique, "we can have the best… of… both… worlds / A little bit of heaven right here on Earth, yeah!"

Tabbed Comparison Table

Here's another recipe for a comparison table for one of those veteran online applications that has the memory of an elephant.

1 Use Table ▸ Insert Table to create a table that includes enough rows for all the content and headers, as well as columns for each of the comparison lists *and for* separator columns between them.
2 Size the columns as needed on the Tables panel or by using the mouse.
3 Like the previous recipe, if you're going to use non-rectangular fills, create them as separate objects and then paste them into the table in their own fields.

4 Copy them one at a time and paste them into their correct locations within the table.
5 Resize the columns or the pasted frames if needed to make everything match.
6 With the Type tool, highlight only the cells in one comparison row, and select Open Table ▸ Table Options ▸ Alternating Fills, and set up your alternating fills as desired. My settings are below.

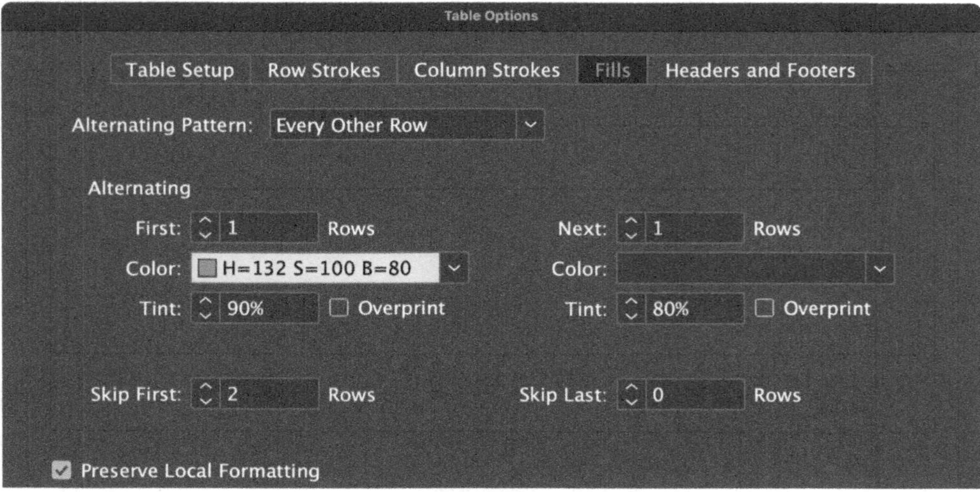

7 Repeat the process for the other two columns. Because of the empty separator columns, you have to do this one column at a time.

Complex Non-Rectangular Tables

	Column 1	Column 2	Column 3	Column 4	Column 5
Facebook	100,000	100,001	120,000	116,000	97,875
LinkedIn	100,000	100,001	120,000	116,000	97,875
YouTube	100,000	100,001	120,000	116,000	97,875
Instagram	100,000	100,001	120,000	116,000	97,875
Pinterest	100,000	100,001	120,000	116,000	97,875

That title doesn't *quite* do it, but after all the cool table stuff we've explored together, it seemed like the best way to describe this tutorial without using a TOC-wrecking title like "Table Designs Using Incongruous Corners, Icons, Nested Objects, and Alternating Fills All Together to Create Something Awesome". Forgive me?

1 First things, first: create your table and fill in the bulk of it.

2 Style the table how you'd like it.

	#	#	#	#	#
#	100,000#	100,001#	120,000#	116,000#	97,875#
#	100,000#	100,001#	120,000#	116,000#	97,875#
#	100,000#	100,001#	120,000#	116,000#	97,875#
#	100,000#	100,001#	120,000#	116,000#	97,875#
#	100,000#	100,001#	120,000#	116,000#	97,875#

3 Create a new text frame to hold the first column header, and fill and/or stroke it the way you'd like.

4 Set the corner options on that frame. To replicate mine, use the below Corner Options settings.

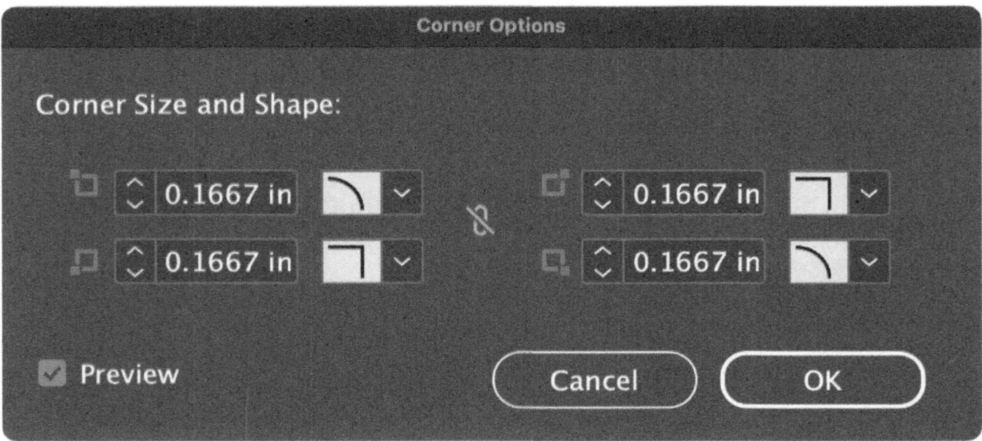

5 Once you're happy with the look of the column header, duplicate it as many times as needed to create all the column headers.

6 Edit the text and then the fill, stroke, or other formatting for each of the individual column header text frames.

7 Now create the text frame for the row headers, setting their fill, stroke, and corner options as needed.

8 Create or place the icons for your row headers. In my case, I created new text frames and used the FontAwesome symbol font to insert the icons for Facebook, LinkedIn, YouTube, and so on.

9 Cut and paste each of them into their corresponding row headings, and set their positioning via Object ▸ Anchored Object ▸ Options.

10 In the end, you should have something similar to my list of row headers (at right).

11 Finally, on at a time, select each of the column and row header objects with the Selection tool, cut it with CMD+X/CTRL+X, switch to the Type tool, click inside the appropriate cell in the table, and paste with CMD+V/CTRL+V.

12 Adjust column widths or row heights on the Table panel as needed, and you'll have a table not limited by the rectangles of table cells.

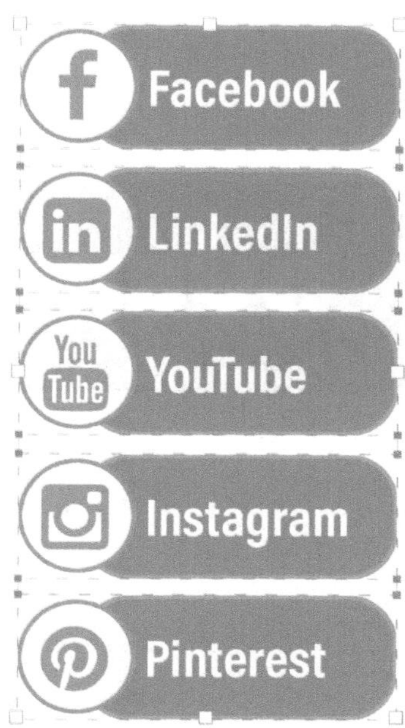

Round Table Cells

Want round table cells? Create an ellipse or elliptical frame, and paste it into your table using the previous technique.

Triangular Table Cells

Triangles can be used for lots of interesting things inside tables. Arrows, directional markers, and pyramids immediately come to mind. But how can you create them? Simple: follow these steps:

1 Grab the Polygon Tool from the Tools panel (it's behind the Rectangle Tool).

2 Click (don't click and drag) on the page to bring up the Polygon (Options) dialog. Set the rest of the fields the way you like, but make sure the Number of Sides field says 3.

3 Click OK, and you'll have a triangle on your page.

4 Resize and rotate it to the size you need in your table, and then cut it with CMD+X/CTRL+X.

5 Switch to the Type tool, click into the table where the triangle needs to go, and paste with CMD+X/CTRL+X.

6 Now fill, stroke, or whatever that triangle to make it part of your table.

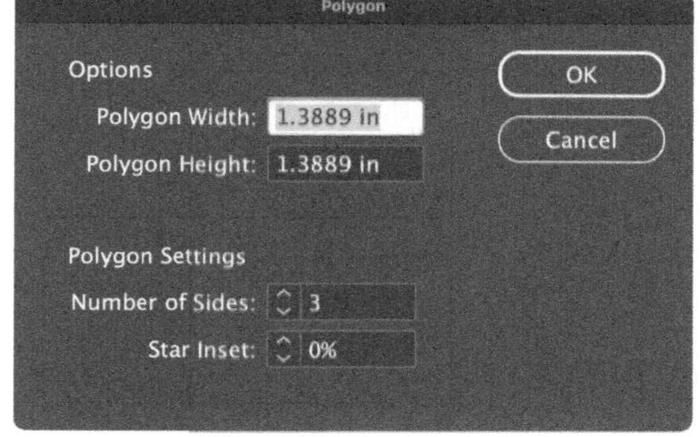

Triangular Table Cells with Text

OVERHEAD

100%

75%

50%

25%

DROPPING!

The previous method of creating triangular table cells works, even with text, *if your triangle will point upward*. If you rotate it to point downward or to the side, any text you put inside it will also rotate, and maybe not in a way you like. For that reason, I present to you a method of creating triangular table cells whose text *won't* rotate in weird ways.

1. Grab the Rectangle or Rectangle Frame tool and create a *rectangle* the size of the *triangle* you want.
2. Switch to the White Arrow (Direct Selection) tool, at which point you'll see the vector path and anchor points of the rectangle.
3. Select the anchor point at the bottom (or top) of the side you want to adjust, and then drag it inward toward the center. When you've reached the exact center of the path you'll see a smart guide appear to tell you that like Jimminy Cricket on your shoulder. Let go of the mouse and drop the anchor point at that location.

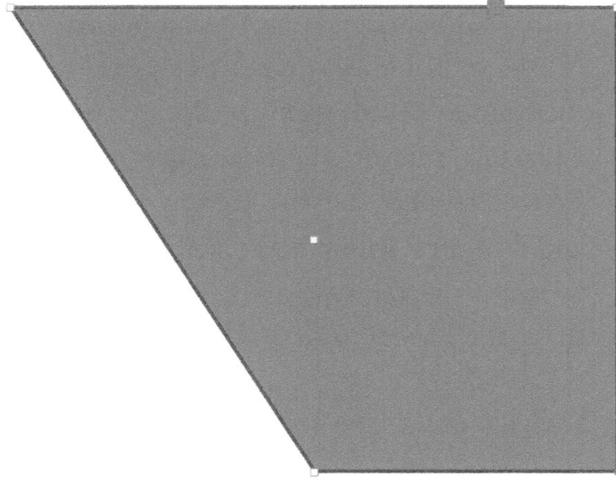

4. Repeat the last step with the anchor point in the opposing corner. You now have a triangle.

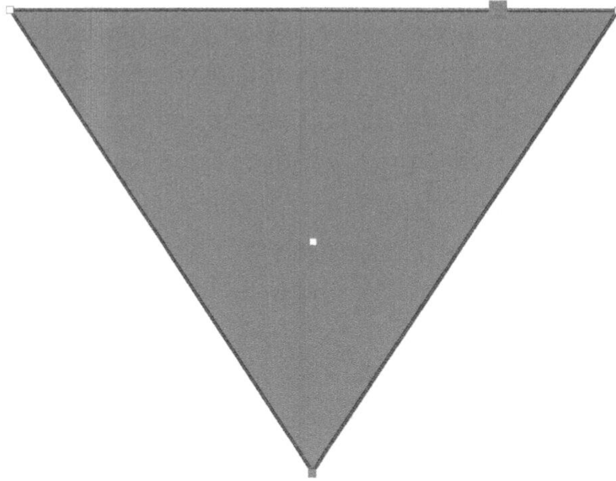

5. Select the Type tool, click inside the triangle, and start typing. Your text will be right side up.
6. Use the Selection tool to cut or copy the triangle, and then paste it into the table with the Type tool.
7. Tweak *et finis*.

Rounded Ends of Rows

	Personal	Pro	Business
Storage Space	100 GB	500 GB	2 TB
Bandwidth	50 GB	500 GB	1 TB
MySQL Databases	Unlimited	Unlimited	Unlimited

To create an LCARS-inspired table look like the image above, with one or both rounded ends on a row or all rows, just follow these steps.

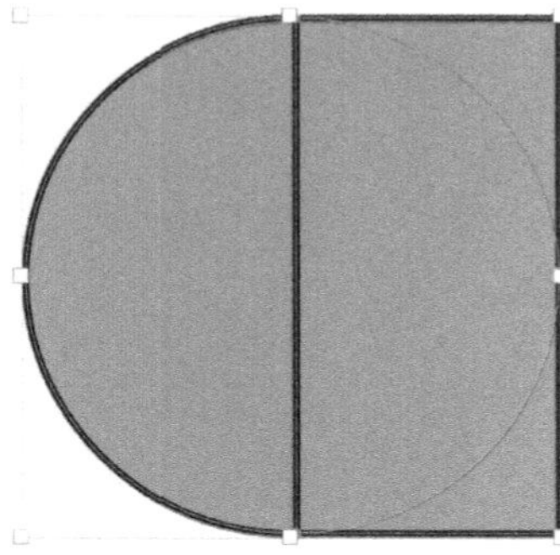

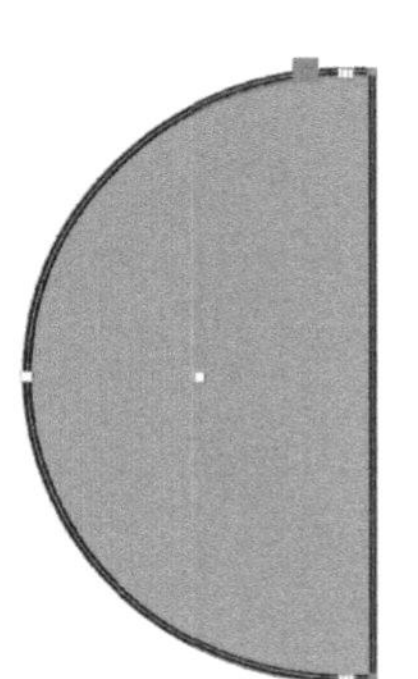

1. Create and style your table.
2. Outside the table, select the Ellipse tool, which is hidden behind the Rectangle tool.
3. Click and drag the Ellipse tool on the page while holding the Shift key on your keyboard to create a perfect circle. When it's about the right size to be the end of your table row, let go of the mouse to create the circle.
4. Switch to the Rectangle tool and, directly on top of the circle you just made, and also while holding Shift, create a square that starts at the center point of the circle and extends to the right. You're creating a square that is the exact same height as the circle, and that blots out the right side of the circle.
5. Switch to the Selection and select both the circle and the square (image at left).
6. Select Object ▸ Pathfinder ▸ Add, or use the corresponding control on the Pathfinder panel, either of which will merge the circle and square to create a shape with a rounded left side and a squared off right side (image at left).
7. If you also want a rounded end on the right side of your table, repeat the last four steps as a new set of objects, but this time, make the square overlap the *left* side of the circle.
8. Match the fill and stroke of the newly merged object with the table cell into which you'll add it.
9. Copy the newly merged object to the clipboard with CMD+C/CTRL+C.
10. Switch to the Type tool and click inside the first column of the table.
11. You'll need a new left column for the rounded end cap, so select Table ▸ Insert ▸ Column, and insert a column to the left.
12. Repeat this process to create a new right-most column if you need the rounded end caps on the right side of the table.
13. Click inside the first cell in the new left column that should receive the rounded end cap, and paste with CMD+V/CTRL+V.

14 If everything was perfect, you're done with that row's first column, but you might need to adjust the size of the pasted object with the Selection tool, remove an existing background color, or change the cell inset values. Do that tweaking now.

15 If you're going to add the same end cap to other rows, repeat the last two steps. Also repeat them if you've adding right-end end caps.

Document Recipes

Modifying InDesign Defaults

Is there a way to change the default font/swatches/hyphenation options/whatever? Collectively, it's probably the most common question I'm asked. Answer: Yes. If you can change the font family and style in the Character Styles panel, you can change the default font. Likewise with creating new default swatches and removing the swatches with which InDesign ships. In fact, if you can do almost anything, you can make it the new default. You just have to override a couple of InDesign's default behaviors, which is easier than it may sound.

Before you can change most of InDesign's defaults, you have to disable something. Follow these steps to prepare InDesign for new defaults.

1. Open InDesign, just the application, without any documents open.
2. While viewing the Home Screen, select InDesign ▸ Preferences ▸ General (Mac) or Edit ▸ Preferences ▸ General (Windows).
3. Disable (uncheck) the very first option, Show Home Screen When No Documents Are Open.

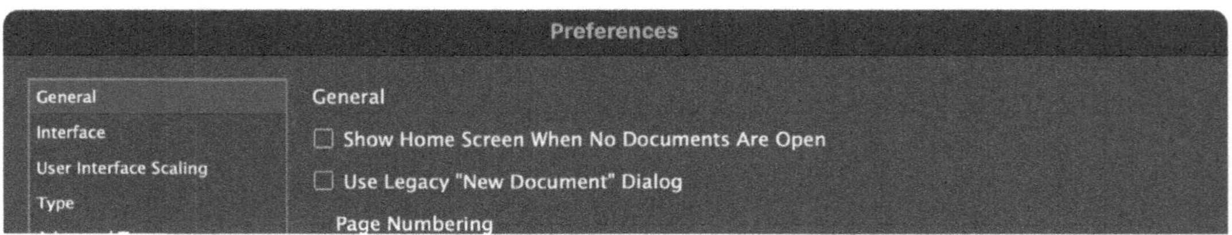

4. Select OK.

Now you're ready to edit defaults. Without the Home Screen, you should see InDesign's panels as if you had a document open. If an option is grayed out, you can't change its default. If it isn't grayed out, you can change its default.

Do you want hyphenation turned off by default instead of on? Uncheck the Hyphenate box on the Paragraph panel (choose Show Options from the panel flyout menu if you don't see it). To remove swatches you rarely use, open the Swatches panel and delete them. Add new swatches you use regularly—like corporate colors—by adding them to the panel with all documents closed. Every new document from that point forward will use only the swatches you see there, or will leave hyphenate unchecked, or whatever change you want to make.

To change the default font, open the Character panel and change the font. Done. Well, not entirely. You see, InDesign has default styles. When you change type options on the Character or Paragraph panels, you are indeed setting new defaults. However, you aren't changing the default styles, which can lead to problems later on if you reapply the default styles to text. If you're sure of your new font (or other type styling defaults), make the changes in the Character and/or Paragraph panels, and then open the Paragraph Styles panel. Highlight the [Basic Paragraph] style, choose Style Options from the panel flyout menu, and then repeat your changes there, making sure to save the style. Do the same with the [None] character style on the Character Styles panel. Now your changes will survive a reapplication of the style.

Experiment with different controls and options. You can set new defaults for a great many things when no documents are opened.

Here I should note three important points: First, after setting your new defaults you should close and restart InDesign to commit those changes to the InDesign preferences saved on your computer drive; if InDesign crashes before you've closed it, you'll lose those changes. Similarly, the second point: Unlike workspaces and keyboard shortcut sets, your newly set defaults are part of the application preferences and can't be saved out to external files. Thus, if your preferences become corrupted and you have to reset them, your typeface, hyphenation, and any other new defaults will be reset to factory default. Finally, you should also realize that setting new defaults makes them the defaults only for new documents—existing documents will use the defaults set at the time of their creation.

Make Italic, Bold, and More Character Styles Automatically Available in Every New Document

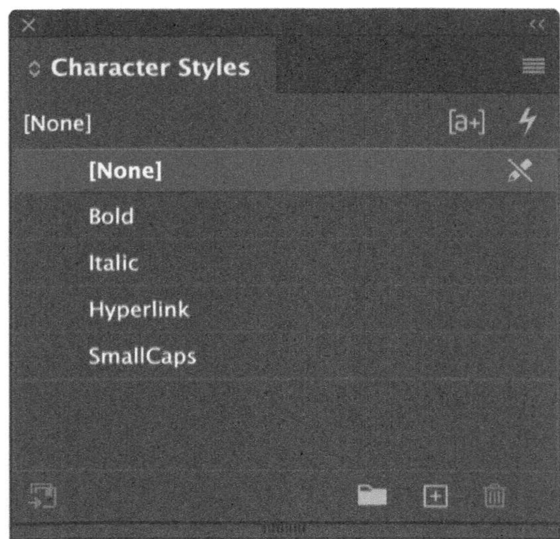

It's extremely common to format small passages of text as italic, bold, strikethrough, underlined, or small caps. The problem is, if you do that ad hoc, highlighting text and changing its formatting, you create overrides that can be wiped away in many ways, intentional and otherwise, returning your text to plain roman. Of course, creating character styles for those formatting options in every single InDesign document is no fun, either. Here's a way to have the best of both world—simple, click-to-apply character-level formatting—without having to create character styles for every document:

1. Start with either a new or existing document, and then apply your would-be character-level formatting to some text. If you want italic, bold, bold-italic, and underlined text, for example, apply those formatting options to four different bits of text.
2. One at a time, highlight each of your formatted bits of text and create a character style from them, being careful to name the styles clearly.
3. Save the document and close all documents.
4. If you land at the Home screen when you close all InDesign documents, follow the instructions for "Modifying InDesign Defaults".
5. Go to the Paragraph panel's menu and choose Load All Text Styles.
6. Navigate to and open the document you just created with the character styles.
7. In the Load Styles dialog, check the box beside the character styles you made and want to be available in all documents. Simultaneously, uncheck any styles you do *not* want in every new InDesign document.
8. Click OK, and you'll see your character styles appear on the Character Styles panel.
9. Quit InDesign to commit those changes to disk.
10. Now, restart InDesign and create a new document. Every new document will now have those character styles—italic, bold, bold-italic, underlined, what-

ever—waiting on the Character Styles panel to be applied to selected text with a single click.

Import and Export User Settings

It would be a terrible shame to customize InDesign to work like you do—maybe even for multiple workflows and projects—only to have them all disappear with a preferences reset or left behind on an old computer when upgrading to a new one. Fortunately, with a minute or two of preparation and simple copying and pasting, you don't have lose any of your InDesign tweaking.

The first method to save and restore your InDesign environment is the easiest. Select File ▸ User Settings ▸ Export User Settings, and InDesign will wrap all your preferences and customizations into a self-contained SQLite database file. That file can be emailed, added to cloud storage, and, through File ▸ User Settings ▸ Import User Settings, restored to InDesign.

Introduced in InDesign 2024, Import and Export User Settings is a new built-in feature that works very well so far, but I'm cautious about making it my only InDesign customization backup method, or recommending you do that. You see, this isn't the first time Adobe has tried something like this. A few years ago, Adobe had InDesign and other Adobe applications backup and synchronize their preferences and other customizations via Creative Cloud servers. It was… an. Epic. Fail. When sync did work, it often worked the wrong way: overwriting all customizations on users' computers with the default, out-of-the-box preferences.

And that's why I have always used, and continue recommend even in addition to Import and Export User Settings, the following backup and synchronization of InDesign (and other Adobe application) settings.

InDesign in Your Pocket

Or, *InDesign on a Stick*—a USB stick/thumbnail drive/flash drive. Although you can fit InDesign and all its component plug-ins on most portable USB flash drives, it won't run from there. (Well, I'm sure somebody could get it to run, but I think that would violate the EULA.) What I mean by the title of this section is taking your InDesign in your pocket, your unique configuration and work habits, and sitting down at any workstation and, in 60 seconds or less, making any copy of InDesign work exactly like your copy of InDesign on your main computer—complete with workspaces, keyboard shortcuts, menus, and even your own autocorrect settings and Find/Change queries.

It's exceedingly simple, really. First, make sure you've created a new keyboard shortcut set, a new set of menus, and a new workspace. Create and save them in their respective manners. Nothing here is permanent, so please don't feel pressured to create the perfect workspace or customize everything right now. Just do something simple for each, save the set, and close InDesign.

Now, open a Finder or File Explorer window and navigate to the InDesign folder:

Mac: `/Users/[your user name]/Library/Preferences/Adobe InDesign/Version [Version]/en_US/`
Windows: `Users\[your user name]\AppData\Roaming\Adobe\Adobe InDesign\Version [Version]\en_US\`

Within those folders, you should see a subfolder for `Workspaces`. Open that, and you'll find an XML file of the workspace you just created. Go back up to the Menu Sets folder to find your recently created menu set. At the same level as both of those folders, you'll find others, called `InDesign Shortcut Sets, Autocorrect, Find-Change Queries, Glyph Sets, Print Presets, Preflight Presets`, and more. Note that you may not see all of those folders; they're created the first time you save a customization in that respective area of InDesign. If you've not yet created Autocorrect replace pairs, saved Find/Change queries, or created a custom Glyph set, you won't have folders for them. All of these folders store personal, per-user settings that are machine- and even platform-independent. You can pick up these files by copying the entire `Version X` folder, carry them to any other installation of InDesign on the same platform (Windows or Mac), copy them to the same locations on the new machine, and have access to them at that workstation just as you would your own. When you launch InDesign, your copied workspace will be on the Window ▸ Workspaces menu, your keyboard and menu sets in the Keyboard Shortcuts and Customize Menu dialogs' Sets drop-downs, and your Autocorrect, Find/Change, and Glyphs sets where they belong (I cover each later in this book). In fact, if you're handy with scripting, you could probably write an AppleScript or VBScript or BAT file that, upon execution on a target workstation, copies the `Version X` folder from the USB drive to the computer's main drive.

You can even store your portable InDesign settings in the cloud, in Google Drive, Dropbox, Box.com, SugarSync, iCloud, or wherever. For that matter, you could even upload and download them from your iPhone. *That* would sell a few copies of this book! I can see the cover line now: *Run InDesign from Your iPhone!* I'll have to talk to my publisher's marketing team…

Resetting Preferences

Now that you know how to save your customizations, you should know how to wipe them out. Why? Because the vast majority of problems that can occur with software from Adobe and other big publishers is often the culprit of something wrong within the preferences, something most often referred to as a corrupt preferences file. Many Mac users are aware of the possibility of preference file corruption, but it can happen on Windows, too. This is why resetting—wiping out—your InDesign preferences is often the first step in troubleshooting.

There are several ways to reset InDesign's preferences, including locating the preference file on your computer and deleting it. That's often tedious, so here are two other easier methods.

1. With InDesign open, select InDesign ▸ Preferences ▸ General (Mac) or Edit ▸ Preferences ▸ General (Windows).
2. Select the button at the bottom-right of the Preferences dialog labeled Reset Preferences on Quit.
3. Select OK.
4. Quit InDesign.

   When InDesign relaunches, it should be as if a fresh install.

The Reset Preferences on Quit is a new method, added into InDesign 2024 at the same time as Import and Export User Settings. The old stand-by method still works, too.

1 Quit InDesign.
2 Locate the InDesign application icon in your Dock or Applications folder (Mac) or on the Taskbar or Start Menu (Windows).
3 Click on the application icon—do not double-click an InDesign document—to launch InDesign.
4 Immediately press and hold the following keys:
   Mac: Shift+Control+OPT+CMD
   Windows: CTRL+ALT+Shift
5 A dialog will appear asking you to confirm resetting InDesign's preferences. Let go of the keyboard keys and answer Yes.

Either of these methods will make InDesign look and behave like a new install. Hopefully it will also cure whatever technical issue you were experiencing with InDesign, but that isn't the only reason you might want to reset the preferences. Another good reason is when handing off the computer to someone else, giving them a clean InDesign they can customize to their work preferences, complete with that new app smell.

See and Count How Many Lines and Words are Overset

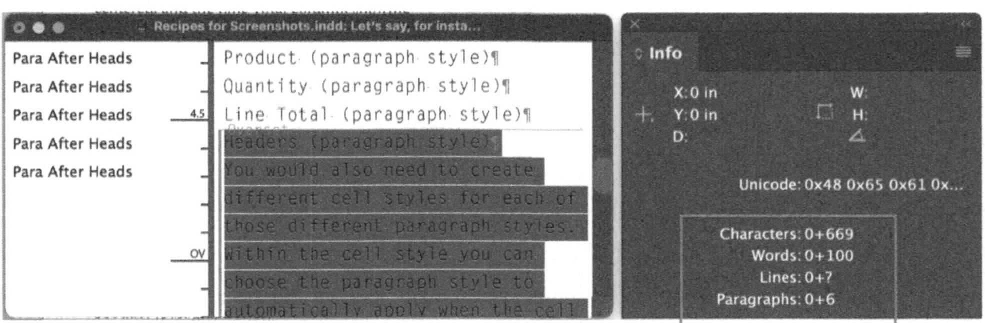

There is an eternal struggle between Editorial and Layout departments that predates InDesign by many millennia. Some say, strife here

on Earth even began out there… among the stars… with space-faring Editorial and Layout ancestors battling across the cosmos.

Editorial sends copy. Layout tries to fit the copy into the prescribed pages or column inches. When it works, space angels sing a choir. When it doesn't work, there starts a conversation wherein the layout artist working in InDesign tries to explain to their Editorial counterpart how much text needs to be cut to fit the story to the hole. Editorial asks how much, Layout says something vague like, "around five or six lines it looks like." Editorial sends a rewrite, which may or may not fit, starting the celestial battle into its next round.

Make it easier for Editorial to make cuts by giving them an exact line, word, or even character count—and without the need to copy and paste into InCopy or Word. Follow these steps next time you have overset text you just can't fit:

1. Select the Type tool and place your cursor at the end of the story, right before it oversets.
2. Select Edit ▸ Edit in Story Editor.
3. Your cursor will be in the same place in the story in Story Editor. After it will be a line indicating the start of the overset text. Press CMD+Option+End/CTRL+ALT+End to select from that point to the end of the story.
4. With Story Editor still open, select Window ▸ Info. Notice that the Info panel now counts the text you have selected, showing the number of characters, words, and even lines (as calculated by the layout line length) of your overset text.
5. Tell Editorial exactly how much needs to be cut from the story.

Just Count How Many Lines and Word are Overset

Even you just need the count of how much copy is overset, without seeing that overset text, don't even bother with Story Editor. Instead, just do this:

1. With your Type tool, click anywhere inside the story that has overset text.
2. Open the Info panel from Window ▸ Info.

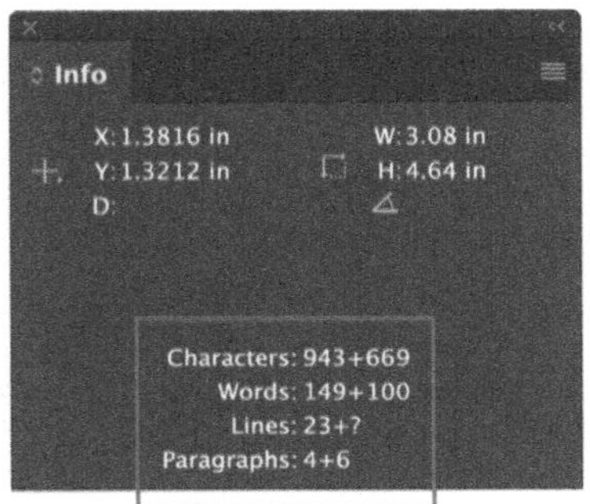

3 There is no Step 3: the information you need is right there on the Info panel. Everything after the plus (+) symbol is overset—characters, words, and paragraphs—though InDesign won't estimate the number of lines that text would occupy.

Prevent Hyphenation of Everyone's Name

~Pariah
~Burke
~Lori
~Naoma
~PariahRocks
~QDogProductions
~MayasMinks
~VickiVicarious
~RobRounding
~RaisedOnDnD
~SamNJerry
~GBurkeThaMan
~SissyAndSons

Hyphenating proper names is a major typographic faux pas. In *InDesign Masterclass: Type & Tables*, Chapter 6, "Stories" I explained how to prevent hyphenation of one name at a time by adding the name to the User Dictionary preceded by a tilde (~). Here's a technique for pre-loading no-hyphenation directives for a batch of names into InDesign.

1 Create a list of all the proper names—people's names, brand names, and other proper nouns—in InDesign, InCopy, Word, TextEdit, Notepad, email, or wherever.
2 In front of every name, add a tilde (~).
3 Save the list to a .TXT file.
4 In InDesign, choose Edit ▸ Spelling ▸ User Dictionary.
5 Select the Import button, and open the .TXT file you just created. InDesign will add your list of names, along with their hyphenation exceptions, to the User Dictionary.

Once you have a list of names with a tilde (~) in front of them, it's easy to add them to InDesign's User Dictionary. What is not always easy is the part of about adding that tilde in the first place. Fortunately, it's not that difficult. I'll show you how to do that in InDesign, Word, and Excel in the next several techniques.

Adding "Don't Hyphenate" to a List in Batch (in InDesign or InCopy)

1. Create a text frame to hold your list of names-that-should-not-be-hyphenated. It might help to create a whole new InDesign document to use for the purpose.
2. Paste or import the list of names into that text frame (or frames, if it's a long list). You'll want to make sure each name is on its own line without any blank lines between.
3. Go to Edit ▸ Find/Change.
4. Switch to the GREP tab.
5. In the Find What field, enter only a caret (^).
6. In the Change To field, put in a tilde (~).
7. Choose Change All.
8. Answer OK to the search completion alert, and you'll have every line of text in your story prepended by a tilde (~), ready for copying and pasting into a text editor like Mac's TextEdit or Windows Notepad, and from there, import into InDesign's User Dictionary.

If you're an InCopy user, this same technique works there. Just substitute "InCopy" where I say "InDesign" in these steps.

Adding "Don't Hyphenate" to a List in Batch (in Microsoft Word)

1. Start a new Word document and paste or type your list of names, one per line, with no blank lines between.
2. Open Advanced Find and Replace.

   Mac: Go to Edit ▸ Find ▸ Advanced Find and Replace.

   Windows: Go to the Home tab of the ribbon. In the Editing group on the Home tab of the Ribbon, click the down arrow beside Find, and select Advanced Find.
3. In the Find and Replace dialog box, select the Replace tab.

4. In the Find What field enter this code: `^p`
5. Add this code to the Replace With field: `^p~`
6. Choose Replace All.
7. When the search completion report appears, click OK.
8. All lines except the first will now start with a tilde (~). Go to the first line and add the tilde to it.
9. If tildes were added to any blank lines at the end of the list, delete those lines.
10. Copy the list and paste it into a text editor like Mac's TextEdit or Windows Notepad, and then bring the list into InDesign's User Dictionary.

Adding "Don't Hyphenate" to a List in Batch (in Excel)

With content such as membership or customer lists, product names from a catalog, or other lists of names managed in a database or spreadsheet, you may want to prepend the tilde (~) to the names in Microsoft Excel directly rather than making a stopover to use the Word or InDesign methods.

1. Open the Excel workbook or sheet containing your list of names, or start a new sheet for the purpose. You'll want to make sure that all the names are in a single column, without any blank rows between them.
2. Select a column where you want the prepended text to appear. This should be adjacent to the column containing the original text. For example, if your original list is in column A, you might choose column B for the output.
3. Click in the first cell of the new column (e.g., B1 if you are using column B).
4. In Excel's Formula Bar, enter the following formula, inclusive of the equals sign and quotation marks, and press Return/Enter: `="~" & A1`

   Inside cell B1, you should now see the contents of A1 prepended with a tilde(~).
5. With B1 still selected, drag the fill handle (the small square at the bottom right corner of the cell) down through the column to fill all the rows containing your list of names. This will replicate the formula through all those cells, adjusting for their own rows, and creating a list of names starting with tildes.

   Note: if you have trouble dragging the fill handle, which is pretty common, you can instead copy the B1 cell and paste it into the remaining cells in the B column. Excel is smart enough to change the row number in the formula as you paste, giving you the same result as if you had dragged the fill handle.

6 Select the entire column B, copy, and then paste the list into a plain text file in Mac's TextEdit or Windows' Notepad. From there, save the .TXT file and import into InDesign's User Dictionary.

Making User Dictionaries Travel with Documents

Adding words to your local User Dictionary does not mean your teammates will benefit from the spelling additions and hyphenation exceptions you've created. You can export your user dictionary and share it to your colleagues, or you can just embed it into the InDesign document. Let's do the latter.

1 Open a document containing spelling or hyphenation exceptions.
2 Go to (Mac) InDesign ▸ Preferences ▸ Dictionary, (Windows) Edit ▸ Preferences ▸ Dictionary.
3 In the User Dictionary section, check the box beside Merge User Dictionary Into Document. InDesign will then make your User Dictionary a part of any document create or edit.

Automatically Format Text as Text Frames are Created

Throughout this book you've been seeing tip and note boxes in the sidebars. I formatted each of them with a single click—title line and body copy—and that click wasn't on the Paragraph Styles panel anywhere; it was on the Object Styles panel. This technique is a little more involved than some, so follow these steps:

1 Choose a text frame for this technique and format it's text.

2 Create paragraph styles from each of the formats. In my tip boxes, for example, the title, the green "Tip" preceded by an icon, is the paragraph style FeatureTip. The body of tips are set to FeaturePara. You can have more than two styles, but start with two while learning this technique.
3 Whichever paragraph style is the first to appear in your text frame, open its Paragraph Style Options.
4 On the General pane, set its Next Style drop-down field to the name of the style that comes after it. For example, I edited FeatureTip and set its Next Style field to FeaturePara, meaning, after the title, the tip box's main text follows.
5 Click OK.
6 We're not going to edit the second paragraph style's Next Style, because we want that to stay as [Same Style], which allows for multiple paragraphs of text in the same style. Instead, switch to the Selection tool and select the text frame.
7 Open the Object Styles panel from Window ▸ Styles ▸ Object Styles.
8 At the bottom of the Object Styles panel click the plus icon-adorned Create New Object Style button.
9 Double-click the new style created to both apply it to the frame and edit the style.
10 In the Basic Attributes list on the left, choose Paragraph Styles.
11 Set the Paragraph Style drop-down to the first style that should appear in the text frame—FeatureTip for me. Don't worry if the entire text frame suddenly looks like the first style.
12 Activate the checkbox beside Apply Next Style, and it should all look right.
13 Click OK.

From now on, all you have to do is apply the object style to a text frame to get it to apply *both* the paragraph styles in order. If you want to include more than two paragraph styles in succession, set them up with their Next Style fields chaining each to its next paragraph style. You can even make them circle back to the beginning by setting the last style in the chain's Next Style field to the name of the *first* paragraph style. One click—on the Object Styles panel—can format your text frame *and* its content.

Even better, you can avoid even that one click by using this technique on the "[Basic Text Frame]" object style, or whatever other style your document uses as its default text frame style. Then, all you have to do is grab the Type tool, drag out a frame, and the paragraph styles are already being applied. Type or paste in text and watch it automatically format.

Fix Hyphenation on All Compound Words

One of the sidebar tips in *InDesign Masterclass: Type & Tables*, Chapter 6, "Stories" was to add a discretionary hyphen in front of any word you didn't want to hyphenate. Another use for the discretionary hyphen is to make sure InDesign wraps compound words—words with ever-present hyphens like in the compound word "ever-present"—at that ever-present hyphen instead of somewhere else like "ev-er" or "pres-ent." By placing a discretionary hyphen inside the word after it's actual hyphen, if InDesign needs to wrap the word, it will break it where it should be broken—at the hyphen. Manually inserting discretionary hyphens in all compound words in a document can be daunting. Here's an semi-automatic way to do it.

1. Go to Edit ▸ Find/Change.
2. Enter in the Find What field this code: `([a-zA-Z]+)-([a-zA-Z]+)`
3. In the Change To field, enter this code: `$1-~$2`
4. Click Change All.

That Find/Change operation finds every regular hyphen that appears between two or more letters—in other words, inside a compound word—without matching other hyphens like where a minus sign or en dash should be used. It then replaces that hyphen with a standard hyphen followed by a discretionary hyphen.

Sort a Comma-Separated List

Sometimes you have a long comma-separated list, such as the list below of radio stations airing *The Hard, Heavy & Hair Show*, my weekly Rock and Metal radio show syndicated around the world. Every month new stations begin carrying the show, and, once in a while, a station needs to be removed from the list because it was merged with another, changed formats, or whatnot. Lists this long can be difficult to sort… Unless you know the simple process.

```
Total Rock, 97 Underground, KRFK Radio, Metal Heart
Radio, The Generator FM 107.7 FM, Bay Ridge Radio
AM 1690, Rock Rage Radio, CBJRadio, Classic Rock
XL, Creative Arts Radio UK, Defiant Radio, Digital
Revolution Radio, EN5 Radio, Fusion109, Get Smashed
Radio, Heat FM Radio, KARL Radio, KBOG 97.9 FM, KXRK
Seattle, LKCB 128.4 Metal Damage, The Manamal, Metal
Mayhem Radio, My Radio Rocks, Rock Mauritius Africa,
OA Radio, ORCA Radio, Radio Diabolus, Radio Lantau,
Radio Playback, Radio Riff, Radio Rock FM, Radio Vegas
Rocks, Radio X Rocks, Rak Rock Radio UAE, Rockcast
Radio, Rock Flame Radio, Rock Radio UK, Savage Radio,
Slick Willy Radio, SNAFU Radio, Sonora Classic Rock,
The Rock Altar, The Shark, Mud Radio, Underground Rock
Radio, Vibe Squad Radio, X-Rock Radio, WCSQ 105.9,
WRSG 91.5 FM, WVWP 101.1 FM
```

I've actually been using this same process in Microsoft Word for decades, but fortunately, InDesign can do it, too.

1. Select the list in its text frame.
2. Go to Edit ▸ Find/Change.
3. Enter in the Find What field, enter a comma followed by a space (`, `).
4. Set the Change To field to the code for a hard return: `^p`
5. Make sure the Search field is set to "Selection," and click Change All. All the individual list items will now be on their own lines.
6. Go to Window ▸ Utilities ▸ Scripts.
7. On the Scripts panel, expand Application, then Samples, then JavaScript.
8. With the text still selected, double-click on SortParagraphs,jsx, which is a script to sort paragraphs in alphanumeric order. Your list should now be alphabetical.
9. Return to Find/Change and reverse the process.
10. Set the Find What field to `^p` and the Change To field to comma space.
11. Click Change All, and you'll have a comma-separated list in alphabetical order.

Automatically Restart Numbered Lists

We are 175 pages into the book. It was all laid out in InDesign, of course, so could you imagine the tedium I'd experience if I had to choose Type ▸ Bullets & Numbering ▸ Restart Numbering for *every single step-by-step list* in this chapter? I'd be tearing out my hair! And if you've seen a photo of me, you know there's *a lot of hair to tear out! Shudder!* Manually restarting numbering for every list in this book?! I'd rather go back to searching the Web with G$$gle, wading through its page after page of paid ads in search of *actual* results relevant to my search.

Thankfully, that is *not* what I had to do. Starting the numbering over again was automatic—after a few seconds of initial configuration.

Follow these steps, and you, too, won't have to deal with such annoyances:

1 In your web browser of choice, go to the Settings menu, which might be in a menu or displayed as a simple three-dot icon.
2 Find and select in the list of settings the option for Search Engine.
3 Change whatever is there (probably Google or Bing) to a non-spammy, non-tracking, non-evil search engine like SearchGPT, DuckDuckGo, or Brave.
4 Confirm the choice.

Bask in the glory of your newfound—Oh! I was supposed to be telling you how to restart numbered lists automatically, not make Web search usable again. I got distracted. It happens. I *am* a graphic designer.

Okay, starting over: to automatically restart your numbered lists, follow these steps (which, you might notice, automatically restarted their numbering without me having to touch my mouse or an InDesign menu):

1 Create a paragraph style for your numbered list, unless you already have one.
2 Edit that paragraph style and go to its Bullets and Numbering pane.
3 In the List field, set or create a list called Numbered Steps, StepUpRevolution, or whatever you want to call the list.
4 Set the Level field to 2. Even if your numbered list is the top level of numbering, set the Level field to 2.

5 Change the Mode field to Continue From Previous Number.
6 And then activate the checkbox for Restart Numbers at This Level After Any Previous Level (spoiler alert: this is the key to the whole technique).

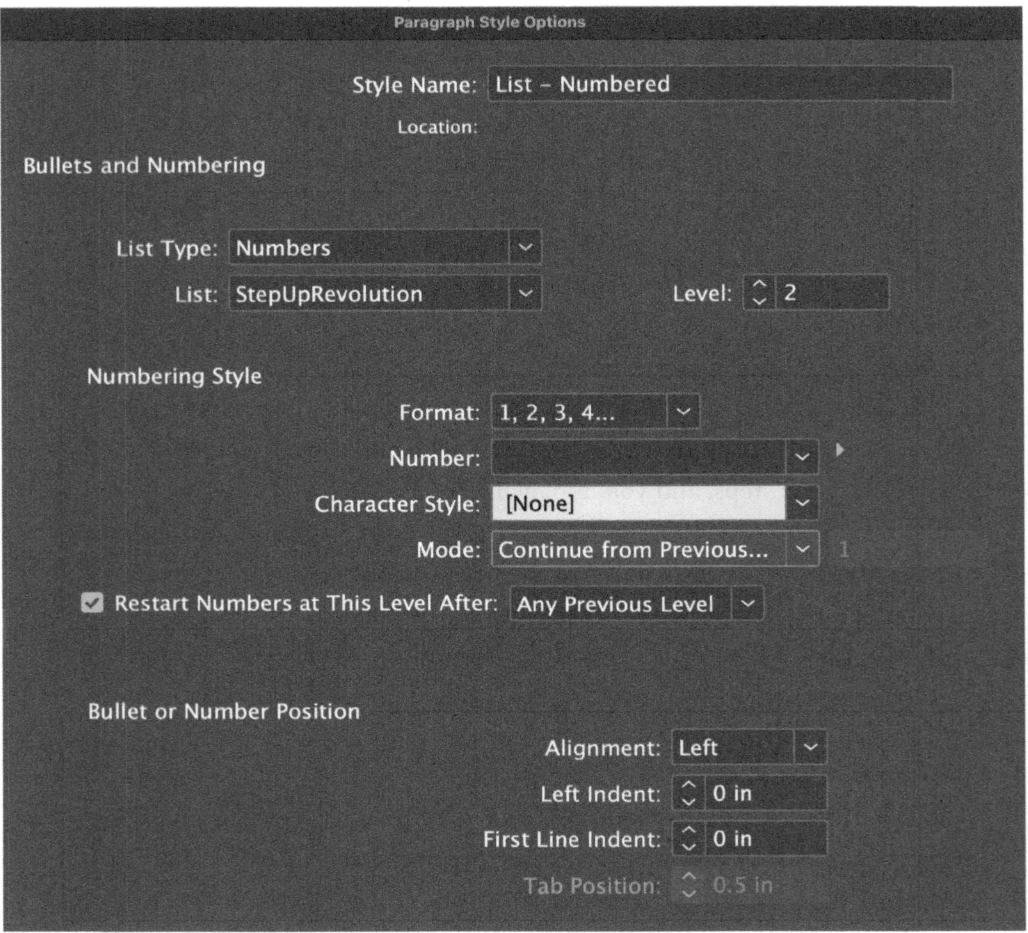

7 Click OK. You're now halfway done with making your lists automatically restart their numbering.
8 Look at your Paragraph Styles panel and figure out some style that always appears before your numbered list. For example, for me, it's Para After Heads, meaning the first paragraph style that appears after a Heading 1, 2, or 3. There is *always* a heading between numbered lists of steps, and always some text tagged as Para After Head between the head itself and the numbered paragraphs (even if you don't see the paragraph). Find some paragraph style in your document like that, one that appears between every numbered list.
9 Edit that always-before-numbered-list paragraph style.

10. Go to the Bullets and Numbering pane in that style.
11. Set the List Type to Numbered Step or whatever you previously chose as your list name.
12. Now wipe out the Number field. Delete anything that happens to appear in the Number field, which is going to be `^#.^t` by default.
13. In the Mode field, choose Start At, and then `1` in the next field.

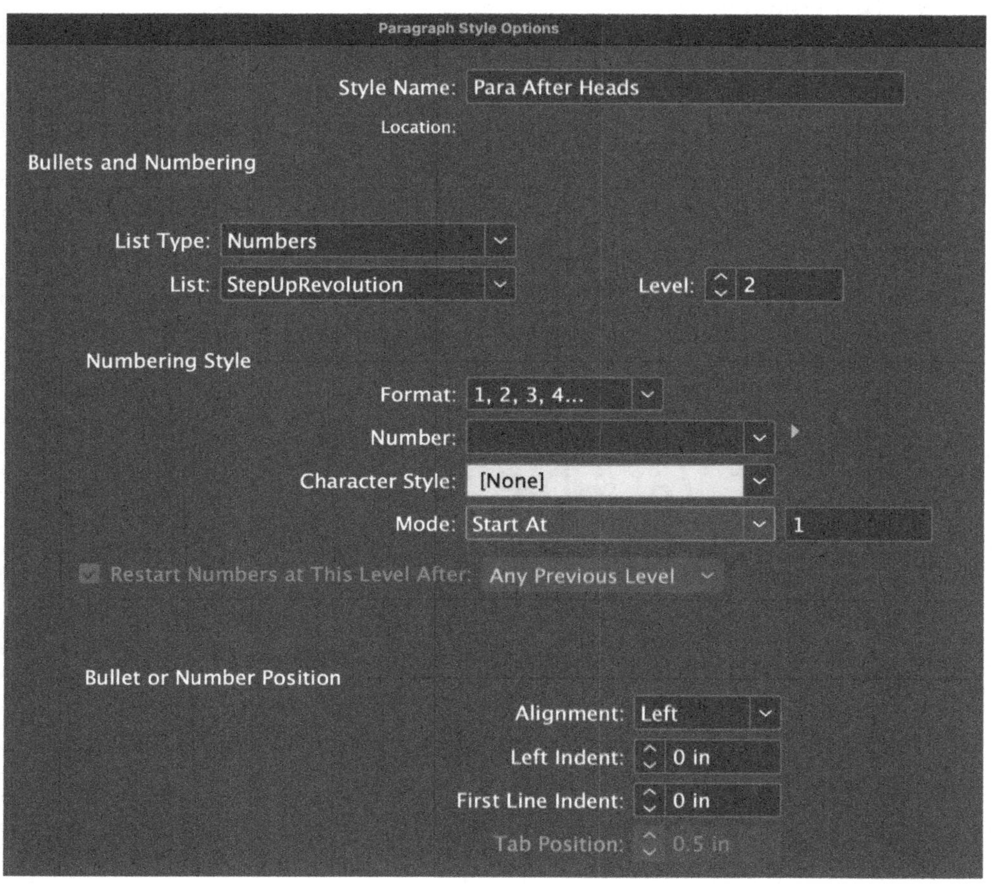

14. Click OK.

And just like that, every time you start a new list, it will automatically start over again at number 1.

Insert Final Page Number

This *InDesign Masterclass: Text Techniques,* "Document Recipes," page 178 of, uh... I dunno. I wish InDesign could give me that last page number somehow. Oh, wait! It can!

If you want the last page number of a document or publication—which is a pretty common need, actually—then it's simple. So simple, I won't even do a numbered how-to. Just put your Type tool cursor where you want the final page number, and go to Type ▸ Text Variables ▸ Insert Variable ▸ Last Page Number. That's it. InDesign will insert a text variable, which we all know by this point at the end of this book, means a dynamically updating piece of text. This particular text variable will be the last page number of the current chapter, or, if used within a book, the last page number of the current chapter or section within that book.

So, welcome to "Document Recipes" page 178 of 193.

Insert Text Variable with Keyboard Shortcut

Although InDesign allows you to assign a keyboard shortcut to many things, a text variable is not one of them. However, you can create a script that inserts the desired text variable and then bind that script to a keyboard shortcut. Here's how to do it:

1 Open your favorite JavaScript or text editor.
2 Enter the JavaScript code below, replacing `Your Variable Name` with the name of your actual text variable from Type ▸ Text Variables ▸ Define...

```
var doc = app.activeDocument;
var textVar = doc.textVariables.itemByName('Your Variable
Name');
if (textVar.isValid) {
    var sel = app.selection[0];
    if (sel && sel.constructor.name == 'TextFrame') {
        sel.contents = textVar.variableOptions.contents;
    }
}
```

3. Save the script with a name like `InsertTextVariable.jsx` in the correct folder for your operating system.

   Mac: /Users/<YourUsername>/Library/Preferences/Adobe InDesign/Version <Version>/en_US/Scripts/Scripts Panel

   Windows: C:\Users\<YourUsername>\AppData\Roaming\Adobe\InDesign\<Version>\Scripts
4. Back in InDesign, open the Scripts panel by selecting (Window ▸ Utilities ▸ Scripts) and verify that your new script is in the User folder of the panel. If not, quit and restart InDesign to refresh.
5. Go to Edit ▸ Keyboard Shortcuts.
6. In the dialog box, select Scripts from the Product Area drop-down menu.
7. Locate your script (InsertTextVariable.jsx) in the list.
8. Click in the New Shortcut field and press the desired keyboard shortcut.
9. Click Assign to set the shortcut.

   Any time you need to insert your text variable, just press that shortcut.

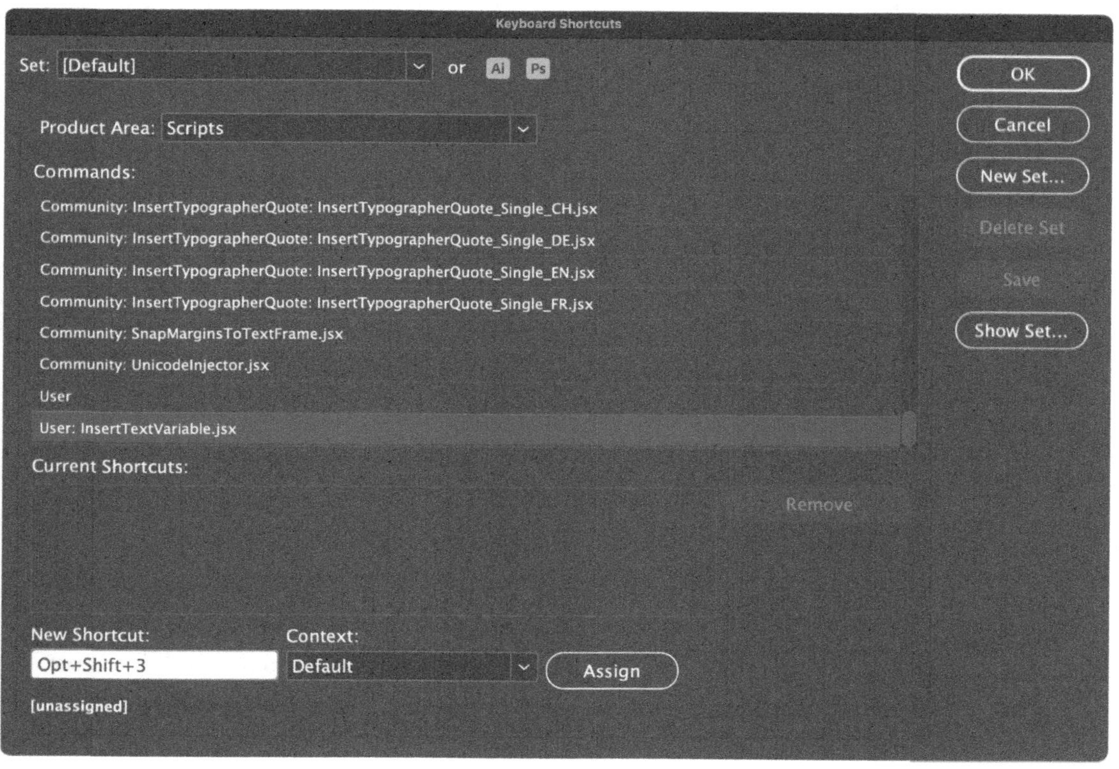

Conditional Images and Objects

As the name implies, the Conditional Text panel only allows us to make *text* conditional. There isn't a Conditional Object or Conditional Image panel with similar functions. But we actually don't need them because Conditional Text can do the job with one simple trick: anchor images and objects you want to be conditional.

Remember: when you anchor an object to a location within text, InDesign considers that entire object to live at the location of the anchor. A graphic frame with an image inside, for example, effectively becomes just a character in a story as far as InDesign is concerned. And that character—specifically the invisible anchor character that looks like a Yen (¥)—can be controlled by a condition or a conditional set. Just make sure you highlight the anchor character when assigning a condition on the Conditional Text panel. That way, you can show different language images only in their correct language text, change out images by region or edition, or personalize the images in VDP projects as well as the text.

Condition Assignment by Language

When working with multi-lingual documents, you may elect to use Conditions and/or Condition Sets to show text in only one language at a time, allowing you to use the same document, same images, and so on while swapping out all the text with just two clicks—one to turn on a language condition, one click to turn off the previous language condition.

Creating text in multiple languages, though, usually involves two steps: first, you have to create the condition for the language, then assign the text to that condition, *and* you have to assign that text an actual language from the bottom of the Character panel or via the Control panel in Character mode. If you don't assign the correct language dictionary, you'll get spelling errors galore, and people using assistive technology such as as screen readers may have a lot of difficulty understanding the text that's being mispronounced to them.

There's a trick I employ, however, to never have to manually assign a condition to text based on a language. All I do is set the language from the bottom of the Character panel, run a Find/Change operation, which I keep in my presets, and let InDesign assign all that text to the right condition. Here's how:

1. Create a document with at least two languages of text in it. I'm going to use English and Spanish as examples for the rest of the steps.
2. Select your first text, English in my example.
3. From the Language field at the bottom of the Character panel or on the Control Panel, choose English: USA.
4. Select the text for the next language (Spanish), and assign that the correct language from the same Language drop-down field.
5. On the Conditional Text panel, create conditions for English and Spanish, but don't bother assigning text to either condition.
6. Go to Edit ▸ Find/Change.
7. On the Text tab of Find/Change, leave both the Find What and Change To fields blank, and set the Search to Story, Document, or whatever suits your current project.
8. Beside the Find Format area, click the Specify Attributes to Find button.
9. Go to the Advanced Character Formats pane.
10. In the Language drop-down, choose the language you want to assign first to a condition. I'm choosing English.
11. Click OK.
12. Beside the Change Format area, click the Specify Attributes to Change button,
13. Go to the Conditions pane, which is pretty low down in the list of panes.
14. There are the conditions from the Conditional Text panel. Turn off the check mark beside [Unconditional] and turn on the checkmark beside English, or whatever other language matches what you just chose to search out.
15. Click OK.
16. Click Change All. Now all text in the language you specified will be assigned only to the condition you selected.
17. Repeat for each subsequent language in your document.

Language Assignment by Condition

In case it isn't obvious, Find/Change also allows you to reverse the previous recipe—starting with text assigned to a language-based condition, and then tagging that text with the correct Language field option. Just follow the same recipe, staring out with conditions instead of languages, and then use the condition in the Find Format and the language in the Change Format.

Condition by Price

Being able to find by condition also opens up other possibilities. In *InDesign Masterclass: Type & Tables*, Chapter 6, "Stories," when we were talking about Conditional Text, one of the examples I gave was a catalog that needed conditional sets for prices relative to three different markets—the United States (U.S. Dollars), the United Kingdom (British Pounds Sterling), and Europe (the Euro). Naturally, those three different currencies have different notations, $, £, and €, respectively. If you haven't already added those currency notations to your prices manually, Find/Change can help you out.

1. Set up a document with prices in U.S. Dollars, British Pounds Sterling, and Euros.
2. Using the Conditional Text panel, create conditions for the appropriate markets, but don't bother assigning the prices to those conditions.
3. Now, select Edit ▸ Find/Change.
4. Switch to the GREP tab.
5. In the Find What field, enter this GREP expression: `\$[0-9]+(?:\.[0-9]{2})?`. That will find every price that starts with a dollar sign followed immediately by one or more numbers, then a period, and then two digits. It won't match values that don't have cents, though. If you want a simpler search for any dollar sign followed immediately by one or more numbers, use this expression: `\$[0-9]+`. Note that will leave out cents.
6. Leave the Change To field blank, but do click on the Specify Attributes to Change button beside the Change Format area.
7. Go down to the Conditions pane and select your condition that corresponds to U.S. Dollars.
8. Click OK.
9. Click Change All. All your U.S. Dollar prices will now be assigned to the condition you chose. When you hide that condition, all the U.S. prices will disappear.

10 Start a new search for British Pounds Sterling, which would be `£[0-9]+(?:\.[0-9]{1,2})?` for prices with decimals, and `£[0-9]+` for prices without.

11 Set your Change Format condition and Change All.

12 For the Euro, which is a notation typically, but not always, written after the price value instead of before it like the other two currencies, you have to search for different expressions based on the Euro symbol's location.

When the Euro precedes the price, use this expression: `€\s?[0-9]+(?:\.[0-9]{1,2})?`

If the Euro is after the price, with or without a space separating them, use this expression: `[0-9]+(?:\.[0-9]{1,2})?\s?€`

Or, if you just want to be efficient and search for both potential locations at once, combine the queries with this expression to find Euros before or after, with or without separating spaces: `€\s?[0-9]+(?:\.[0-9]{1,2})?|[0-9]+(?:\.[0-9]{1,2})?\s?€`

13 Change All.

When finished, your prices should all be assigned to their correct conditions. Turning on one condition via the Conditional Text panel or via a conditional set will show only the prices appropriate for that currency. If you need additional currencies such as Yen (¥), Rupee (₹), Australian Dollar (A$), or whatever, use my GREP expressions as a guide to create your queries. If you typically work with multiple currencies and conditional text, I suggest you save each of these as a query in the Find/Change dialog, making future operations as simple as selecting the list from the Query drop-down and hitting Change All.

Fill Type with Imagery

This is another technique that never fails to wow people at conferences and training classes. Way, way back, I figured out how to fill text with imagery, like the above example. Word of this fun and useful InDesign technique spread faster than news of that Oscars slap-heard-round-the-world. If you haven't learned it yet (the fill type with imagery technique not the Will Smith thing) here's the tutorial:

1 Create a text frame with a word or short phrase in it. This does work with any amount text that can be contained within a single text frame, but it has the most impact when the text is short.
2 Style that text to be big and thick for best effect. You can see mine below.

3 Switch to the Selection tool and select the text frame.
4 Go to Type ▸ Create Outlines. After a brief pause—and perhaps a progress bar—InDesign will have broken your type down into its constituent vector shapes. Remember: fonts are merely software filled with vector shapes they serve up in response to the operating system's request for a letter, number, or other glyph. The Create Outlines command strips away that filter and special treatment, revealing the vector paths within.

5 Keep the shape-that-was-text selected with the Selection tool, not the White Arrow (Direct Selection) tool, which is what I used to give you the above image. Then choose File ▸ Place.
6 Find and choose an image, and it will fill your text. At which point you can use the fitting commands or Direct Selection to adjust its placement in the text, and add any finishing touches.

Fill Type with Type

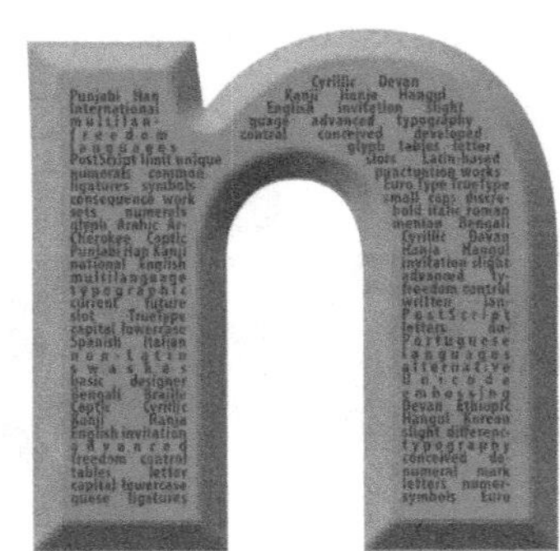

You don’t *have to* put an image inside type you’ve outlined. It could be text with which you fill it.

1 Follow the instructions for “Fill Type with Imagery” up to the point of selecting Place.

2 Instead of Place on the File menu, choose the Type tool on the Tools panel and click within the shape-that-was-text. That will convert the path to a text frame.

3 Now type, paste, or place text, or use Type ▸ Fill with Placeholder Text, and style as desired.

Fill Every Character of Type

Another thing you can do once you've converted text to outlines is to further break it up, putting a different image in each letter.

1. Follow the instructions for "Fill Type with Imagery" up to the point of selecting Place.
2. Select the shape-that-was-text with the Selection tool and choose Object ▸ Path ▸ Release Compound Path. This will break down the letterforms even more into their actual separate paths, which is why the counters (holes) filled in, too.
3. If your design has any filled counters you wish weren't filled, select them one pair at a time with the Selection tool.
4. Open the Pathfinder panel from Window ▸ Object & Layout ▸ Pathfinder, and click the Subtract button to knock the counter out of the letter once more. Repeat as needed for other letter-counter pairs.
5. Once everything has been fixed, select one letter at a time, and use File ▸ Place to bring in an image that fill just that letter. Conversely, you could put type in each individual letter.

Fill Type Counters

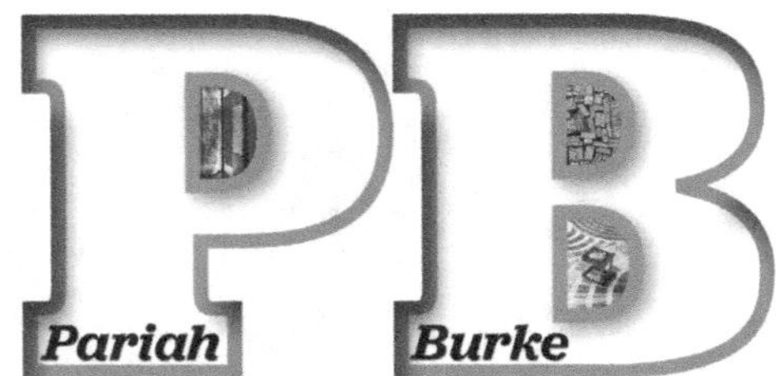

You may have already figured this out, but if you haven't, those counters that were so recently filled with color? Yeah, you can fill those with images and text, too. Sometimes, filling the counters is better than filling the characters.

Blur Text in InDesign

AFTER 16
HOURS
WORKING IN
INDESIGN

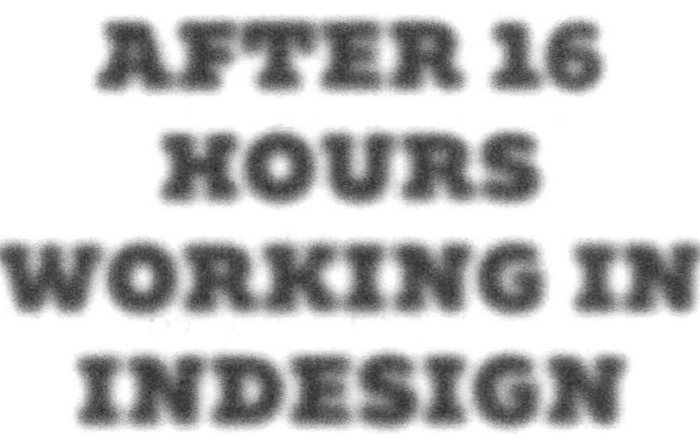

This one really... blurs the line... between text and image effects (*ba-dum-tsh*), and I wasn't sure if I should save it for *InDesign Masterclass: Images & Objects* rather than this *Type & Tables* book. But... let's do it!

In Photoshop and Illustrator you can apply blur effects, like Gaussian Blur, to just about anything. InDesign does not have that ability, leaving some designers to have to have to create the effect in one of InDesign's siblings. However, you can simulate blurry text in InDesign with a little Effects work.

1 Create your text to be blurred.
2 Select it with the Selection and choose Object ▸ Effects ▸ Basic Feather.

3 Apply the Basic Feather effect that looks good to you. To blur even more, you might try adding an Outer Glow—with the color set to be the same as your text, and a blending mode that compliments the color of the text. Below are my settings for the first blurry text above.

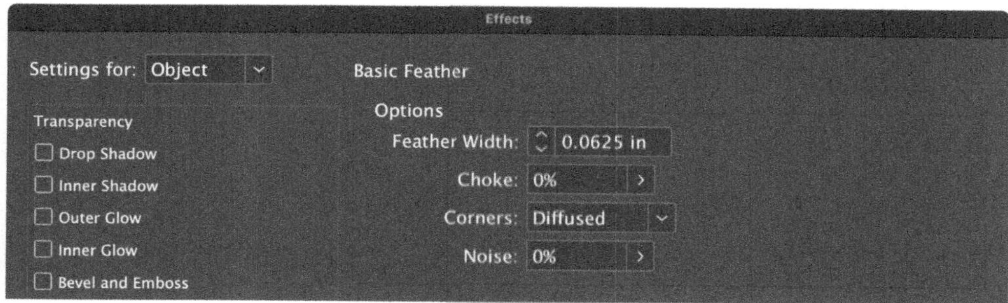

For the second blurry text, the one on the right, I added an Outer Glow effect using these settings.-

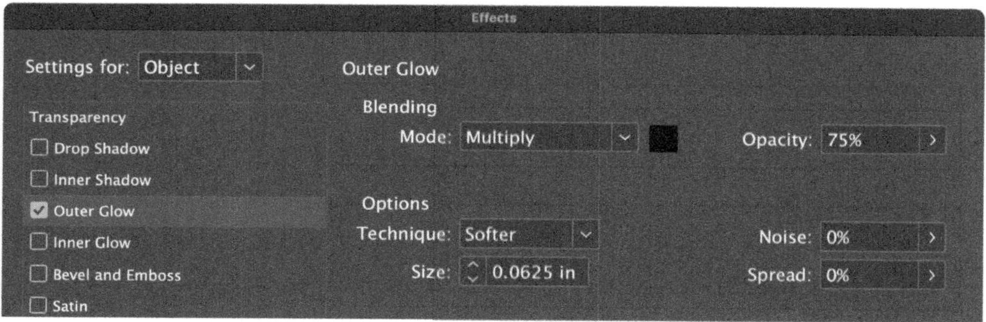

Two-Click Formatting of an Entire Document

Perry Mason
(503) 555-1212
pmason@perrymasonlaw.com

Jennifer Walters
(617) 555-1212
meangreen@glkh.law

Harvey Specter
(503) 555-1212
hs@pearsonspecterlitt.com

Alicia Florrick
(503) 555-1212
aflorrick@sternlockhartgardner.com

Saul Goodman
(503) 555-1212
mcgill@saulgoodmanatlaw.com

Elle Woods
(617) 555-1212
ewoods@harvard.edu

Matt Murdock
(503) 555-1212
matt@nelsonandmurdock.com

Analise Keeting
(503) 555-1212
akeating@keatingnassociates.law

Criss Angel, David Copperfield, David Blaine, Siegfried & Roy, and all the world's other top magicians and illusionists belong to the International Magicians Society (IMS), an organization that, among other things, enforces amongst it's members the policy that a magician never reveals the secret to their tricks. Thankfully, there is no similar body governing InDesign masters, because what I'm about to reveal to you is, without exaggeration, one of, if not *the*, best kept secrets of the top InDesign gurus. It's often the big finale trick at conferences, and it's rarely shared in mass consumption media like a book or blog post because, well, knowing the trick is one of the reasons people call us InDesign masters. You know me, I won't hold back any knowledge from you; the other gurus, though, might come gunning for me. If I suddenly have an "accident" you'll know the truth.

Here's the Prestige of the trick, the payoff: An entire document—from one to 1,000 pages—can be formatted with multiple paragraph styles in only two clicks of the mouse.

Like all great magic tricks, this one is achieved through preparation and misdirection. The preparation part is a matter of using cascading paragraph styles and the Next Style field. With projects like the directory of fictional attorneys I created, every line carries a different paragraph style. By setting the Next Style field to every successive style required for the listing, and then looping the last paragraph style back to the first of a listing's styles, you can perpetually type directory listings that automatically style. But this trick isn't about automatic formatting as you type; this is about applying multiple styles instantly to a story already written. The preparation is the same, though; set up your Next Style fields, but don't actually apply any paragraph styles to your text.

1. If you don't have a document ready, create a membership directory like my example—just three lines per entry, no need to overly complicate things.
2. Now create three paragraph styles, one per line for each entry. For example, I created Directory Name, Directory Phone, and Directory Email paragraph styles for mine.
3. Edit the Next Style field in each of them so that they move down the line like so, with the last style looping back to say the first style in the Next Style field:
    - Directory Name, Next Style: Directory Phone
    - Directory Phone, Next Style: Directory Email
    - Directory Email, Next Style: Directory Name

This technique will work on any number of lines with cyclic formatting, so feel free to go for more than three lines and three paragraph styles per entry.

Now that the trick has been prepared, you're ready for the Pledge (the setup) and the Turn (the performance of the trick). Remember to practice it in front of a mirror before attempting it before a live audience.

1. Begin by setting the stage with the Pledge—pour your unformatted or improperly formatted text into InDesign. Although not absolutely necessary, for dramatic effect, simply because overset text can't be seen, you'll want to make sure that the entire story is placed on one or more pages, that there isn't any overset text.
2. Allow the audience to inspect the text, to see that the text is normal and not rigged in any way.
3. Inform the audience of the extreme difficulty and terrible danger involved in the following trick. Ask for total silence.
4. Place the text cursor somewhere within the story and press CMD+A/CTRL+A to select all.
5. Careful to use misdirection to draw the audience's attention away from the movement of your mouse cursor, go to the Paragraph Styles panel and right-click on the first style in the chain of styles—the Directory Name style in my

example. Up will pop a context sensitive menu you may think you know inside and out, top to bottom.

6 Around the middle of the popup menu there will be a new command you've never seen before, one that is available nowhere, nowhen else in InDesign than when you have multiple paragraphs selected and have right-clicked on a paragraph style that has a Next Style attribute set to something other than [Same Style]. There is the secret to the best trick of the greatest InDesign masters—Apply [This Style] and Then Next. Click that command, and your entire document will instantly, automatically, format to the amazement and delight of your audience.
7 Bask in the applause.
8 Curtain down.

The way the trick works is that the Apply [This Style] and Then Next command applies the first style—the one on which you right-clicked—to the first paragraph in the selected text. It then applies whatever style is defined in the first style's Next Style field to the second paragraph, then continues applying Next Style paragraph styles to every subsequent paragraph. Because the last style—Directory Email, in this case—loops back to the beginning of the chain, InDesign keeps applying the paragraph styles in a loop, one at every hard return, until the entire story is formatted. Thus, you can format 1,000 pages of unformatted directory listings—or any type of document that uses successive paragraph styles—with two clicks.

Even a document like a newspaper or magazine article, one that isn't cyclic and doesn't loop the last style back to the first, can be formatted with this trick. Just make sure the last style—probably one for body copy—has [Same Style] set in the Next Style field. Then, after the kicker, headline, deck, byline, first paragraph, and first body copy paragraph are styled, every subsequent paragraph will also be assigned to the body copy style.

Now that you know the secret, don't tell anyone else. Sure, encourage them to buy their own copies of this book (my family has to eat), but until they do, let them think of you as the magician, as the InDesign master, formatting multiple paragraphs, multiple pages, even whole documents, in only two-clicks.

Now *you* are one of the keepers of the secret.

Welcome to the hidden society of the InDesign Illuminati.

Curtain down.

Glossary

A

508 See *Section 508.*

accessibility In the context of InDesign the document formats it can produce, this is the practice of removing barriers to reaching, using, and perceiving content for people with disabilities (permanent, temporary, or situational). In the United States, accessibility of electronic documents is mandated of certain organizations primarily by Section 508 of the Rehabilitation Act of 1973 (see *Section 508).*

ACE Depending on context, the acronym ACE refers to two very different things in the world of Adobe.

First, ACE is an acronym for the Adobe Color Engine, which handles color management in and between the Creative Suite applications like InDesign, Photoshop, Illustrator, and others.

Second, ACE is an acronym for Adobe Certified Expert, a certification of expertise in Adobe applications earned after passing an independently administered exam. There are ACE exams available for InDesign, InCopy, Illustrator, Photoshop, and virtually all Adobe products.

This book's author has also authored or co-authored ACE exams for InDesign, InCopy, and Illustrator.

alpha channel An alpha channel is a special color channel within pixel-based images containing transparency. Opacity is measured in 256 levels and generally represented in the onscreen alpha channel as 256 levels of gray. Although applications such as InDesign will read, interpret, and display the transparency of an alpha channel, there is no way to specifically view or directly manipulate the alpha channel without an interface such as Photoshop's Channels panel. Image formats that support alpha channel transparency include Photoshop documents (PSD, PSB), PDFs, and PNGs.

Adobe Sensei One of Adobe's generative artificial intelligences used within InDesign and other major Adobe applications to automate and enhance processes like Auto Style (see *generative artificial intelligence* and *Auto Style*)

alpha transparency See *alpha channel.*

anchor point Vector drawings are made up of paths—more specifically, coordinates on a two-dimensional grid. An anchor point is the path-defining point plotted on the grid. It contains an x-axis horizontal location coordinate and a vertical coordinate on the y-axis; it may also contain angle and curvature data, which control the angle and curve of path segments emanating from either side of the anchor point. When a second anchor point is plotted on the grid, a path segment may be drawn between the two points to create a path. Repositioning the anchor point alters the shape, angle, and length of the path, and manipulating the anchor points' curve handles changes the curvature or angle of attached path segments.

anchored object An anchored object is any object—graphic frame, text frame, or other object—that is tethered to a specific point in another frame or story. The anchored object is actually tied to a special, invisible marker placed inside the other frame or story, and the anchored object will follow the marker to maintain a specific relative distance. If page recomposition causes an anchored object's marker to flow from page 2 to page 6, for instance, the anchored object itself will also jump from page 2 to page 6 automatically. Inline images, those pasted into text, are also anchored objects. The relative position, alignment, and numerous other options regarding the placement of anchored objects relative to their markers, columns of text, the page, and document spine are available in the Anchored Object Options dialog.

ascender The portion of a glyph that extends above the x-height (the height of a typeface's lowercase *x*). Glyphs with ascenders include f, *h*, *l*, and *t*.

ASCII (Acronym for American Standard Code for Information Interchange) This is the computer language that represents human-readable text. The English-based ASCII contains 95 characters, including the Latin alphabet and standard punctuation. TXT files are ASCII-encoded and thus are often referred to as ASCII files. More robust text-based file formats such as RTF and DOC are based on, but extend beyond, ASCII.

assignments Within InDesign and its sister application InCopy, an assignment is a collection of one or more text or graphic frames separated from an InDesign publication and made available for work by an InCopy user or another InDesign user. Only one user may have any one InDesign INDD document opened for editing at a time. When assignments are used to apportion the document into linked and semi-autonomous sections of content, however, that single document may be edited by several people concurrently. A bidirectional check-in/check-out system further assists by maintaining version control and preventing double-modification of assigned content.

Auto Style A tool powered by *Adobe Sensei* and using style packs to automatically style stories.

B

baseline The invisible line on which type stands. Glyphs such as *j*, *g*, and *y* have lower portions—called *descenders*—that descend below the baseline.

Bézier In vector drawing, paths are created by placing *anchor points* on a virtual grid and then connecting those anchor points with *path segments*. In the Bézier drawing system of vector illustration, path segment angle and curvature are controlled by the anchor points rather than by the path segments. Bézier curves are parametric, meaning that the curvature in one end of a path segment affects and interacts with the curvature in the other end.

The vector drawing tools in all of Adobe's applications—InDesign, Illustrator, Photoshop, and others—use Bézier curves.

blow out When a device such as a printer or camera cannot render low percentages of color (in subtractive color models) or high percentages (in additive color models) and the result is a jump to 0% color, or pure white, the color is said to "blow out." For example, many offset presses cannot render less than 4% of a given ink, thus an area painted in 3% of a color will blow out and become no color at all. *Plugged* is the opposite of blow out; when very dark the values become 100% color, or black.

C

calibrate To calibrate a device is to bring its color rendering or capturing ability as close as possible into alignment with the actual colors presented to the device.

caliper The thickness of a sheet of paper expressed in thousands of an inch. For example, the caliper of 20 lb bond paper is 0.0038-inches.

CALS CALS is a model for representing tables and tabular data in XML. (See *XML)*

camel case Originally termed "medial capitals," camel-case refers to compound words or phrases where, instead of spaces, hyphens, or other separators, the words are joined together with each component word bearing a capital letter, often in the middle of the combined word. Common examples of camel-case include "InDesign," "QuarkXPress," and "iPod."

cap height The distance between the baseline and the top of the average capital letter in a given typeface.

carry-over A notation to readers that the current point in a threaded story is not the beginning of the story, that it continues here from an earlier place. For example, "continued from page 10." Also known as carry-over line, continued line, or continue head. See also: *jumpline.*

CJK Shorthand for Chinese, Japanese, and Korean; most often used to describe a group of fonts containing glyphs for one or all three languages.

clipping path A vector path embedded into, or attached to, an image or object that causes parts of the object to appear transparent. Unlike alpha transparency, clipping-path transparency does not offer levels of opacity; areas of color are either completely transparent (clipped) or fully opaque. Clipping paths may be added to images in Photoshop or Illustrator and are understood by InDesign and other page-layout applications. If an image does not contain a clipping path, one may be created inside InDesign to mask out (render transparent) parts of the image.

CMS (Abbreviation for Color Management System; also for Content Management System and for the *Chicago Manual of Style*) A color management system connects calibrated color capture or render devices and their respective profiles, translating color data from one device to the next in an attempt to ensure consistently accurate portrayal of colors at each step.

CMYK (Abbreviation for Cyan Magenta Yellow blacK) CMYK is a subtractive color model wherein the more color added, the further the mix moves from white. CMYK, or process ink, is the standard for printing in North America and most of the world. Although CMYK has an extremely limited color *gamut,* it may be augmented through the use of spot color inks.

color profile When a color rendering or capture device such as a computer monitor or scanner is profiled, its unique color interpretation characteristics are examined and recorded into a color profile and saved as an ICC or ICM file to be read by a color management system that translates and maintains consistent color between several devices' color profiles.

color ramp The continuous tone display of the hues, tints, and/or saturation and lightness levels available within the selected color or *gamut,* such as you might find at the bottom of the Color panel for examining or selecting available colors.

color stop An indicator showing the location of a color, usually within a gradient.

compound path Two or more vector paths behaving as one.

compound shape Two or more complete shapes (closed paths) behaving as one shape.

content-first A method of designing a page wherein you bring in your content—text, images, and other elements—before deciding where on the page they will be and how they will fit together. It is the opposite of a *frame-first workflow.*

contextual orphan An orphan is the first line of a paragraph left behind at the bottom of a column or page while the rest of the paragraph flows to the next column or page. A contextual orphan is what the author calls a short or single-line paragraph that, in context, should remain in the same column and on the same page as the paragraph it precedes but is instead left behind at the bottom of the previous column or page. For example, a single-line heading is its own paragraph but should always appear in the same column and page as the first paragraph it describes. (See also *orphan.*)

contextual widow Similar to a contextual orphan, a contextual widow is a term coined by the author to describe a single-line or short paragraph pushed to the next column or page even though logic dictates that it should remain directly beneath the preceding paragraph. For example, a contextual widow would be the final, single-line paragraph of a bulleted or numbered list. (See also *widow.)*

counter The holes or large open spaces within letter forms—for example, the holes in the letters *o* and *g*.

creep Your neighbor with the telescope that always seems to be pointing in the direction of your bedroom window. In the world of print, creep refers to the fact that the mass of sheets of paper displace other sheets of paper folded together. The edges of interior sheets stick out from the edges of enclosing sheets.

creep-in Also called push-in, a creep-in is a negative inside or spine-side adjustment meant to push the page image inward toward the bound edge of a document to adjust for *creep*.

crossover A crossover is bleeding ink into the spine of a bound document similar to the way the outer edges of ink are set to bleed off the page edges.

cross-reference A directive advising the reader to reference a different section of, or item within, the current document. For example, directives to "See Figure X.Y" or, in an *index, "See also: CMYK,"* are cross-references because at one point in the document they direct a reader to a different point in the same document. In InDesign cross-references are made of two parts: the destination text and the source cross-reference. Cross-reference is often referred to by the shorthand *xref.*

CSS Cascading Style Sheets, the means by which styling is accomplished online. CSS style definitions and attributes such as font size, color, and much more are applied to HTML content tagged or named a particular way.

curve handles In vector drawing, anchor points contain angle and curvature data to affect path segments. Curve handles are always present but only visible when the anchor point has more than 0° of curvature and/or more than a 0° angle. Dragging curve handles alters the angle and depth of curvature of path segments emanating from an anchor point.

D

data source file When creating variable data printing (VDP) documents using InDesign's mail merge features, the set of comma- or tab-delimited variable data is stored in a data source file (a CSV or TXT file).

dek The subhead or explanatory paragraph immediately below a headline in an article or news story.

descender The portion of a glyph that extends below the text baseline, such as with the lowercase letters *g*, *q*, and *j*.

destination text The target of a *cross-reference* directive's source cross-reference.

dialog box Utility boxes that offer access to settings and features. Unlike *panels,* when a dialog box is open, you cannot select objects on the page, change pages, or otherwise interact with the document or panel-based features.

direction lines (See *Curve Handles)*

drop rule A vertical rule or line separating columns or rails.

duplexing Printing on both sides of a piece of paper.

E

em A relative measurement equal, in theory, to the width of a typeface's capital *M* and to the cap height of the typeface. For example, type set in 12 pt should theoretically have a 12 pt em measurement; 10 pt type should have a 10 pt em. In practice, with digital fonts, the capital *M* is rarely the width of a full em, although an em is still usually same in width as the cap height of the font.

em dash A horizontal dash one em wide.

emoji An emoji is a small digital image or icon used to express emotions, objects, or ideas in electronic communications. Originating from Japanese mobile phones in the late 1990s, emojis have become a universal language in texting and social media, allowing users to convey complex feelings and concepts succinctly. The term "emoji" comes from the Japanese words "e" (picture) and "moji" (character). In InDesign, emoji may refer to this classic definition as well as to "emoji fonts," meaning fonts whose primary or entire purpose to insert digital imagery or icons.

en A relative measurement equal, in theory, to the width of a typeface's capital *N* and slightly more than half width of an *em.*

en dash A horizontal dash one en wide.

endpoint An anchor point at the beginning or end of an open path.

ePUB The file extension and format of the XML-based ebooks standardized on by digital book readers such as Apple's Books, Amazon's Kindle, Adobe Digital Editions, and other e-reading platforms.

F

flat-file database A collection of data stored in an ASCII-based format such as a comma- or tab-delimited TXT file rather than in a traditional database.

flattening The process of removing transparency and generating opaque objects from the areas of color created by overlapping one or more transparent objects with nontransparent objects.

flush The clean edge of type. For example, this page is printed with type flush left, meaning that the type aligns along the left to create a clean edge.

flush left Text aligned uniformly to the left margin.

flush left and right See *force justified.*

flush right Text aligned uniformly to the right margin.

folio A page number. Also refers to the page itself and to large sheets of paper that are folded once and bound.

force justified Text aligned to flush, clean edges on both the left and right sides of the column is justified. In most justified paragraphs, last lines that are too short to fill the width of the column remain left, right, or center aligned. However, when even short last lines are made to justify, creating a uniform rectangle but with large gaps possibly introduced between words or letters, the paragraph is called force justified. Some newspapers, for example, force justify text.

format building blocks Components of cross-reference formats, which may include static text, dynamic text such as the page number `<pageNum/>` building block, styling directives such as the `<cs name=""></cs>` building block that assigns a character style to one or more building blocks, and other types. See *cross-reference.*

FPO (Abbreviation for For Position Only) Temporary content—text or imagery—placed to estimate size, position, or usage of other content to be inserted later.

frame-first A method of working in whch the geometry of a page or document is mapped out using empty or *FPO* frames before the actual text, imagery, and other content is ready to be placed into InDesign. It is the opposite of a content-first workflow wherein the layout is built from a blank page using the actual content that will be on the page. The frame-first methodology is also called wireframing, especially among designers who also produce Web and mobile app designs.

G

gamma The frequency of radiation that turned Dr. Bruce Banner into the Hulk. Also the luminescence value of color as measured in tones of gray.

gamut The range of color values possible in a particular color space, device, or color-production process.

gang Printing multiple pages from one or more jobs on a single, large sheet of paper to save production time and costs.

ganged See *gang.*

generative artificial intelligence Generative artificial intelligence (AI) refers to a type of AI technology that can generate new content, such as text, images, audio, and video, based on patterns and data it has learned from existing content. This technology uses algorithms to synthesize new material that is coherent and contextually relevant, often creating outputs that mimic human-like creativity.

glyph A single character, pictogram, mark, or entity within a font or language.

gradient ramp The preview of a gradient, sometimes showing *color stops.*

greeking Content—usually text—that is used in place of final copy (aka FPO text). In InDesign, when text appears onscreen below a size limit set in the preferences, the text is replaced by black-and-white patterning, which is also greeking. The term derives from the expression "it's all Greek to me," indicating that something cannot be read or is gibberish.

GREP GREP, originally a Unix command line search application in 1973 by Ken Thompson, is regular expression query or search language used within InDesign and many other applications. GREP allows for not only verbose queries (e.g. finding all instances of the word "the'), but also queries of regular expressions, or fuzzy searches, wherein the user looks to find patterns, such as any three letters beginning with "t," or any digit, any letter, and so on. GREP is used within InDesign in the Find/Change dialog box to enable searching for, and possibly replacing, virtually any text. It is also used in GREP Styles, which enables applying character styles to type that matches patterns or regular expressions. Although GREP has all but completely separated as its own word independent of its original longer form, GREP is indeed an acronym for "global / regular expression / print", which translates to search globally amongst the text for a regular expression and return (or print, in old Unix) the result.

gutter Traditionally either the space between pages in a spread or the space between columns or both. In InDesign, the gutter is only the space between columns.

H

hanging punctuation Punctuation and parts of glyphs allowed to shift in part or wholly beyond the flush edge of text to create a more optically balanced flush edge instead of a physically clean flush edge.

hard proof Any printed version of a document short of the final output.

HSL (Abbreviation for Hue, Saturation, and Luminosity [or Lightness]) A color model that describes a color in terms of its hue, saturation, and luminosity values; interchangeable with HSB (Hue, Saturation, and Brightness).

I

ICC profile See *color profile.*

IDML An abbreviation for InDesign Markup Language, an XML-based, tagged format version of a document. Also, the file extension of such documents when exported to InDesign Markup Language. IDML files are often used when it becomes necessary for users on different versions of InDesign to collaborate as IDML files are version-agnostic within InDesign.

imposed (See *Imposition)*

imposition Sometimes called "digital stripping" or pagination, imposition is the process of placing pages into the correct order for printing such that, when folded, a sheet containing multiple pages will make the pages readable in the correct order. (See *Printer's Spreads* and *Reader's Spreads)*

in port The place on a threaded text frame through which text flows into the frame. The in port is located near the upper-left corner of a text frame and on the left end of a type on a path object. Opposite the in port is the out port.

inset A margin on the interior of a text frame that pushes type inward from one or more edges of the frame.

J

IPTC Abbreviation for the International Press Telecommunications Council and the label for a set of metadata defined by that body as the most important for general and editorial usage imagery and other content. (See *Metadata)*

JSON JSON (JavaScript Object Notation) is a lightweight, text-based format for data interchange that is easy for humans to read and write. It is commonly used to transmit structured data between systems, applications, and languages. JSON represents data in a standard format using key-value pairs, arrays, and primitive types like numbers, strings, and booleans, making it widely used for APIs and data serialization.

jumpline A directive to readers that a threaded story resumes at a later point. For example, "continues on page 83." Also known as continue line or jump head. See also: *carry-over.*

K

kerning The relative distance between a pair of letters. Kerning values are adjusted on the Character panel or the Control panel's character mode to reduce or increase space between two characters whose shapes create awkward gapping or collision.

knockout When two or more colors overlap, the foreground color can either *overprint,* which often causes mixing of colors from the background into the foreground color, or knockout such that the lower or background ink is removed, punching a hole through it in the shape of the foreground color area, thus preserving the appearance of the foreground color.

L

layer comp In Photoshop, a layer comp is a recording of the state of an image's layers at a given moment in time. Layer comps register the visibility, opacity, blending mode, and position of individual layers and may be used to switch between design variations without the need for creating multiple documents. InDesign honors and employs layer comps stored in Photoshop PSD documents such that design variations created in Photoshop may be placed and changed on the InDesign page without a return trip to Photoshop.

leader Marks, glyphs, or symbols representing or preceding a tab. For instance, in many tables of contents, entries are connected to their page numbers by a series of dots/periods or a continuous rule (really underscores). Those dots or underscores are the leader.

leaf (See S*ignature.)*

left-read In a bound publication or facing-pages document, the page to the left of the spine. In English- and other Latin-based-language publications, the left-read pages are even numbered. In Japanese, Hebrew, and sinistral publications reading from right to left, left-read pages are odd numbered.

ligatures Two or more letters tied into a single character. Generally, when certain pairs, triplets, or quartets of individual letters or glyphs are combined, their shapes cause awkward collisions—for example, *f-i* and *f-t.* In old metal and block type as well as older *TrueType* and *Type 1* fonts, ligatures were extra, single characters added to fonts that combined the shapes of individual colliding letters in a way that voided collision. In modern *OpenType* fonts, ligatures are created by combining special variants of each individual character drawn to accommodate such combinations and avoid collision while maintaining the individuality of each letter.

live area Approximately 1/8 inch inside the trim, the "safe" area of a page inside of which content should be safe from harm in the event of a slight paper shift on the cutting machine.

LPI (Abbreviation for lines per inch) A measurement of the resolution of printed output that is the number of halftone dots per linear inch. The greater the number of dots, the higher the resolution. Also known as screen ruling or screen frequency.

LTR Shorthand for left-to-right written languages such as Latin-based and Cyrillic languages.

M

marker In InDesign, markers are invisible but important characters that act as placeholders or tethers for different types of content. For example, anchored objects are tied to their descriptive text via markers, as are footnotes.

master page (See *Parent page)*

merged document When variable data documents are created via InDesign's mail merge feature, the merged document is the ready-to-print result of combining the source document containing variable data markers with the data source document that holds the variable data.

metadata Information stored within a special layer of a document to identify, categorize, or define the file. Metadata do not print with a document but are accessible to numerous XML-aware applications and databases for file management, asset management, and other purposes.

misregister Inadvertently registering for Early European Economics 301 instead of for Early European Arts & Culture 301 because you woke up on the dormitory roof with a hangover. Also, when plates fail to align perfectly on a printer, colors fall out of register or alignment and are said to misregister.

mixed ink In InDesign, a mixed ink is one that is a combination of two or more spot color inks or one spot color ink and one or more process color inks.

mixed ink group Multiple swatches generated as incremental tint variants resulting from mixing spot and process inks.

more often than not A mantra by which efficient designers live. If you do something in InDesign—use a particular document setup, need certain colors, and so on—more often than you don't do it, whatever it is should be automated or made the default value.

O

nut fraction Horizontally stacked fractions where the numerator and denominator are separated by a horizontal rule. All together, their shape resembles a nut. Nut fractions often are more compact than standard fractions.

onomatopoeia A special kind of word named to closely approximate the sound described by, or associated with, the subject of the word. For example: bang, pow, smash, and numerous other examples from the 1960s *Batman television show.*

OpenType The latest, er, *first* generation, in my not so humble opinion, of intelligent font software. Based on *Unicode*, OpenType fonts (or simply OpenTypes) have predefined spaces for more than 65,000 glyphs from more than a dozen languages. These fonts often contain variant designs such as true small caps, swashes, contextual alternates, ordinals, and several versions of numerals in a single file, replacing several separate fonts required to achieve the same functionality in Type 1 or TrueType fonts. OpenType fonts are identified on a computer by the extension `.otf`, although in many cases they bear the old TrueType `.ttf` file extension revealing the fact that, at their cores, OpenType fonts are structured as either Type1 or TrueType. OpenType fonts are 100% cross-platform; the same font functions and renders identically on Windows, MacOS, iOS, Android, and several flavors of Unix.

OpenType-SVG Also called "Color Fonts," "Emoji Fonts," "Picture Fonts," and other names, OpenType-SVG fonts take advantage of OpenType's large spaces and Unicode nature to include full vector illustrations, often including multiple colors and gradients, to allow typing with, effectively, complete illustrations standing in for characters, though many times those illustrations are drawn to resemble the characters, numbers, and punctuation they replace. If you have inserted emojis into any text messaging app updated since 2014, you have used OpenType-SVG. InDesign is one of the few applications that fully supports typing in OpenType-SVG.

OPI (Abbreviation for Open Prepress Interface) The process of inserting a low-resolution or FPO image to be exchanged automatically further on in the production process for a high-resolution or final image. Using InDesign, OPI image substitution can be performed at output time or left to be done in-RIP.

orphan In a paragraph, a line left behind at the bottom of a column or page while the rest of the paragraph flows to the next column or page. Bringhurst limits the definition of orphan to the paragraph's first line ending a page, although common usage has expanded the definition to also include the paragraph's first line ending a column. (See also *contextual orphan.*)

out port The place on a threaded text frame through which text exits the frame to connect with and enter another text frame. The out port is located near the lower-right corner of a text frame and on the right side of a type on a path object. Opposite the out port is the *in port.*

overprint When two or more colors overlap, they can be printed over one another, each color layed down successively, which usually results in the colors mixing to form a new, combined color. This is overprinting. Conversely, the uppermost ink can be set to *knockout* lower inks to preserve the appearance of the foreground color.

override In terms of styles, an override is a formatting option not specifically defined in the style assigned to the text, object, table, or cell. For instance, using the CMD+Shift+I/CTRL+Shift+I keyboard shortcut to apply italic to text is an override of a paragraph style in which the text is defined to be roman, or not italic. Overrides are indicated by a plus sign (+) beside the style name in Paragraph Style, Character Style, Object Style, Table Style, and Cell Style panels.

overscore A rule above text, as opposed to an underscore. Also called overline or overbar.

overset When a text frame (or type on a path object) is not large enough to hold all of the text placed into it, any overage is said to be overset. A frame containing overset text displays a red plus sign (+) in its out port.

P

pagination (See *Imposition)*

palette The long ago name for the floating utility boxes that contain the majority of InDesign's functionality, now called *panels.*

parent page Called "master page" until InDesign 2022 (version 17.0), a parent page is like an in-document template for printable pages, called document pages or, increasingly "child pages" following the change from "master". Objects such as backgrounds, headers, footers, or anything else placed on a parent page automatically appear on any and all document pages to which the parent has been associated. Changes to those objects on the parent are automatically inherited by the "children" document pages.

panel Name for the floating utility boxes that contain the majority of InDesign's functionality; formerly called palettes. InDesign cc 2025 has 62 panels. Unlike *dialog boxes*, you can select content on the page while one or more panels are open.

path A vector drawing consisting of anchor points and path segments.

path segment Segment of a path connecting one anchor to another.

perfect bound A bindery process whereby pages are grouped together and printed into *signatures*, and then the signatures are collated and glued together with a wraparound, squared spine. This book is an example of a perfect bound document.

pilcrow Paragraph mark (¶).

plugged When a device such as a printer or camera cannot render high percentages of color (in subtractive color models) or low percentages (in additive color models) and the result is a jump to pure black, the resulting color is said to plug. For example, many offset presses cannot render ink tints greater than 95%; thus, an area shaded in 97% black will plug and become solid black. *Blow out* is the opposite, when very light color values become 0% color.

polyglot A person or computer application fluent in more than one language, or a book or other long publication that prints the same information in more than one language.

PostScript The printer language that translates computer-drawn graphics and text into high-quality printed output on a PostScript-enabled printer or other device. PostScript was created by Adobe Systems, Inc., founders John Warnock and Chuck Geschke and was the foundation technology for that company. Coupled with a computer—the Apple Macintosh—and printer—the Apple LaserWriter—both with onboard PostScript interpreters, Adobe's PostScript launched the Desktop Publishing Revolution in 1985.

preflight Preparing a document for print output.

printer's spreads *Signatures* containing pages printed in *imposition* rather than sequential order such that, when the signatures are folded, the pages can be read in sequential order.

prosumer Coined in 1980 by the futurist Alvin Toffler—in his book *The Third Wave*—as a blend of producer and consumer, the term prosumer was used to describe a possible future type of consumer who would become involved in the design and manufacture of products so they could be made to individual specification. The term also refers to amateurs or hobbyists who use professional-grade tools such as InDesign.

push-in See *Creep-In*

Q

quad Spacing added to align text to the left, right, or center. Also often used to describe simply the flush edge of text. See *flush*.

quad left See *flush left*.

quad right See *flush right*.

R

rag The uneven side of flush left or flush right type, as in "the rag edge."

rag left See *flush right*.

rag right See *flush left*.

ragged The uneven side of flush left or flush right type.

rail A column. The term is most often used in newspaper publishing.

reader's spreads Spreads with pages printed in sequential order rather than *imposition* or bound order. Documents are designed in reader's spreads, with pages following each other consecutively, but are later imposed into printer's spreads.

rebate On photographic film, the margin surrounding the image area. In desktop, object, and certain other printers, the area of the substrate required to be gripped by the printer's rollers or grips; no image may be printed in the rebate.

rendering intent When a color management system must convert colors from one *gamut* to another, and when some of the colors in the source gamut do not fit into the destination, the rendering intent determines how out-of-gamut colors are brought into gamut. For instance, are out-of-gamut colors clipped to the nearest values in the same range, are they converted based on their relative distances from the color space's white point, or is another method used?

RGB (Abbreviation for Red, Green, and Blue) An additive color model encompassing the visual portion of the radiation spectrum. The more color added, the closer the combination moves toward pure white. RGB has a vastly wider *gamut* than *CMYK* but is smaller than the Lab color gamut.

rich black Black created by mixing a percentage of cyan, magenta, yellow, and/or black process inks. Rich black is so named because it is a richer, deeper black than pure black process ink; however, because it requires the use of at least three different inks, its use increases the risk of misregistration. Nearly every press, prepress, and graphics professional has a different opinion of the ideal formula to produce rich black, and the formula often varies depending on the print image and the substrate in use.

rich text Based on but an extension to ASCII text, rich text incorporates basic word processor–level formatting such as bold and italic, color, underlines, wrapping lines, tabs, indents, and an expanded character set. (See also *RTF.)*

right-read In a bound publication or facing-pages document, the page to the right of the spine. In English- and other Latin-based-language publications, right-read pages are odd numbered. Right-read pages are even numbered in Japanese, Hebrew, and southpaw publications.

RIP (Acronym for Raster Image Processor) When digital artwork is sent to press, it often includes pixel-based raster images, resolution-independent vector type and paths, transparency, and Z-order stacking of objects. Printers—including imagesetters, platesetters, digital printers, and desktop laser and ink-jet printers—can only render two-dimensional, flat images and in screened raster form. The job of the RIP is to convert all data in the document to screened rasters at the resolution of the output device.

river An unsightly optical effect created by white space gaps between words or letters aligning, or nearly aligning, vertically. Rivers are prevalent especially among justified type and narrow columns such as one finds in newspapers. InDesign's composition engine, particularly effective when using the paragraph composition option, all but eliminates most rivers.

RTF (Abbreviation for Rich Text Format) A universal format based on rich text content. RTF files can be read and created by all modern word-processors, page-layouts, and many other applications. RTF files are cross-platform.

RTL Shorthand for right-to-left written languages such as Japanese, Hebrew, and Arabic.

run-on Extra copies run at the end of a print job to provide a buffer in case some earlier pages turn out to be unsuitable for delivery to the client. Also known as run-out and run-down. Also, what the ersatz informant Huggy Bear always gave Starsky and Hutch.

run-in head A subhead with text immediately following it on the same line.

runt A runt is a single word residing on a line by itself within, or at the end of, a paragraph. In the case of forced justified text, runts space out their constituent glyphs horribly to fill the entire column width.

run-up Extra sheets printed at the beginning of a job to prepare a press to print the actual job and to test ink and press accuracy and readiness. Run-up is typically done with cheap, low-quality paper such as newsprint or paper left over from a previous job rather than the paper actually ordered for the job, thus not risking the stock required to complete the job.

S

SaaS Pronounced sæs, SaaS is the acronym for Software as a Service. (See *Software as a Service.)*

saddle stapled (See *Saddle Stitched.)*

Section 508 Section 508 of the Rehabilitation Act of 1973 is a law passed by the Congress of the United States of America requiring most government entities, contractors, and even non-government organizations meeting certain criteria produce all their electronic content in a way that eliminates or minimizes barriers to people with disabilities. Although Section 508, as it is typically called or simply "508", is policy specific to the U.S. government, many other nations' governments have adopted similar requirements based on the same framework for making documents created on or for electronic devices accessible. This framework, which is incorporated into Section 508 by attribution, is the international standards known as the Web Content Accessibility Guidelines (*WCAG*). (See also *accessibility.)*

saddle stitched A bindery process quite common with magazines, catalogs, and other periodicals in which a stack of pages is folded at the center and then bound together by means of stitching in thread or stapling along the stack's spine or centerfold. The "saddle" is the wedge or surface on which the stack of folded paper sits open so that it's centerfold is accessible to the stapler or stitcher.

separations Digital, film, paper, or other material wherein each ink used in a job is created as its own image distinct and separate from other inks.

seps Slang for *separations. (See separations.)*

signature The printed sheet after it has been folded, also often called a *leaf.*

slug Any piece or set of information placed in a document outside the trim and bleed area of the page. Slugs will appear on film and, generally, even on the printed substrate but will be trimmed off during finishing. Common information inserted as a slug includes the job name and number, client information, name and contact information for the designer, color scales, and special instructions to the pre-press or press operators.

slug area The area of the InDesign document in which slugs may be placed. The dimensions of the four sides of the slug area are defined together or individually in the New Document and Document Setup dialogs in InDesign.

snippet InDesign objects—text frames, paths, placed assets, or other objects—or portions or whole pages saved as external files. Snippets are XML-based chunks of layout data that may be reused, restoring InDesign objects into any document, and shared with other InDesign users.

soft proofs A digital version of a document used to check the document on screen.

solidus The unique slash appearing between the numerator and denominator in a fraction; often called simply the fraction slash (for example, 9/10). The slope of the solidus is not as steep as the virgule—the so-called "forward slash" found on keyboards and used as a substitute for the words *or, and/or,* and *per* in English grammar. The solidus is not found on computer or typewriter keyboards (see also *virgule*).

OpenType fonts have separate virgule and solidus glyphs. Through InDesign's Glyphs panel, or by activating the Fractions OpenType option, InDesign will convert a virgule between two numbers into a solidus (and make the numbers properly sized and positioned numerator and denominator).

source cross-reference The directive in a *cross-reference* that advises the reader to go to a different point in the document, to the destination text.

spot colors (Also known as spot inks, spots, or PMS colors after the PANTONE Matching System, the most widely used set of spot color inks in North America) Premixed ink colors that expand upon the limited *gamut* of *CMYK* process inks. Spot colors come in a rainbow of colors, including some—such as neons and metallics—that cannot be rendered onscreen.

spread What Mom lays out for Thanksgiving dinner. Also, any set of consecutive pages in a document meant to be viewed concurrently.

Stacking order See *Z-order.*

sticky settings When options and settings entered into an application or one of its dialog boxes remain as set between sessions, the settings are said to be sticky settings. An example is InDesign's Print dialog, where basic options set once will be retained for the next print operation.

SVG Abbreviation of Scalable Vector Graphics, an open source file format that replaced Adobe Flash SWF as a cross-platform, application-agnostic vector-based graphic format free from licensing fees. SVG artwork can be created and/or imported by most major graphic and office applications, as well as viewed in any web browser.

substrate Any material on which an image may be printed. Paper is, of course, the most common example of a substrate, but others include plastic, metal, and wood.

super-family A set of typefaces that includes multiple families, such as serif and sans serif, built around a core design. Type super-families are designed to work harmoniously together when used in the same document.

T

text wrap The process of causing text to move away from another object automatically or the result of that process.

thread A thread is a story that flows freely between several text frames. The frames themselves are said to be threaded.

tittle A diacritic most often seen as the dot over the lowercase *i* or *j*.

transparency flattening See *flattening.*

trapping Because offset printing applies only one ink color to the page per run, slight misalignment of the substrate on any subsequent pass may cause misregistration and gaps between adjacent colors. Trapping, also called choking and spreading, is the process of overlapping inks slightly to hide minor misregistration and to eliminate gaps.

U

Unicode An international standard in which glyphs from all the world's written languages are encompassed and included in a form understandable by computers. In Unicode, every glyph from each language has its own predefined and inviolable position in the table of glyphs. OpenType fonts are built on Unicode.

V

variable data printing The process of customizing each copy of printed output to include unique text, imagery, or both.

VDP See *variable data printing.*

virgule The proper name for the "forward slash" found on keyboards and used as a substitute for the words *or, and/or*, and *per* in English grammar. The *virgule* is the proper punctuation to use in shorthand dates (e.g. "3/18") while the deeper-angled solidus, or fraction slash, is the correct separator in a fraction (see *solidus*).

W

white-label trainer Me, for 20-something years. An independent, freelance trainer and/or expert in a field who fully represents themself as a member and/or employee of an employing training company without trying to promote their own brand, projects, or agenda. Contact me (https://iampariah.com) to discuss how this book's author, one of the top Adobe trainers, can be *your* branded instructor.

widow A paragraph's last line appearing as the first line in a new column or page. Bringhurst limits the definition of widow to only the paragraph's last line beginning a page, but the definition has expanded through common usage to also include the last line beginning a new column. (See also *contextual widow.)*

wireframe A skeletal representation of the shape of a three-dimensional object.

workspaces In InDesign and other Adobe applications, the workspace is the entire environment of the application interface, including menu configurations and panel arrangements. Most such applications enable the user to save, recall, and often even share their environment settings as a "workspace" file. InDesign comes with several predefined workspaces on the Window ▸ Workspace menu.

WYSIWYG (Acronym for What You See Is What You Get) Basically, what you see onscreen is what will print. InDesign is the first page-layout application to offer true WYSIWYG, particularly with regard to transparency, vector graphics, and object interactions on the page.

X

x-height The distance between the baseline and the top of any given typeface's lowercase *x*, which is indicative of the height of all lowercase letters without ascenders or descenders, making it a static unit of lowercase measurement for the typeface regardless of point size or vertical scale. Even the height of characters with ascenders or descenders can be determined from the x-height because either the bottom or top of those characters typically match the bottom or top of the *x*.

xref Shorthand for cross-reference. (See: *cross-reference*.)

XMP (Abbreviation for eXtensible Meta Properties) A technology coauthored by Adobe that allows *metadata* to be embedded in file formats based on XML or containing an XML layer. Common XMP metadata include author and copyright holder information, camera settings (for photographs), licensing restrictions, and archival data such as categories, description, and keywords. The extensible part of XMP is its ability to go beyond predefined metadata fields and include any information a file author sees fit to store in the XMP layer.

XSLT An abbreviation for XML Stylesheet, a set of rules defining how XML data will be transformed into another data format such as HTML.

Z

Z-order Three-dimensional (3D) space is plotted on three axes: X (the horizontal plane), Y (the vertical plane), and Z (the depth plane). Within two-dimensional or pseudo-three-dimensional applications such as InDesign, full understanding of, and support for, the z-axis and 3D objects is not available. Out of necessity, however, objects can be stacked above or below, in front or behind, one another. This stacking is done along the z-axis and is referred to as the Z-order of objects.

Made in United States
North Haven, CT
26 March 2025

67271688R00117